CRITICAL AESTHETICS
AND POSTMODERNISM

Critical Aesthetics and Postmodernism

PAUL CROWTHER

CLARENDON PRESS · OXFORD

Oxford University Press, Walton Street, Oxford OX2 6DP

Oxford New York
Athens Auckland Bangkok Bombay
Calcutta Cape Town Dar es Salaam Delhi
Florence Hong Kong Istanbul Karachi
Kuala Lumpur Madras Madrid Melbourne
Mexico City Nairobi Paris Singapore
Taipei Tokyo Toronto
and associated companies in
Berlin Ibadan

Oxford is a trade mark of Oxford University Press

Published in the United States
by Oxford University Press Inc., New York

British Library Cataloguing in Publication Data
Data available

Library of Congress Cataloging in Publication Data
Crowther, Paul.
Critical aesthetics and postmodernism / Paul Crowther.
p. cm.
Includes bibliographical references and index.
1. Postmodernism.   2. Aesthetics.   3. Aesthetics, Modern—20th century.
I. Title.
BH301.P69C76   1993   111'85—dc20   92–29734
ISBN 0–19–824037–6
ISBN 0–19–823623–9 (Pbk.)

Printed in Great Britain by
Biddles Ltd.
Guildford & King's Lynn

This is the first work in a multi-volume project. Each volume is an independent work clarifying different aspects of art and the aesthetic's philosophical significance. Such a project, of course, involves a philosophy of art; but, more than that, it involves consideration of the historical and conceptual relations of art and philosophy in the context of broader patterns of social change. In *Critical Aesthetics and Postmodernism* aspects of all these issues are addressed in terms of the debates concerning contemporary sensibility. In *Art and Embodiment* (Clarendon Press, forthcoming) an ecological definition of art will be formulated. It will draw its bearings from a specific tradition—or rather *counter*-tradition—in Continental philosophy. The third volume—*Philosophy in Art*—will address some of the complex historical and conceptual interactions between philosophy and twentieth-century art criticism and practice. Finally, in *Philosophy After Art*, I will consider aspects of the history and future of philosophy in the light of ideas broached in all the preceding volumes.

PAUL CROWTHER

Pittenweem, Fife
29 August 1991

For Sophia Fahrenholz
in memoriam

Preface

As its title suggests, this text addresses both problems of aesthetics, and of contemporary culture. Its basic strategy is to clarify the nature of the latter by investigating the former. To set the scene for this, I shall make some preliminary observations about the relation between modern and postmodern culture, and then about the nature of aesthetics.

The first stirrings of Modernism can be traced to new patterns of production inaugurated by the industrial revolution. At the heart of these is a single phenomenon—the division of labour. In the productive processes which embody this relation, artefacts are not made by a single producer. Rather, the process of production is rigidly compartmentalized into stages and tasks, which are assigned to different individuals. This division of labour brings with it a quantum leap of *efficiency*. Likewise in the sphere of knowledge and culture. From the late eighteenth century (notably in the work of Kant), attempts are made to radically separate different forms of knowledge and experience from one another: to separate, say, metaphysical thinking from scientific method, or aesthetic experience from ethical judgement. By isolating and defining what is unique and distinctive to each mode of knowledge and experience, such modes can then be understood or pursued all the more efficiently.

Something of this impulse also finds its way into art in the late nineteenth and twentieth centuries, in the form of a tendency to emphasize the importance of formal values at the expense of overt narrative content. This, of course, reaches its high point with the rise of non-objective art. Here—according to its apologists—art reaches a stage of 'autonomy'. Its production is motivated and justifiable in purely artistic terms. It is no longer dependent upon factors—bound up with social utility—which are external to art. The basic impulse of Modernism, therefore, is optimistic. By dividing labour and modes of knowledge and experience into distinctive and separate segments, the human species' control and understanding of the world is immeasurably advanced. Indeed, the possibility of unlimited progress, and (given time) ultimate emancipation from want and ignorance is opened up.

The Modernist impulse, however, now seems to have lost its authority. There are many symptoms of this. In the economic and social sphere, patterns of industrial production have changed radically with the introduction of new technologies. In turn, familiar social structures (such as class identity) and political groupings have undergone fragmentation and complex realignment. In the sphere of knowledge and culture, the rigid categories established by Modernism have been questioned by the various strains of poststructuralism. Poststructuralists hold (characteristically) that the boundaries between such things as philosophical, literary, and historical knowledge are shifting and ill-defined. Any attempt to make such boundaries fixed and absolute is regarded as an instance of 'closure' (to use a term of contemporary jargon). Such 'closure', on the poststructuralist view, can usually be traced to some power-group wishing to consolidate or enforce its own interests and preferences.

This scepticism concerning the rigidity of categories has also extended to art-practice. The abstractions of the New York 'Neo-Geo' artists exist alongside conceptual art, neo-classicism, and a 'Neo-Expressionism' which combines both figurative and abstract tendencies, and heavy borrowings from the imagery of popular culture as well as past art. The 'style' of the present is eclectic. It admits of even the most incongruous combinations. This eclecticism, indeed, has led to much talk of art having come to an end, in the sense of having exhausted its potential for real innovation and creativity. The orderly divisions of the Modernist epoch, then, have given way to much more fragmented and shifting ways of ordering and expressing the world. The old hopes of unlimited progress and ultimate social emancipation have been replaced by uncertainty and scepticism. We have entered a *postmodern* age.

This raises the question of how much such changes should be evaluated. Some theorists, such as J.-F. Lyotard, have welcomed them, arguing that Modernism's rigid categories and striving for efficiency and control have an ultimately authoritarian outcome. They lead to the excesses of Hitler and Stalin. In contrast to this, the complexities and pluralism of postmodern culture are anti-authoritarian in impulse. They demand that we respect difference and diversity and transience. Other commentators, however, have been much less sanguine about Postmodernism. Neo-conservatives such as Peter Fuller, Roger Scruton, and Daniel Bell, for example, see contemporary culture as afflicted by a loss of meaning and direction which can only be compensated for by a return to traditional, more 'spiritual' values. Neo-Marxists such as Jürgen Habermas and Frederic Jameson share the same worries but offer a more complex solution. This consists in continuing the Modernist impulse to enlightenment and emancipation, by formulating practical and theoretical strategies of an appropriate sort.

None of these evaluations of Postmodernism is wholly adequate. Lyotard, and the poststructuralists, have drastically overemphasized both the fluidity of modes of knowledge and experience, and their status as social 'constructs'. Such views treat the human subject, indeed, as though his or her consciousness were little more than the sum of shifting societal influences upon it. In so doing, they fail to engage adequately with the possibility of there being *flexible constants* in knowledge and experience. The neo-conservative view moves to the opposite extreme. It supposes that it is possible to dismiss the radical changes in contemporary society, and return to a more homogeneous and 'spiritual' sense of community and value. On these terms, culture will be preserved by, as it were, forgetting the fragmented dimensions of contemporary existence. A society, however, cannot forget its own history—no matter how difficult that history may be. The neo-Marxist approach recognizes this. Where it falls short, however, is its failure to formulate concrete strategies of response. This reflects fundamental problems which have always bedevilled Marxism; namely its continuing failure to articulate theoretically a positive theory of the relationship between the individual agent and broader socio-historical forces; and to clarify the relation between the cultural superstructure and socio-economic infrastructure of society.

This outline of the Modernism–Postmodernism debate is, of course, a sketchy one; and my reservations about the theoretical standpoints involved have been asserted rather than argued. However, in the essays which constitute this text, these standpoints will be addressed in more depth and a broad response to them will be formulated. The clue to this response is to be found in the domain of aesthetics. Traditionally, the term 'aesthetics' has been used in an 'essentialist' sense. This sees the basic task of aesthetics as consisting in a search for both a once-and-for-all definition of art and aesthetic experience and, also, the formulation of definite criteria of aesthetic excellence. This essentialist view is strongly

linked to Kant and the rise of Modernism. Recently, however, it
has been radically questioned by poststructuralism and feminist
thought. The very attempt to define art and the aesthetic is seen as
a case of 'closure'—in the sense noted earlier. For example, the
dominant tendency in essentialist aesthetics is that of formalism.
On this view, what defines art is its embodiment of balanced and
subtly harmonious formal qualities; what defines aesthetic experience is an elusive 'disinterested' attitude which must be taken up in
order to appreciate such qualities. According to poststructuralists
and feminists, however, this approach is profoundly inadequate. It
makes art and the aesthetic the prerogative of a privileged few
who have the time and 'sensitivity' to pursue them. Indeed, by
defining art and the aesthetic in terms of formal qualities and disinterestedness (respectively), the artefacts and experience of working-
class and non-European people, are by implication, degraded.
There are two aspects to this. The first is exclusion: such artefacts
and experiences are deemed 'commonplace' or of mere social or
tribal 'utility', and, thence, not worthy of the status of art or the
aesthetic. The other aspect (somewhat rarer) is that of colonization:
such artefacts and experiences are not taken on their own
terms—in the social context in which they were produced—but are
judged rather as configurations of form which can give rise to the
elusive 'disinterested' experience. In either case, here, the attempt
to define art and the aesthetic serves the interests and reinforces
the identity of white, middle-class patriarchy. This fact is not just
undesirable in ethical terms. It also invites more general sceptical
questioning. Why, for example, should formal qualities be invested
with so much prestige? Why is the pleasure derived from them
deemed to be 'higher' than other forms of pleasure? Given, indeed,
the individual's location within a society and ideology, can there
ever be a wholly detached and 'disinterested' way of appreciating
things? These sceptical questions have not been adequately dealt
with by essentialist aesthetics. Hence, poststructuralists and feminists have argued that aesthetics must be replaced by modes of critical discourse which address the socio-historical issues surrounding
the production and reception of art. This means, in effect, an
investigation of the varying conditions under which 'art' and the
'aesthetic' are (to use the relevant jargon) 'socially constructed'.

Contemporary aesthetics, then, involves a body of sceptical
critical discourse which exists in direct opposition to the more

traditional essentialist view. It is my contention that these view-points are both inadequate and unnecessarily polarized. Critical discourse theorists fail to comprehend the continuities—bound up with the fact of human embodiment—which underlie socio-histori-cal transformations; whilst the essentialists fail to deal with the ways in which aesthetic experience is modified by such transforma-tions. These shortcomings can be rectified by critically engaging with, and extending, the aesthetic theories of two philosophers. The first of these is Maurice Merleau-Ponty. In his later texts Merleau-Ponty attempts to articulate the complex relation which holds between the creative embodied individual being and the broader world. This, however, remains an incomplete project. One reason for this is Merleau-Ponty's untimely death in 1961. But the more fundamental reason is that the Sixties' fad for intellectual change—amplified by the 'revolutionary' impetus of May 1968—diverted creative attention to other fields, notably structuralism and the nascent poststructuralism. An opportunity was thus lost. For Merleau-Ponty's analyses of embodiment offer the basis of a foun-dational but flexible philosophy of perception and art, which avoids the sceptical reductionism of poststructuralist approaches, yet without falling into naïve philosophical realism. It sets out the basis of those continuities in human experience which underlie socio-historical transformation.

Now, just as Merleau-Ponty has been neglected, so the work of Kant—and in particular his *Critique of Judgement*—has been mis-understood. Most participants in the Modernism–Postmodernism debate acknowledge his project as Modernist *par excellence* in so far as it seeks to draw strict lines of demarcation between philo-sophical knowledge, scientific method, ethics, and aesthetic experi-ence. However, whilst the establishing of such divisions is admittedly central to Kant's project, there is a further dimension of complexity and comprehensiveness to it which has barely been understood. For the central task of the *Critique of Judgement* is to show that (whilst being a distinctive category in human experience) the aesthetic is also a unified *complex* of varieties, whose enjoy-ment is intimately linked to both theoretical reason and ethical freedom. The majority of commentators, however, have concen-trated on his arguments concerning the distinctiveness of aesthetic experience, rather than those concerning its complex varieties and the dimension of integrative comprehension. In particular, the real potential of his theory of art and his analysis of the sublime has hardly been touched upon. By developing the former, essentialist aesthetics can be modified so as to find a role for socio-historical transformations; and by developing the latter, some of the potentially disruptive complexities of postmodern culture can be articulated in a unified and positive way.

The chapters in this text, then, will expound and/or freely adapt ideas from Merleau-Ponty and Kant so as to provide the basis of a viable Critical Aesthetic. In so doing, they will offer a theoretical standpoint from where some of the antagonistic positions in the modern and postmodern culture debate can be overcome. Most of the chapters were originally written as self-contained essays and clearly retain this character. However, they have all been arranged and substantially modified so as to present my position in clear, logically progressing stages. Its overarching theme will be stated at the end of my Introduction.

In the most general structural terms, my text is organized as follows. In the Introduction I articulate the nature of postmodern experience through a critical appropriation of ideas from Walter Benjamin. In particular, I argue that contemporary sensibility is one which is orientated towards experiences of novelty and shock, which are the province of art and the sublime, respectively. Part One, accordingly, addresses the nature of art and the significance of our responses to it, whilst Part Two gravitates around the sublime and its relevance to postmodern culture. In Part Three I consider developments in contemporary art on the basis of ideas broached in previous sections. More specific chapter content is as follows.

Chapter 1 is a critique of Derrida's approach to language. The critique focuses on an extended reappraisal of the notion of *différance*, and stresses the continuity which exists between perception and our reading of symbolic formations. This continuity stabilizes presence and meaning, and is grounded on the reality of our existence as embodied subjects. The ideas from Merleau-Ponty which informs this chapter are given a more systematic and extensive development in Chapter 2. Here his account of the complex relation between perception and art is clarified, and placed in a broader context. Issues raised here receive further development in Chapter 3, which deals with Kant's theory of art. In particular, attention is paid to the subjective conditions of artistic creativity.

The objective dimension is then taken up in Chapter 4, by means of a critique of Benjamin and Adorno, on the basis of Kant's theory of art. The chapter seeks especially to clarify the relation between political effects, artistic merit, and aesthetic experience. It ends with an exposition of my notion of Critical Aesthetics, and its relation to Postmodernism. Chapter 5—Violence in Painting—draws on ideas broached throughout preceding chapters, so as to defend the aesthetic dimension of violent representation from reductionist feminist approaches.

Part Two commences with Chapter 6, where Burke's existential sublime is outlined, critically revised, and applied in relation to the socio-political aspects of postmodern experience. Chapter 7 presents the basic tenets of Kant's theory of the sublime. It rejects Thomas Weiskel's attempt to revise it on the basis of concepts from structural linguistics and psychoanalysis. An alternative revision—extending the approach taken in my book *The Kantian Sublime*—is proposed and defended against critics. Chapters 8 and 9 apply my revised version of Kant's theory as part of a critique of several aspects of Lyotard's hugely influential work on postmodern art and culture.

Part Three begins with Chapter 10. Here I address Arthur Danto's claim that in the postmodern era art has come to an end, through having exhausted its creative possibilities. The claim is then rejected on the basis of an alternative account of the relation between Modernism and Postmodernism which draws on ideas broached throughout this book. In Chapter 11 I investigate scepticism about artistic creativity based on Roland Barthes' notion of the text. The scepticism is appraised and rejected on the basis of a discussion of contemporary art. As a conclusion to this chapter and the book as a whole, I elaborate the notion of a Critical Aesthetics.

Contents

List of Plates

between pages 176 and 177

---

1. Malcolm Morley, *S.S. Amsterdam at Rotterdam*
   Reproduced by courtesy of the Saatchi Collection, London

2. Anselm Kiefer, *Die Meistersinger*
   Reproduced by courtesy of the Saatchi Collection, London

3. Julian Schnabel, *The Sea*
   Reproduced by courtesy of the Saatchi Collection, London

4. Peter Suchin, *With Yellow Cross*
   Reproduced by courtesy of the artist

5. Peter Suchin, *The Golden Code*
   Reproduced by courtesy of the artist

6. Thérèse Oulton, *Second Subject*
   Reproduced by courtesy of Marlborough Fine Art Ltd.

7. Thérèse Oulton, *Counterfoil*
   Reproduced by courtesy of Marlborough Fine Art Ltd.

Introduction

Experience and Mechanical Reproduction

> During long periods of history, the mode of human percep-
> tion changes with humanity's entire mode of existence. The
> manner in which human sense perception is organised, the
> medium in which it is accomplished, is determined not only
> by nature but by historical circumstances as well.[1]
>
> Walter Benjamin

It is often remarked how, in recent times, the general quality of
human experience has changed. One of the key factors in this
change is the impact of technology and, in particular, modes for
mechanically reproducing and transmitting information. In this
general introductory discussion I shall address these issues by
means of a philosophically informed exercise in social theory. The
philosophical dimension will gravitate around key arguments
broached in Walter Benjamin's study *Charles Baudelaire: A Lyric
Poet in the Era of High Capitalism*,[2] and from his essay 'The Work
of Art in the Era of Mechanical Reproduction'.[3] The choice of
Benjamin is apt for two main reasons. First (as the epigraph
shows), he has a profound and incisive awareness of the phenomenon which lies at the heart of the enquiry; and second, he uses
a theory of experience which foregrounds those features most

This Introduction is based on a series of lectures entitled 'The Philosophy of
Postmodern Experience' given during my tenure of a Visiting Fellowship at the
Centre for Research in Philosophy and Literature, Warwick University, in 1988. I
extend my thanks to all those who attended, and, in particular, to those whose
comments have influenced the present text.
[1] Walter Benjamin, 'The Work of Art in the Age of Mechanical Reproduction',
in *Illuminations*, trans. H. Zohn (Fontana–Collins, London, 1982), 219–53. This
ref., p. 224.
[2] Trans. H. Zohn (Verso, London, 1983).   [3] In *Illuminations*.

susceptible to transformation by mechanical reproduction and which pertain most directly to the *quality* of human life.

It must, however, be noted at the very outset that in this discussion I will not be offering a scholarly exegesis of the fine details of Benjamin's ideas; nor will I be considering their role in his literary criticism or in the more distinctive Marxist aspects of his thought. I will be concerned, rather, to extract, amplify, and criticize a central line of argument, so as to illuminate the more general problem of how experience has been transformed by techniques of mechanical production and reproduction. In section I, accordingly, I will extract the logical core of Benjamin's theory of experience and will buttress it with insights drawn from the work of Merleau-Ponty and with refinements of my own. In section II, I will consider how Benjamin historicizes this model in relation to pre-capitalist and modern industrial societies. In particular I shall emphasize and develop that relation, between mechanical reproduction and the decay of 'aura', which Benjamin sees as central to Modernism. In section III, drawing on more insights from Benjamin and also from Baudrillard (and, to a lesser extent, Lyotard), I shall outline the way in which techniques of mechanical reproduction arising in the modern epoch prove ultimately decisive for postmodern experience. I will further suggest that the decay of aura is compensated for by the development of a sensibility orientated towards shocks. In conclusion, I will briefly relate this to the project of Critical Aesthetics, and the strategy of this book as a whole.

I

For Benjamin, consciousness is a direct awareness of sensory stimuli. Its function is to prevent the self from being overwhelmed by the super abundance of stimuli that forever crowd in on it and which threaten debilitating shocks to the system. By intercepting these and preparing us for them, the shock effect is moderated. As Benjamin puts it, 'The more readily consciousness registers these shocks, the less likely they are to have a traumatic effect.'[4] At the heart of this cushioning effect is the relation between consciousness and 'voluntary memory'. For, if a stimulus is registered at a con-

---

[4] *Baudelaire*, 115.

scious level, it is rendered amenable to immediate and voluntary recall. Such registering, according to Benjamin, 'would lend the incident that occasions it the character of having been lived in the strict sense'.[5]

On these terms, in other words, the conscious registering of an event serves to schematize it and locate it within an immediately legible temporal continuum. We can recall it as such and such a thing which happened to us at such and such a time in our lives. It takes on the character of voluntarily retrievable fact or information. There is, however, another dimension to memory as well. This is because a great number of the stimuli and energies swarming through our perceptual field elude the net of consciousness. These form the domain of what Benjamin (following Proust) calls 'involuntary memory'. The defining feature of this mode is that it does not deal with schematic facts subject to immediate recall, but involves, rather, more indirect and profound senses of times, places, feelings, and situations, which are involuntarily triggered in response to items or events associated with those times, places, feelings, etc. The most familiar example of this form of memory in action is, of course, Proust's famous *madeleine*—a cake the taste of which evokes the author's childhood in Combray, with a fullness that the exercise of voluntary memory could not begin to attain. Involuntary memory serves, in other words, to represent personal experience with a degree of sensory richness and affective plenitude.

Given this analysis, one might say that 'involuntary memory' is the depth factor in human experience. This is not only because it involves a profound evocation of the past, but also because it impresses itself upon our present. This impression, i.e. 'the associations which, at home in the *mémoire involuntaire*, tend to cluster round the object of a perception',[6] is what Benjamin calls 'aura'. His more detailed articulations of this notion are, however, startingly cryptic. We are told, for example, that 'Experience of the aura . . . rests on the transposition of a response common in human relationships to the relationship between inanimate or natural object and man . . . To perceive the aura of an object means to invest it with the ability to look at us in return. This experience corresponds to the data of the *mémoire involuntaire*.'[7] Now, the

---

[5] Ibid.   [6] Ibid. 145.   [7] Ibid. 148.

idea that inanimate things have, in some sense, a capacity to return our gaze is a familiar motif in the theories of painters and poets. But isn't this all that there is to it? Isn't Benjamin cryptically elevating poetic insight to the level of philosophical truth? The answer is, of course, 'yes'; but this elevation does have a high degree of philosophical justification. To show this we must draw upon the work of Merleau-Ponty. In the essay 'Eye and Mind', for example, we are told that

Visible and mobile my body is a thing among things; it is caught in the fabric of the world and its cohesion is that of a thing. But because it moves itself and sees, it holds things in a circle around itself. Things are an annex or prolongation of itself; they are incrusted into its flesh, they are part of its full definition. The world is made of the same stuff as the body.[8]

Merleau-Ponty's point, then, is that in so far as we are embodied beings, things have an essential relation to us. We are of the same ontological order; we are 'of' them. Each perceived object occupies a position from which we too could in principle be seen. Our human mode of belonging to the world, in other words, involves a recognition of our affinity and reciprocity with things. When this intuition is most keenly felt, therefore, we might very aptly express it in terms of a sense that inanimate objects are returning our gaze. Now, of course, when this deep intuition of affinity and reciprocity informs our everyday perception, it is not generally registered at a conscious level. Rather, it echoes out from its foundations in childhood, where we first learn the palpability of things by exploring them and dwelling amongst them. This, of course, is the origin of some of the involuntary memory's most crucial data.

This set of associations, however, does not provide a complete explanation of Benjamin's notion of aura. Rather, he supplants it with these 'We define the aura . . . as the unique phenomenon of a distance, however close it might be. If, while resting on a summer afternoon, you follow with your eyes a mountain range on the horizon or a branch which casts its shadow over you, you experience the aura of those mountains, of that branch.'[9] The meaning of this passage hinges on how we interpret the phrase 'unique phe-

[8] Maurice Merleau-Ponty, 'Eye and Mind', *Aesthetics*, ed. Harold Osborne (Oxford University Press, Oxford, 1972), 58–9.
[9] *Illuminations*, 224–5.

nomenon of a distance'. I would suggest the following approach. When Benjamin uses the terms 'unique' or 'uniqueness' in relation to nature or human artefacts, he means the total fabric of an object's appearance and physical being—in other words, the quite particular way in which it fills out its own little portion of the spatio-temporal continuum. This could be said to involve a phenomenon of distance in two different senses. First, when we attend to those aspects and details which define an object's sensuous particularity, we are very much tied to the immediate experience of it. When the object is not present, we may be able to recollect or imagine salient aspects of our experience of its particularity, but much of the richness—the sensuous and affective depth of the direct experience—will be lost. This loss, of course, will tend to increase in proportion to the experience's recession into our past. With mundane, commonplace objects this will not matter. But with those whose sensuous particularity has engaged us in aesthetic or affective terms, it will be a matter of deep import. I am suggesting, in other words, that if we are attracted by the uniqueness of an object's presence, we are also distanced from it in the sense that the features which define its particularity are destined to slip gradually from the grasp of voluntary memory. We may attempt to combat this distancing effect by perpetually renewing our perceptual contact with the object, but this in itself bears witness to the potency of the distance. In perception, objects transcend us. In order to retain the experience of their unique presence, it is we who must move out to them. One might say, then, that distance features in the aura in so far as the object's presence attracts us but cannot be completely assimilated by voluntary memory.

The second way in which distance features in the aura is rather more straightforward. In relation to the artwork, Benjamin informs us that 'the existence of the work of art with reference to its aura is never entirely separated from its ritual function. In other words, the unique value of the "authentic" work of art has its basis in ritual, the location of its original use value.'[10] Benjamin's point, here, is that the artwork always retains some manifest sign of its function in relation to the original context of its production. This introduces a sense of overt cultural distance into our experiences of the work in so far as the revelation of this function will demand

---

[10] Ibid. 225–6.

interpretation, or (in the case where the function is familiar to us) because it embodies it in a medium, format, or style that differs from those which are customary in our own present culture. One can, of course, extend this notion of distance to artefacts in general. Buildings and monuments in foreign countries (or from our own or other cultures' pasts) can often have an aura of the strange and distant. Likewise nature, when it has been utilized in ways alien to our cultural present. One might even extend the point to 'raw' nature itself. For there are some cultural perspectives in which nature is distanced from us because it strikes us as not simply there, but as open to alternative interpretations of its 'meaning'. This, of course, is especially the case in times of competing rival cosmological schemes. Thus, the traveller in eighteenth-century Europe might be fascinated by the Alpine avalanche precisely because it is a site of mystery and questioning. Is it, for example, simply a sign of the Old Testament God's awesome wrath, or is it better understood as unfolding on the basis of Newtonian mechanics designed by a benevolent Creator? Could it be both?[11] (At this point the aura palpably thickens.)

I have argued, then, that Benjamin's notion of aura is complex (in fact, rather more complex than he himself realized). We should see it essentially as an interplay of three factors: our sense of promixity to and reciprocity with objects; unique presence and the scope of voluntary memory; and the distance which cultural perspective gives to the relation between experience and object.

Now the experience of aura is positive and gratifying, but how can we explain this? I would suggest as follows. Factor (*a*), our affinity and reciprocity with things, is an intuition which always informs and sustains our intercourse with the word, but is rarely experienced in itself. However, if encountered through the aura, it is felt as a profound sense of belonging—of secure immanence in a hospitable world. In the case of factor (*b*), namely the distance between the full immediacy of an object's presence and the scope of voluntary recall, we are moved in a different direction. Here we find that the human being cannot retrieve the richness of its immediate experience of the world by an act of will alone. If we did have some total recall capacity and could fully reinvoke past experience at will, we would be entirely different beings. But, of course,

[11] The origins of the experience of the sublime in relation to nature is clearly tied to the latter.

we are not like this. The immediacy of our experiences of the world fade with the passing of time. We can only enjoy such immediacy again if we ourselves are prepared to seek out a re-encounter with the object which provided it. Factor (*b*), in other words, involves the poignant combination of both a felt sense of the transience and mutability of experience and of our necessary transcendence towards the world. Factor (*c*) in the aura—namely a sense of distance arising from our cultural perspective—proves to be a special, indeed privileged, case of this latter tendency. For, unlike other animals, our transcendence towards the world is not simply aimed at modifying it so as to procure the means of subsistence and survival. It is also a transcendence towards the creation and/or discovery of meaning. Now, the fact that some artefact or object seems mysterious (and thence distant) according to our cultural perspective means that it can vividly signify the demand for understanding—our basic transcendence towards meaning itself.

Given all these points, then, one might claim that the experience of aura in its fullest (complex) sense is a kind of self-gratification of experience itself. It is an affective overflow or plenitude arising from a vague but felt response to those features which—in concert—are fundamental to human experience. The uniqueness and distance of the object evokes aura, in other words, because it awakens an echo of what is unique to our own species and its particular relation to the world. Hence, if the experience of aura is common and widespread in a society, we might say that it gives that society a general ambience of health and humanity. It signifies an accomplished quality of life.

II

The historicization of the foregoing theory of experience involves a mapping out of the key relations which hold between its various elements in different historical epochs. A useful starting-point here is Benjamin's own usage of the term 'experience'—a usage which is highly specialized. For example, we are told that

Where there is experience in the strict sense of the word, certain contents of the individual past combine with material of the collective past. The rituals with their ceremonies, their festivals . . . kept producing the amalgamation of [the] . . . two elements of memory over and over again. They

are triggered recollection at certain times and remained handles of memory
for a lifetime. In this way, voluntary and involuntary recollection lose their
mutual exclusiveness.[12]

Benjamin's point here is that in certain forms of society the individual fully identifies with its institutions and culture. His or her
whole hearted participation in collective as well as private existence shapes the very structure of personal experience. In a co-
operatively based society where the 'rat race' type of competition
does not occur, there is a relaxation of the degree of vigilance and
tense concentration which is necessary in order for consciousness
to adequately register and protect against threatening stimuli.
Indeed, in such a society, there will be fewer threatening stimuli
about. At the same time, however, because we identify our own
needs and interests so closely with those of other people (and with
the surrounding culture and environment), we will attend to stimuli with heightened care and receptivity. This attention, indeed,
will be focused by appropriate symbolic acts such as ceremonies
and festivals. Linking these points together, one might say that in a
co-operative society consciousness registers stimuli in a more
relaxed and receptive way. We can retrieve a rich sense of our personal past and history—and thus achieve a fully integrated and
whole notion of self—on the basis of voluntary acts. Unlike Proust,
in other words, we are not tied as closely to chance fragmentary
triggerings of recollection in order to comprehend the depth of our
own identity. Rather, this sense of depth is recovered at will. We
truly possess ourselves.

   Now, whilst it is an analysis on these lines which is implicit in
Benjamin's concept of experience, he does not historicize it in any
specific way. However, what he at least means in historical terms
is pointed towards by a certain convergence in the thought of
Schiller and Heidegger. In the work of both those thinkers, for
example, ancient Greek society has a quite special significance. For
Schiller, it embodies a state of being wherein the various human
intellectual capacities and sensuous inclinations are wholly integrated in a harmonious way. For Heidegger, the philosophies and
artefacts of pre-Socratic Greece embody a profound openness to
the Being of beings as such. (Indeed there are elements in his
thought which link this openness to the pattern of life in village or

---

[12] *Baudelaire*, 113.

peasant communities in general.) However, what makes the thought of Schiller and Heidegger so especially relevant here is that they see this fully integrated mode of human existence as being disrupted by the development of those specializations and techniques which are required in order for various human capacities—such as technology—to be developed to a full level of efficiency. What this means, in effect, is that fully integrated existence—'experience' in Benjamin's sense—should be understood as a somewhat idealized model of experience in pre-capitalist societies, and one which is transformed under specific historical conditions.

It is on the question of such transformations, of course, that Benjamin becomes much more specific. For it turns out that, for him, the rise of capitalist production and society brings about an 'atrophy of experience'. At the heart of this atrophy is the fact that life in modern industrial society is orientated fundamentally towards the containment of shock, rather than towards a receptiveness to stimuli and the experience of aura. The worker at the machine, for example, must drill or regiment his or her behaviour so as to accommodate the jolting rhythms of the conveyor belt, or whatever. Behaviour must likewise be regimented in relation to the environment of the big city. Negotiating city streets, for example, involves a permanent alertness to traffic and traffic signals. Such alertness is also required in order to deal with buffeting by city crowds, and to find a way through them. It is also required in order to process the competing media images and messages which bombard us on all sides. For these do not solicit our attention as narratives which embody the experience of the person who produced them. Rather, they assault us as so many fragmented and conflicting items of information which, more often than not, are designed to induce specific sorts of responses in us. On these terms, then, whereas in the best pre-capitalist societies consciousness is generally receptive to stimuli, in capitalism it is assaulted, and has to selectively register and schematize in the face of a fragmented and fragmenting bombardment. Now, according to Benjamin, advanced means of mechanical reproduction also bring about a 'decay' of the aura. This claim can be explained as follows. First, in a modern industrial society, the dominant mode of orientation towards the world is appropriative. Reality is construed fundamentally as a network of resources or data with a use-value determined by human interests. Now, at first sight photography and film appear to have an ambiguous relation to this appropriative drive, in so far as whilst they provide images which are of immense use-value, they also seem to embody a more detached yet personal vision of things. We can, as it were, stand back and view the world, in a way which enables us to select and preserve those aspects of things and events which are of great significance to us. However, the decisive point here is that this detached and personal selection from the continuum of the phenomenal world can be achieved immediately by mechanical means, rather than by the painstaking effort and experience which is demanded, say, by painting or sculpture. This means that our detached personal vision is not won through a continuing interchange with the world at a level of affinity and reciprocity with it. Rather, it is an out-and-out mode of direct appropriation.

I am suggesting, in other words, that, far from being divergent with the basic appropriate drive of modern industrial society, photographic images consolidate and extend this drive. They corrode that aspect of the aura which involves a sense of affinity and reciprocity with things. This corrosion, of course, is also manifest in relation to that sense of distance between us and the world which is due to the fact that the immediate experience of an object's unique presence eludes the scope of voluntary recall. For, as Benjamin points out, 'The perpetual readiness of volitional discursive memory [is] encouraged by the techniques of mechanical reproduction.'[13] Indeed, with the advent of photography, 'The touch of a finger now sufficed to fix an event for an unlimited period of time.'[14] The point is then, that in the modern epoch it becomes possible to extend voluntary recall by mechanical means so as to preserve something of the immediacy of our experience of sensible objects. Surfaces and fragments of the past are now immediately and permanently retrievable. We know in advance that the flow of stimuli and moments can be arrested and frozen for retrieval at our convenience. This means, of course, that our sense of the world's transcendence, and the uniqueness of the passing moment, are diminished. Something fundamental about the finitude of human experience itself begins to change.

The final way in which modern society brings about a decay of the aura is in relation to the phenomenon of cultural distance. For

---

[13] *Baudelaire*, 146.   [14] Ibid. 132.

example, techniques of mechanical reproduction constitute a substantial attack on the uniqueness of the items they reproduce. Such items no longer occupy their own portion of the spatio-temporal continuum in a wholly secure manner. Rather, those fundamental aspects of their appearance which admit of reproduction are at the disposal of the viewer. He or she can engage with them in such places or at such times as he or she deems convenient. This domestication means that the reproduced item's alien identity—its salient demand for interpretation—is neutralized through immersion in its new surroundings. Indeed, techniques of mechanical reproduction also facilitate a quantitative shift in our relation to culturally alien artefacts or environments. Because we seek so many of these through photographs in books, or magazines, or whatever, our sense of acute difference is diminished. We see, indeed actively search out, points of contact—shared universal characteristics which hold between the products of different cultures. Thus, one might suggest that it is no accident that the rise of formalist attempts to define art transculturally on the basis of purely aesthetic qualities coincides with the accelerated availability of photographic reproductions in the late nineteenth century.

Following Benjamin, then, I would hold that in the era of modern industrial society, 'technology has subjected the human sensorium to a complex kind of training'.[15] Specifically, experience in a modern society is orientated fundamentally towards the containment of shocks arising from an abundance of adverse stimuli in the industrial work process and big-city environment. Techniques of mechanical reproduction facilitate this containment through extending the scope of voluntary recall, but this too has its negative effect in so far as it brings about a decay of the aura.

We are now in a position to make the transition towards an understanding of the salient aspects of experience in the postmodern epoch. The basis of this experience, as I shall now argue, consists in an amplification of the effects of mechanical reproduction, together with a reaction against the decay of the aura.

III

Perhaps the pre-eminent feature of Western society since the late 1950s is the huge quantity of information made available by

[15] *Illuminations*, 224.

mass-media of communication—especially television. This not only means that we are bombarded with greater quantities of information, but also that these are thrust upon us more immediately and efficiently. Indeed, that technology which facilitates this optimal transmission itself begins to shape the content of such transmissions. 'Hi-tech' is invested with glamour and high social status for those who are shown to possess it. At the same time, the way in which human consciousness and actions, and social interactions, are interpreted is increasingly founded on models, statistical norms, and stereotypes, derived from technology, cybernetic, and 'communication' theory. A whole culture of 'input', 'feedback', and 'participation' develops in such a way that, as Baudrillard puts it, in relation to 'the response of the polled to the poll-takers, the native to the ethnologist, the analysed to the analyst, you can be sure that . . . circularity is total: the ones questioned always pretend to be as the question imagines and solicits them to be'.[16] Even objective events reported in newscasts often seem geared in themselves towards media presentation or, at least, strike us simply in terms of being 'media events'. As Baudrillard again observes, 'all hold-ups, hi-jacks and the like are now as it were simulation hold-ups, in the sense that they are inscribed in advance in the decoding and orchestration rituals of the media, anticipated in their mode of presentation and possible consequences. In brief . . . [they] function as a set of signs dedicated exclusively to their recurrence as signs, and no longer to their "real" goal at all.'[17] On these terms, experience becomes 'hyperreal': in other words, reality and signs or simulacra of reality are fused in an indistinguishable mass. Our criterion of the 'real' is reduced to operational efficiency—such as matching up with some statistical norm, or stereotype, or model; or being processable into computer data or some structure of media discourse.

Now, this hyperreal implosion of the real and its simulacra—this merging of medium and message—brings about a narrowing of experiential possibilities. In this respect, Baudrillard notes that 'Every image, every media message, but also any functional environmental object, is a test—that is to say, in the full rigour of the term, liberating response mechanisms according to stereotypes and

[16] Jean Baudrillard, *Simulations*, trans. P. Foss, P. Patton, and P. Beitchman, semiotext (New York, 1983), 130.
[17] Ibid. 41.

analytic models'.[18] This tendency to consumer-conformity, however, must be located in relation to another effect of the hi-tech transmission of information which Baudrillard somewhat underplays. This consists in what—following Jean-François Lyotard—one might call 'immaterialization' (a notion which I will address in detail in Chapter 9). Hi-tech increases the volume and vividness of information at such a rate that existing categories and classifications rapidly immaterialize into overlapping and shifting complexes. Consider, for example, how complex so concrete and familiar a notion as 'the body' is now becoming under the impact of our new awareness of sexual difference, genetic engineering and dietetics, and in the face of such direct interventions as life-support machines, organ transplants, and the possibility of cryogenic resuscitation. Likewise, in the socio-political sphere, traditional notions such as class and political party are resolving into rapidly changing and diverse groupings with no overarching sense of fixed identity or ideology to stabilize them.

All in all, then, one might say that postmodern experience is being pulled in two different directions. On the one hand, the mingling of medium and message—the advent of the hyperreal in Baudrillard's sense—involves an increasing conformity of experience to models and stereotypes determined by technoscientific interests; yet, on the other hand, this technoscientific thrust brings about a profusion of such models and stereotypes—each rapidly receding into obsolescence as new forms are produced and reproduced. One might say, therefore, that postmodern experience hinges not just on conformity, but on manic conformity.

Let me now consider these developments in relation to the model of experience outlined earlier. First, given the widespread, domestic availability of techniques of mechanical reproduction, it is clear that facts about one's past and about the world in general are now made enormously retrievable. The scope of voluntary recall, in other words, is augmented to an unprecedented degree. However, the question of what is recalled here is somewhat complex. The data yielded by television and video pictures, for example, may have a quasi-corporeal character, but it is only a partial one, holding at the level of audio-visual surface alone. The traces yielded by mechanical reproduction, then, constitute simulacra of

---

[18] Ibid. 120.

stimuli combining both schematic and corporeal elements. Now, increasingly, these simulacra are providing the contents of experience itself—either through being used in productive processes, or through their provision of images to occupy our leisure time. (One only has to think here of the amount of time spent watching television.) Indeed, even those human interactions which are not explicitly mediated by simulacra are, as noted earlier, increasingly organized or interpreted on the basis of models and stereotypes drawn from such simulacra. This means that techniques which augment voluntary recall are now determining what is recalled. In other words, a substantial proportion of the contents of memory are themselves founded on simulacra.

To clarify one of the major changes at stake here, one might make the following contrast. In pre-capitalist social formations, the individual deals with other persons and institutions at a level of direct acquaintance and participation. He or she, indeed, closely identifies personal interests with those of the community at large. For such a person the self as a quite definite sense of unity in terms of *meaning*. The past and the domain of the other are both felt to be organically connected with the present experience of the individual. One feels oneself to be an active participant in an ongoing process of collective struggle and realization. One's choices and deeds, in other words, are meaningful beyond the immediate personal present. They are inscribed with a sense of effective history. They become a narrative of reciprocity—a free, balanced interchange between self, other, and world. In the postmodern era, however, one's sense of self is very different, in so far as experience is fundamentally that of a consumer related to others and institutions on the basis of norms and stereotypes. Indeed, the content of one's experience is as much an interaction with simulacra as it is with real people. This issues in two predominating models of the self. The first involves the character of an episodic sequence of exchange transactions and events—a mere chronology. One's past consists, in effect, of decayed self-contained presents, each perhaps of some value but with no real significance in relation to the rest, or to the immediate present. The true model of the self here is that of the photo-album—a chronologically arranged sequence of posed fragments. This illustrates the negative dimension of the relation between mechanical reproduction and voluntary recall. For, whilst the former indeed augments the latter, what is recalled is a mere fragment stripped of its immediate experiential roots and bonds.

The other model of the self hinges upon a narrative of the simulacrum. One organizes one's life on the basis of 'career goals'— dividing it up into stages of transition and advancement etc. The availability of media information means that one's life can be shaped and directed as though it were an artefact. One manipulates one's experience in order to make it match up with prevailing norms and stereotypes. One's criterion of meaning in life becomes quantitative—that is, the degree of success in realizing norms and stereotypes of success. At the heart of this experience is a paradox. For it brings about a felt division of subject and world, in so far as the world is reduced to the arena of one's projects. Yet this division arises from the largely unrecognized colonization of the self by norms and stereotypes prevailing in the world. All in all, then, in the postmodern epoch the self tends to be structured as a episodic chronology, or as a narrative of the simulacrum.

Now, as one might expect, in relation to the question of aura, postmodern experience accelerates and amplifies its decay, in so far as our affinity and reciprocity with things and the distance between them and our powers of voluntary recall and interpretation are further narrowed by the ubiquity of mechanical reproductions. However, one must also note the development of a crucial response to this decay. In order to understand its ramifications, let us return to some critical issues raised by Benjamin's analysis of Modernism and the shock experience. (I shall follow him by interpreting 'shock' in very broad terms as any kind of affective jolt.) These issues converge on his approach to work processes in capitalist society. We are told, for example, that 'The shock experience which the passer-by has in the crowd corresponds to what the worker experiences at the machine'.[19] Benjamin also likens the work experience to the shocks experienced by the gambler at the gaming table, or to the jolts received in the dodgems at the funfair. Indeed, he even goes so far as to say that 'In a film, perception in the form of shocks was established as a formal principle. That which determines the rhythm of production on a conveyor belt is the basis of the rhythm of reception in a film.'[20]

Now, the reason why Benjamin can viably link the experience of

---

[19] *Baudelaire*, 134.   [20] Ibid. 132.

the man in the crowd to that of the worker at the machine is because both involve a drilling and regimentation of behaviour. By adapting themselves to the jolts of the crowd or the machine they are able to parry shocks. Benjamin's linking of the worker's experience to that of gambling, or dodgem rides, or the reception of film, in contrast, is much more problematic. For these latter cases do not—as in the work process—embody a preparedness to parry shocks, but rather an active solicitation of shock effects. The nearest Benjamin comes to acknowledging this is in his remark that film answers 'an urgent need for stimuli'. However, he also says that

The film is the artform that is in keeping with the increased threat to his life which modern man has to face. Man's need to expose himself to shock effects is his adjustment to the dangers threatening him. The film corresponds to profound changes in the apperceptive apparatus—changes that are experienced on an individual scale by the man in the street in big-city traffic, on a historical scale by every present day citizen.[21]

Hence, whilst Benjamin here acknowledges that the experience of film involves a receptivity to shocks, it turns out that this is to be understood as a forearming—a kind of getting in practice for dealing with the actual dangers of modern life. It is, in other words, a propaedeutic for coping with *real* shocks.

Now, Benjamin's whole line of reasoning in these areas is clearly meant to assign a primacy to the economic infrastructure of society. The shock-parrying dimension of the actual work process of capitalist production determines or is repeated indirectly at the superstructural level—as, for example, in the experience of film. This exemplification of Marxist orthodoxy, however, hinges on claims which are open to question. For one might argue that the receptivity to shock embodied in film, gambling, or the dodgem ride, or whatever, is not an indirect mode of parrying shocks echoing the work process, but is, in fact, a direct oppositional response to the process. The reason for this is that the drudgery and regimented work patterns of a society founded on the division of labour involve a profound suppression of stimuli. Hence, shock experiences are sought out both to compensate for the monotony of the work process itself, and to compensate for the general impoverishment of being that is involved in the decay of the aura.

---

[21] *Illuminations*, 252.

One can already see the origins of this response in both the growth of the music hall and vaudeville variety bills in the late nineteenth and early twentieth century, and in the growth of a popular press. Here we find a juxtaposition of incongruous acts or items of information whose very juxtaposition brings the surprise of the unexpected in addition to their intrinsic entertainment value. Now, whilst such phenomena as these originate in the modern industrial epoch, they cannot be regarded as definitive features of it. This is because (a fact unnoticed by Benjamin) the modern epoch retained substantial vestiges of experience and aura in a restricted context. In working-class communities, for example, shared economic hardship engendered an ethos of mutual aid and responsibility, and a characteristic culture of participation—as exemplified in working men's clubs, sports teams, brass bands, and the like. Hence, even if the work process and general urban life were orientated towards the parrying of shocks, in leisure hours at least there remained room for 'experience' and 'aura' in something like Benjamin's sense of those terms. Since the Second World War, and with the rise of postmodern consumer society, however, such communities have been in decline. The clubs and local football teams remain, but the ethos has gone, and hours of leisure are now organized fundamentally around media images and information. This engenders a kind of culture or sensibility of shock which is definitive of postmodern experience. But why should shocks be enjoyable? How can they compensate for the decay of aura? To answer this, we must now analyse in turn three broad patterns of shock response.

The first pattern of shock-response to be considered pertains to the phenomenon of aura itself. For, whilst in modern and postmodern times it has undergone widespread and accelerating decay, this has not been a blanket phenomenon. Rather there are certain contexts where it has survived—in a concentrated form, even. The best example is the extraordinary boom undergone by the art market and gallery system since the late 1950s. Original works now command unparalleled prices, major galleries draw increasingly large attendances even for mediocre exhibitions. At the heart of this lies an astonishing practical reversal of Benjamin's logic. For it is precisely because we are so accustomed to reproductions of visual artworks that our encounter with an original takes on the shock-value of a privileged experience. Indeed, it may well be that through being reproduced in such quantities, the unique presence of the original undergoes what Gadamer calls 'an increase of being': in other words, the existence of multiple reproductions signify and expand the existential potency and aura of the original. Indeed, those aspects of nature which have *not* been appropriated, signposted, and packaged as 'tourist resources' perhaps retain some aura precisely because their survival as pure nature is so unexpected. Ironically, Benjamin himself tacitly acknowledges these counter-examples to his main thrust of argument, in a quite memorable remark. We are told that 'the sight of immediate reality has become an orchid in the land of technology'.[22] Exactly: we prize the orchid of an immediate original reality—be it a painting, a musical performance, or a landscape—precisely because it is out of the ordinary. Its aura is preserved and enhanced through the shock-value of the unusual. (I shall address the relation between art and originality in Chapters 3, 4, and 5 of this book.)

The second broad patter of shock-response is bound up with the thrills and surprises of such things as adventure films, television quiz shows, sport, and the like; and from the sensational events— scandals, riots, warfare, disasters, etc.—which are reported in the various news media. In relation to our responses to these, Edmund Burke's theory of the sublime proves instructive, and I will discuss it at length in Chapter 6. Before that, it is worth briefly pointing out Burke's claim—namely that just as labour is requisite in order to keep the 'grosser' parts of the body healthy, so too is stimulation required for those 'finer parts' upon which the mental powers act. This arises when we experience mild pain or shock in contexts where the objects giving rise to these feeling do not immediately threaten us. In such contexts, shock acts as a stimulant to the working of the mental powers, and takes on the character of delight.

The third broad pattern of shock-response endemic in postmodern society is structurally more complex. It arises from the sense of bewildering and awesome complexity and infinite developmental possibility that characterizes hi-tech itself. In this respect, it will be recalled that earlier on I spoke of the 'immaterialization' of reality—the way in which familiar surfaces and categories of experience are broken up into webs of astonishing complexity under the impact of hi-tech's profusion of data. The shock of this experience

---

[22] *Illuminations*, 235.

can, however, be of positive significance. An important clue here is provided by Kant's theory of the mathematical sublime. For Kant, this involves some perceptually or imaginatively overwhelming aspect of the phenomenal world making vivid the superiority of our rational being. This occurs because no matter how overwhelming an object may seem from the point of view of our perceptual and imaginative capacities, it can always be comprehended *as* a totality in rational terms. In Chapters 7 to 9 I shall outline this theory in great detail, and trace its relevance to the postmodern context.

Let me now summarize the arguments of this section. (1) In postmodern times, techniques of mechanical reproduction (exemplified by the mass-media) have increasingly shaped human experience. (2) This brings about increasing conformity to models, statistical norms, and stereotypes, derived from technoscience. (3) At the same time, these models and stereotypes succeed each other rapidly in so far as existing categories and classifications are immaterialized by the profusion of new data brought to bear on them. (4) Given these phenomena, the distinction between schematic and corporeal memory is blurred. Our experience is reduced fundamentally to that of a consumer, and our sense of self becomes a chronology of largely self-contained private episodes or a narrative of the simulacrum. (5) The general decay of aura is accelerated but is compensated for by the development of a postmodern sensibility orientated towards shocks.

Now the question arises as to how we should more generally describe such a sensibility. Is it alienated, or is it a stage in the general evolution of the species? The basic thrust of Benjamin's insights is towards the former interpretation. Modern life involves an atrophy of experience, and (quite clearly) postmodern sensibility is a continuation of this. However, matters are rather more complex than Benjamin's (or a Benjamin-type) position would suggest. In the first place, we will recall that Benjamin's notion of experience is, in effect, an idealized evocation of life in a pre-capitalist society. This means that it will not come again. Now, of course, as a Marxist, Benjamin could claim that in a classless society where the division of labour is abolished, experience in something like its pre-capitalist mode will be restored. However, in Benjamin's account the sources of alienation are traced not so much to social relations and ideology, but rather to the large-scale effects of technology on the human sensorium. Now, if this account is correct, we might expect the problem to be exacerbated rather than diminished in a classless society. The reason for this is that if the means of subsistence are to be efficiently obtained and equitably distributed on a local and international basis, we can expect the sphere of technology to be expanded accordingly. The individual sensorium, in other words, is likely to become more subject to the effects of mechanical reproduction. Given this, it seems that modern and postmodern experience are either irredeemably alienated, or (if we want to put as brave a face on it as possible) have evolved to a new complex and problematic stage.

There is, however, another consideration to be taken account of. Earlier I argued that contemporary experience has responded to the decay of aura. Such a sensibility is orientated towards affective jolts or shocks from three sources. These are through a continuing interest in art, through an orientation towards Burke's existential sublime, and through an orientation towards the Kantian sublime. Now the question is, are these, as it were, simply cheap thrills—the characteristic pleasures of a passive consumer sensibility—or are they in some way redemptive? In my Preface it was suggested that a Critical Aesthetics derived from Merleau-Ponty and Kant would be able to reconcile contemporary, antagonistic viewpoints concerning art and sensibility. I can now go further. A Critical Aesthetics is one which articulates all aspects of aesthetic experience as an interplay between constants in subjectivity (bound up with embodiment), and historical transformation. It construes art and the aesthetic as modes of *synthesis*—in the sense of actively bringing together different capacities, in relation to different sets of objects. The relation of subject to object in such experience is not one of passive contemplation. Rather, we are bonded to the world and other people in a way which draws on all aspects of our embodied historical existence. The experience is integrative. Even if there has been a general decline in the quality of life, art and the aesthetic can restore it to a substantial degree.

The task which this work addresses, then, is the justification of postmodern sensibility on the basis of a Critical Aesthetics. To reiterate and clarify my general strategy (as outlined in the Preface): Part One will proceed from an affirmation of embodiment to an investigation of the art-object, its relational context, and the positive nature of our responses to it. Part Two will address the aesthetics of the sublime and the (rather more ambiguous) question of its positive aspects. In Part Three, I will address contemporary art on the basis of the foregoing material, and, at the end of my final chapter, will draw together and expand themes explored throughout the work. Critical Aesthetics will be shown to have a key role to play. For, through their experiences of art and the sublime, many people enjoy heightened and redemptive states—but without knowing why. If, therefore, what is felt intuitively can be articulated on an adequate theoretical basis (i.e. become an object of knowledge as well as feeling), our hold on the world is strengthened accordingly.

To commence this task, I shall, in Chapter 1, criticize a mode of poststructuralist scepticism which might otherwise call a project such as mine into question at the outset. The critique will take the form of an argument which establishes the primacy of embodiment.

Part One

1

From *Différance* to Embodiment

Subjectivity and Symbolic Formations

At the heart of many recent debates in intellectual circles has been a scepticism concerning the fixity of categories, meaning, and notions of the self. Much of this scepticism stems from a relatively unthinking acceptance of the work of Derrida. In this opening chapter I will subject Derrida's basic philosophical position to critical scrutiny on the basis of ideas derived very loosely from Merleau-Ponty. Section I will expound the essentials of this position by fixing on the key notion of *différance*. In section II I shall indicate a basic flaw in Derrida's position, and will offer an alternative account which grounds *différance* in our embodied relation to the world. Specifically, I will show that presence in perception, and meaning in symbolic formations, are stabilized by reference to embodiment. On the basis of this account I shall go on in section III to offer a decisive critique of Derrida's theory. Finally, in section IV, I shall extend my approach further by briefly but explicitly drawing on ideas from Merleau-Ponty's late work.

I

Let us commence with Derrida's attack on the 'metaphysics of presence'. Derrida—in common with practitioners of post-Wittgensteinian Analytic philosophy—is hostile to the view that when we speak what we are doing is transposing some contained unit or sequence of thoughts into a publicly accessible idiom. In terms of this prejudice, writing is simply a debased form of such a transposition, in so far as it strives to repeat that perfect congruence of signified and signifier already attained at the level of speech. In the absence of the utterer, this inscribed echo of speech relations is doomed to ambiguity and the need for complex apparatuses of interpretation. Derrida, however, rejects this view wholesale. For him the relation of thought or representation to its mode of utterance or referent cannot be one of perfect congruence, i.e. 'self-presence' or direct correspondence. This is because all language—spoken or written—is a function of complex differential relations. As he puts it:

The play of differences supposes, in effect, syntheses and referrals which forbid at any moment, or in any sense, that a simple element be *present* in and of itself, referring only to itself. Whether in the order of spoken or written discourse, no element can function as a sign without referring to another element which is not simply present . . . Nothing, neither among the elements nor within the system, is anywhere ever simply present or absent. There are only, everywhere, differences and traces of traces.[1]

For Derrida, then, any utterance or inscription is only possible in so far as it ambiguously defines itself within an inexhaustible network of other utterances and inscriptions. The congruence of language—spoken or written—with the world, therefore, is not an exact correspondence of presence to presence. It is shifting and elliptical in so far as any particular instance of a semantic relation bears the trace of an infinite number of other semantic relations from whose inexhaustibility it emerges. This network of deferral and difference (i.e. différance) is not just a neutral background. For it will exert various pressures on individual instances or individual types of linguistic formulation. Consider, for example, the case of philosophy. The dominant 'logocentric' orientation of this discipline strives to attain a purified form wherein its propositions and arguments will adequately correspond or cohere with ultimate general facts about how the world is. This discourse of 'pure reason', however, is, for Derrida, contaminated. Its texts are amenable to deconstruction, in so far as at key points in their striving for absolute objectivity they ingest and manifest precisely those more playful and metaphorical uses of language which they seek to exclude. Much of Derrida's deconstructive work is concerned with the mapping out of just these intersections in particular philsophical texts. The upshot of this project is that there is no autonomous discourse of philosophy wherein a perfect adequation of language, and how the world is, will be achieved. More generally, any attempt to secure some specific form of meaning from meanings

---

[1] Jacques Derrida, *Positions*, trans. Alan Bass (Athlone Press, London, 1981), 26.

which are ostensibly excluded by it will not succeed to any absolute degree. The closure of a concept will always be somewhat arbitrary.

Now, if language is shaped by the play of *différance* which sustains its particular formulations, *différance* must also shape self-consciousness. This is because self-consciousness cannot be conceived of as independent of language. Derrida remarks that

. . . the a of *différance* also recalls that spacing is temporization, the detour and postponement by means of which intuition, perception, consummation—in a word, the relationship to the present, the reference to a present, the reference to a present reality, to a being are always *deferred*. Deferred by virtue of the very principle of difference which holds that an element functions and signifies, takes on or conveys meaning, only by referring to another past or future element in an economy of traces.[2]

On these terms, consciousness cannot be present to itself or to its objects in any kind of perfect congruence. Self-consciousness is not self-presence. It is rather distributed somewhere in and between the field of language and other sign-systems, with which we engage with the world. My use of the spatial metaphors 'somewhere', 'between', and 'field' here is symptomatic of both our inability to articulate the self in purely abstract philosophical terms and, also, how unamenable the self is to our common-sense way of thinking about it—as some underlying substance in which our different moments of consciousness inhere.

There is perhaps a single insight at the heart of Derrida's notion of *différance*. It is the fact that the network of signifying units and relations from which any state of consciousness emerges is not an enclosed system. It is shifting, opaque, and semantically inexhaustible. Hence, any element within the network will not be positioned absolutely. Meanings will, as it were, flicker, rather than function as 'solid' presences defined within a fully determined totality.

II

First, let me note what is of real worth in Derrida's account of *différance*. This consists in the fact that, after it, there can be no

___

[2] Ibid. 28–9.

naïve notion of presence in the province of either language or consciousness. Any meaningful item in experience can only be recognized as meaningful in so far as it is mediated by at least tacit reference to other such items. That is to say, our thoughts, utterances, and writings are only intelligible in the context of something like Derrida's *différance*. However, the qualifying clause here is crucial. For Derrida's *différance* is not as rigorous a notion as it seems. The reason for this is his privileging of linguistic *différance*. In this respect, we are entitled to ask, 'How is language itself possible?' Of course, given the fact that consciousness is a function of language, it might seem that such a question does not admit of any answer. After all, we cannot step outside language to give a reply. However, whilst language is a necessary condition of consciousness, it is not a sufficient one; indeed, whilst *différance* is a necessary condition of language, it is not a sufficient one. The extra dimension which has to be considered in both these cases is that of physical embodiment. Without the tongue, throat, and brain, there is neither consciousness nor language. Indeed, consciousness and language do not simply spring from these organs. They are a function of the socially mediated growth of the body's total hold upon the world. If the full ramifications of language's origins in embodiment are considered, the shortcomings of Derrida's approach will begin to emerge.

Let us, then, consider the two vectors of *différance*, namely difference and deferral. The child learns difference before it learns language in so far as, in its protocognitive and motor activities, it divides the world into a foreground of items accessible or amenable to inspection, manipulation, and consumption, and a background of items which are inaccessible, or access to which entails bodily exertion. It is, of course, this learned dimension of sensory fulfilment, and bodily effort as the means to such fulfilment, which enables the child to learn spatialization and temporalization, in all, 'deferral' in its most basic sense. Before the child can speak, therefore, the co-ordination of its sensory-motor capacities into a unified field serves to articulate a proto-world. Things are concretely present as items for inspection or consumption, but they have this character only in so far as they emerge from a background determined by the scope of the body's developing co-ordination. Language grows from this matrix of achieved co-ordination, at once articulating it and rendering it more complex and abstract. The child, in other words, learns a language only because it has already learned the vectors of *différance* through its achieved co-ordination with a world of things. This means that we must posit a kind of *archédifférance* on the basis of presence as bodily accomplishment.

Now, this *archédifférance* is not only a function of the body's relation to its immediate object of perception and the surrounding field. It is enriched and articulated by what I shall call *latent existential space*. Every perceptible item is located within a schema of possible positions which the body might take up in relation to it. This schema is further refined through the acquisition of language. Most significantly, the subject learns to accommodate the fact that the physical space it inhabits is shared by beings with competences and interests similar to its own. This sense of shared physical and existential space goes hand-in-hand with initiation into a social world of values and conventions. Hence, the immediate object of perception is one charged with meaning. Its presence focuses possibilities of action that are at once of personal and more general social significance for the particular embodied subject.

On these terms, then, *archédifférance* comprises the perceived object's relation to the immediate field and also a latent existential space continuous with it. For the adult, the field of *archédifférance* gravitates around *body-hold*. By this term I mean those possibilities presented by the individual's awareness of both his or her body's relation to the world and also the scope and significance of embodied action in general. It is by reference to body-hold that terms present to perception are defined and given meaning.

Similar considerations hold in relation to our engagement with symbolic formations—those artefacts such as written texts or modes of visual representation which are created for purposes of communication. Of course, to *read* (using that term globally) such a formation can, in psychological terms, be discontinuous with immediate experience to the degree that the semantic space which it opens up engrosses us. However, in other respects, reading is continuous with the immediate. The act of reading itself, for example, is an integral part of our present. Poststructuralists such as Derrida and Barthes radically underplay the significance of this bodily act. For it is not simply a causal interaction with a physical object. Rather, to decipher the basic convention of reference which determines a symbolic formation (i.e. to read it as a specific configuration within a specific semantic–syntactic code) is to recognize what kind of state of affairs the formation is positing. Of course, symbolic formations always have dimensions of meaning which are unstable, and a function of the particular formation's historical circumstances of production and reception. (It is this level, indeed, which has been made so much of by Derrida and Barthes, especially in the latter's notions of 'text' and *signifiance* which I shall discuss in the final chapter of this work). But before a formation can be interpreted on the basis of such circumstances, it must be intelligible at a more universal level. It must be read as referring to determinate *kinds* of phenomena, concepts, or sets of relations. This basic level of meaning—let us call it the *proto-symbolic*, or, in visual representation, the *proto-iconographic* (to be discussed in chapter 5)—is presupposed by any more specific act of interpretation. Now, to read a formation at the proto-symbolic level is not simply some cognitive act. It is to posit in the broadest sense possibilities of action for embodied subjects; or sets of circumstances which are relevant to such actions; or more general relations which explain or condition the two preceding features. Formations such as works of fiction, for example, will be orientated towards the significance of possibilities of action. Others, such as landscape painting, will address contexts relevant to such actions. Others still, such as philosophical works or scientific texts, consider conditions governing the broader world in which humanity is situated. Some formations, indeed, can combine all the features just referred to—for example, religious narratives.

This positing of the proto-symbolic through the very act of reading is a direct continuation of what I earlier termed latent existential space. Indeed, the proto-symbolic is a fundamental level of meaning which constellates around and is stabilized by body-hold. To recognize such a content is at the same time to be existentially positioned in relation to it. In reading Celan's *Todtnauberg*, for example, we find a way of articulating experience which—even if we do not know the circumstances under which the poem was written or the personal significance to Celan of particular words—still engages our interest. The narrative line juxtaposes imagery shot through with both private and collective hopes. Celan's melancholy has determinate origins in both the tragedy of his past and his fateful encounter with Heidegger. But, made into a poem, these origins declare a more universal human significance. For it is open to any embodied subject to find an analogy or focus for private grief in the contours of the landscape. This dimension of general significance even encompasses some of the most overtly biographical material in the poem. Consider the following stanza

> the line
> —whose name did the book
> register before mine?—
> in that book about
> a hope, today
> for a thinking man's
> coming
> word
> in the heart.[3]

Here, in effect, the poet locates himself in relation to tradition viewed as a passage to hope and personal redemption. Of course, the book in question is simply Heidegger's famous visitors' book. Hence, a biographical fact is recorded. But, in recording it, Celan betrays the general possibilities of the incident. His particular inscription is part of a continuity of inscription—the project of finding truth and redemption through writing.

This leads us to the decisive point. Every particular event or situation in the life of an embodied subject is imbued with a more general significance which the subject may not recognize. If such a person later undergoes similar experiences in similar or (even) different contexts, his or her response will be shaped by these earlier experiences. An overt knowledge of them may even clarify and enrich the current situation. Likewise for the observer of that embodied subject. Even though we may only encounter such experiences or events through their being posited in a symbolic formation and even though there may be much about them which is culturally alien, yet there is still something in them *for us*. They will present likenesses of context, strategy, and response to those available in our own personal and social circumstances. Indeed, whilst the general significance of embodied actions is usually overlooked in a causally direct encounter, the positing of them (or contexts for them) in a symbolic formation foregrounds this general significance. For once ideas and experiences have been made into an

---

[3] In *Poems of Paul Celan*, trans. Michael Hamburger (Anvil Press, London, 1990).

artefact as its proto-symbolic content, they become ontologically independent of the contingencies surrounding their creation. We simply have *a* formation which presents states of affairs of general human significance. To determine more exact inflections of meaning, or to trace the particular way in which circumstances of production have determined the artefact's structure, requires collateral information external to its immediate physical presence. (In Chapter 5 I will develop the implications of these considerations in relation to aesthetic experience.)

Let me now summarize my major argument. To read a symbolic formation is (at least) to posit its proto-symbolic content, that is, what kind of actions or contexts are being referred to. To posit such a content is, at the same time, to be positioned in relation to it by body-hold. This is because the posited content delineates possibilities or contexts for action which find analogies or parallels in the reader's own embodied situation. The proto-symbolic content is thence a continuation of his or her latent existential space.

The consequences of these arguments are considerable. For they hold that, just as perception's archedifferential relation to the overall field gravitates around and is stabilized by our sense of embodiment and its possibilities, so too is the reader's relation to a symbolic formation. Indeed, the account I have offered shows how our intercourse with such formations is continuous with immediate perception. Body-hold is always *present*. Now, this is not a refinement of, or a mere out-and-out alternative to Derrida. Rather, it overcomes tensions within, not to mention downright *silly* aspects of his strategy. I shall now proceed to a detailed exposition of this overcoming.

III

First, Derrida's scepticism about presence is based, as we have seen, on the fact that nothing is *simply* present; it is a function of the play of *différance*. However, he offers no account of the relation between the articulation of *différance* in perception and its articulation in symbolic formations. But the two must have some connection. My account of *archédifférance* as constellated around body-hold fills this gap. Presence is not found—rather, it is achieved and stabilized as a focus of actual or possible action. This does not simply fill a gap. Rather, it reverses the whole dynamic of Derrida's strategy. For his notion of *différance* is, paradoxically enough, a reification of the relation between subject and world; it represents it in static and philosophically idealized terms. What this effectively negates is the fact that our inherence in the world as embodied subjects is primarily pre-reflective. That is to say, it forms a phenomenologically unified continuum of experience, wherein the carrying out of action *x* does not at the same time demand that we are explicitly and self-consciously aware that 'I am currently carrying out action *x*'. Of course, there are occasions when we do have such awareness. One such mode of reflective awareness is the *analytic* attitude, wherein we analyse some given whole into its parts in order to explain—and thence control—its behaviour or function. Once such knowledge has been realized, it is able to inform our subsequent actions. It forms a part of the latent existential spaces which we project around and upon the immediate field of embodiment. The analytic attitude, therefore, is at the service of, and secondary to, our pre-reflective inherence in the world. Many philosophers, however, make the mistake of supposing that the phenomenological unity of our pre-reflective engagement with the world can be adequately reconstructed on the basis of models derived from the analytic attitude. Bergson succinctly expresses the dangers of this. 'For the living unity, which was one with internal continuity, we substitute the factitious unity of an empty diagram as lifeless as the parts which it holds together.'[4]

Derrida's notion of *différance* ultimately emerges as such a lifeless empty diagram. It is the breaking up of language and consciousness into a network of logical relations. From this viewpoint, such notions as meaning and presence appear as unstable and lacking a point of reference. Paradoxes result. But this is hardly surprising, since all that Derrida has done is to freeze language and consciousness and dissect the cross-section. Now, when a biologist dissects an organism, he or she can better understand the nature of the individual parts and their relation to the whole. But the *living* whole is prior to this dissection. Indeed, the qualitative unity of that whole cannot be adequately reconstructed on the basis of the dissected material. This is also true of our pre-reflective phenomenological experience of the world. It is prior to the structures

---

[4] Henri Bergson, *Matter and Memory*, trans. N. R. Paul and W. Palmer (Harvester Press, London, 1978), 239.

revealed by analysis, and cannot be adequately grasped as a function of them. Yet it is precisely this latter point which Derrida gives priority to. Instead of deriving *différance* from embodiment, he posits *différance* and then derives presence and meaning as unstable functions of it. This is not a case of him simply inverting the priority of phenomenological over logical issues. Rather, he collapses the former into the latter and thence distorts our understanding of both elements.

Consider, for example, enjoying the mellow flavour of a piece of cheese. In order to enjoy this mellow flavour we must logically presuppose the capacities to distinguish mellowness from other characterizations of flavour, and to distinguish flavour from the other modalities of sense such as touch and smell. However, at the phenomenological level of enjoyment, whilst these distinctions—'traces' in Derrida's sense—may be logically presupposed, and whilst indeed they may impinge upon our enjoyment (for example, through the cheese's texture and smell enhancing its taste), the mellow flavour is not just the 'play' or precarious sum of these logical traces. In phenomenological terms, it is a cohesive and undifferentiated whole of experience determined by a specific bodily act. The mellowness of the flavour is a principle of cohesion about which traces of one sort or another constellate in a hierarchical sub-system. Here, in other words, immediate presence-to-body is the conditioning fact.

Similar considerations apply in relation to the presence of meaning in symbolic formations. Consider, for example, two such diverse items as an instruction manual for a microwave oven and Spinoza's *Ethics*. Here the act of reading is substantially pre-reflective. We study the instructions so that we can take appropriate steps to operate the oven. We read Spinoza's text so as to comprehend arguments concerning the broader context of human actions and aspirations. In both these cases, proto-symbolic content posits possibilities of, or contexts for, action. Of course, there may be ambiguities in either formation which demand rereading and analysis, or which provoke more diverse trains of thought. But, nevertheless, there is a central and stable core of meaning, which our more subjective responses flow out from, and—if they are more than free association—return to, in order to clarify. This is also true of our intercourse with symbolic formations of an artistic character. For, as I showed earlier, the proto-symbolic content of such works finds its echo in our own experience on the basis of body-hold. Again, the subjective associations which this gives rise to may be considerably more than an arbitrary free-play. Kant's notion of the 'aesthetic idea' (which I shall discuss in more detail in Chapter 3) provides a crucial insight into what such responses involve. He sees them as offering an 'aesthetically unbounded expansion' to those concepts embodied in the formation whilst remaining cognate with them. Here, subjective responses articulate the possibilities of the original concept; that is to say, they draw out its general relevance to experiential contexts beyond those envisaged by the creator.

My argument, then, is that our pre-reflective phenomenological engagement with the world and symbolic formations embodies stability of presence and meaning. Derrida's notion of *différance*, however, is a logical structure abstracted from this. By deriving presence and meaning as unable functions of *différance*, he thereby misrepresents the nature of our fundamental embodied inherence in the world.

Now, by failing to understand the relation between the logical and phenomenological aspects of meaning, Derrida not only distorts the latter, but also misunderstands the former. It will be recalled that in our enjoyment of the cheese's flavour, our enjoyment may be enhanced by the texture and smell of the cheese. Our phenomenologically undifferentiated whole of experience, in other words, may involve 'trace' elements—in this case data of touch and smell—which are logically different from flavour. However, whilst our experience here is a complex whole of logically different elements which we do not clearly differentiate at the phenomenological level of consumption, this does not mean that these elements are not autonomous. Flavour may be informed by data from other senses, but this phenomenological intertwining in no way diminishes the fact that, logically speaking, the senses are independent of one another. Neither, indeed, is this independence negated by the fact that we can only recognize them individually by virtue of difference—for example, we can only talk of flavour in so far as we are talking of something which is *not* a visual or tactile surface or a sound or a smell. For taste cannot simply be defined as what is left if we remove all reference to the other senses. If it were, we would be in the absurd position of having to allow that a person possessed of all the senses except taste could nevertheless have a full understanding of what the sense was, simply by thinking of it as 'not the ones which I do have'. Consider now the example of philosophy. Philosophical understanding is often enhanced by uses of language—such as metaphor—which, in striving for objective purity, it seeks to exclude. However, the fact that in the act of doing philosophy metaphorical elements impinge—positively or negatively—on our more abstract use of language does not of itself call into question philosophy's claim to logical autonomy. Indeed, whilst it may be that we can only talk of distinctively philosophical concepts in so far as we see them as, say, not mathematical or historical concepts or terms of poetry, this is a necessary but not a sufficient condition for defining philosophy. To put all these points more generally, the fact that some form or element of meaning is 'contaminated' by the trace of other forms or elements at the direct level of phenomenological experience does not in any way detract from their claims to logical autonomy. (This point will be of recurrent significance in this work—most notably in chapter 4.)

I am arguing, then, that Derrida's notion of *différance* involves a confusion of phenomenological and logical issues which leads him to misunderstand both. Specifically, he treats logical relations—the play of traces—as though these were a sufficient condition of our phenomenological experience of presence and meaning; and treats the undifferentiated wholeness of phenomenological experience as though it 'contaminates' the logical autonomy of the strands within it. In so doing, in other words, he misses out on both the cohesion determined by our embodied and social interaction with the world, and also the logically autonomous layers of sensory receptivity which are aligned *in* this interaction.

The origins of Derrida's problems, then, are clear. *Différance* is a logical structure. But logical structure is parasitic upon a more fundamental contact with the world—exemplified in perception itself, and our intercourse with symbolic formations. This contact is a function of embodiment. In focusing on logical structure, however, Derrida reduces the human subject itself to a purely logical status—a mere manipulator of signs. Now, poststructuralists such as Derrida are often taken to have 'shown' that the 'subject' itself is as fragile and indeterminate as meaning and presence. It is a 'play' amongst relations of *différance*. But as I have shown, Derrida's approach involves an abstract model which is wholly secondary to our embodied inherence in the world. His basic philosophical position is a semiotic Idealism which entails a notion of subjectivity that is—literally—disembodied. To affirm the fashionable doctrine of the 'death of the subject', in other words, is to embrace the ludicrous view that subjectivity can be sufficiently described without reference to embodiment.

Now, against this it might be claimed that at various points in his work (such as *Spurs: Nietzsche's Styles*) Derrida does have something to say about embodiment. Indeed, even if he does not give it enough emphasis himself, there are poststructuralists (with a view of language and subjectivity akin to his own) who do. A notable example is Roland Barthes. Barthes, however, exemplifies the general paucity of poststructuralist approaches to embodiment. The following remark summarizes this position with great lucidity. 'Does the text have human form, it is a figure, an anagram of the body? Yes but of our erotic body.'[5] And this is the problem. Derrida's and Barthes' treatment of the body is determined primarily by an unquestioning acceptance of basic tenets of Freudianism. Overlooking the philosophical absurdity of most of these tenets, let us consider the basic one—namely the decisive role of sexuality and the erotic in human experience. Against this, one must assert that to foreground the sexual function is to foreground what is of secondary significance. Sexuality is one aspect of body-hold; but our general orientation towards the world is a function of embodiment *per se*, i.e. all the senses operating together in a unified field. Of course, questions of sexuality, gender, and the erotic pervade many aspects of human experience, but they are not, philosophically speaking, its fundamental pivot. Consider in this respect the frequently remarked upon division of experience on the basis of gender. Can a man ever understand the experience of a woman, or vice versa? Of course not—or at least not in any absolute sense. But this is only a variant of the more fundamental fact that *qua* finite embodied subject, no human being can fully understand what it is to be another such being. It is this gap which impels us to create and develop modes of symbolic formation. As noted earlier, the protosymbolic level of such works is the fundamental point at which the divide between people is bridged. For, irrespective of one's gender or sexual orientation, to recognize what is being posited in a symbolic formation is to recognize a set of general

[5] Roland Barthes, *The Pleasure of the Text*, trans. R. Miller (Hill and Wang, New York, 1975), 17.

possibilities of body-hold. At this level there is something for everyone. Even the most rigidly sexist conservative male, for example, can recognize or come to recognize what a poem celebrating lesbian love is 'about' and how it is being characterized, even if he cannot identify with the situation in sexual terms. Indeed, the alien quality of the poem does not involve some blackout of meaning. Rather it is encountered *as* an embodiment of alien experience.

The point to gather from this is that embodiment in a general rather than specifically sexual mode is the decisive factor in our engagement with both world and symbolic formations. What we require is a theory which will express this decisiveness. Fortunately, one is at hand. It is the philosophy of Merleau-Ponty, and, in particular (*vis-à-vis* the notion of *différance*), a distinction made in his late work between the 'visible' and 'invisible'. I shall now conclude this chapter with a brief exposition of this distinction.

IV

For Merleau-Ponty items only become visible—i.e. explicitly present to visual awareness—in so far as they are defined against a complex background of other visual items and relations such as colours, light-levels, and the traces of such items in memory. Indeed, things would not take on the character of being visibly present without an at least tacit awareness on our part that we who see are ourselves visible—that is, are embodied subjects who occupy part of the visual field. Vision is a reciprocity with the visual. Now, whilst this background network of items, relations, and tacit awareness is the flesh which sustains and enables us to recognize specific visual presences, it is not generally noticed. It is invisible from the viewpoint of immediate awareness. Were this not so, vision would be swamped and paralysed by an excess of data.

Let me now qualify and develop Merleau-Ponty's distinction. First, it should be noted that his use of the visible–invisible pairing is as a metonym. The reciprocity of the two terms characterizes not only vision as such, but also the unified operation of all the senses. To express his insight in more general terms, one might say that the presence of any item in experience is only possible in so far as it is defined against a network of other items, relations, knowledge, and beliefs of which we are not immediately aware.

But, reciprocally, this network of 'traces' is only there in so far as it arises from the embodied subject's striving for, and successful achievement of, a consumption of presence. Putting this in even more general terms, the presence of any specific item of meaning in experience presupposes the traces of items not present, but reciprocally this system of traces is itself organized and, indeed, only made possible, by the fact of achieved meaning. The great utility of Merleau-Ponty's visible–invisible pairing as a metonym for this more general reciprocity is that vision most lucidly expresses both the foundation in embodiment, and the logical autonomy of its elements. Indeed, this provides us with the crucial antidote to Derrida's linguistic *différance*. For, whilst language is founded on *différance, différance* itself, as I have argued, is an outgrowth of the embodied subject's more global and concrete interaction with the world. Language is a crucial but abstract articulation of this *archédifférance*, wherein presence is not something fragile and elusive, but concrete and achieved. Merleau-Ponty, in other words, returns us to the philosophically more fundamental level. Indeed, Derrida's own approach requires this. For, as Derrida admits, the pull of the 'metaphysics of presence' is strong—inescapable, even. But why is this? Why is even his analysis not immune from it? One reason is that rigour, consistency, the formulation and following of a strategy, all presuppose a certain constancy of meaning and definiteness of sense. The stability of presence is, logically speaking, just one element in the play of *différance*, from the viewpoint of embodied social being—the demands of human existence in the broadest sense—the achievement of meaning and presence is a stabilization and *raison d'être* of the whole system.

Having, then, introduced a crucial theme from the work of Merleau-Ponty, I shall now, in Chapter 2, offer a critical exposition of his account of the transition from perception to art. As well as preparing us for an understanding of the artwork, this exposition will also expand on many of the themes broached in my critique of Derrida.

2

Merleau-Ponty

Perception into Art

Since Heidegger's *Being and Time*, the fundamental intent of phenomenology has been to burrow beneath the edifices of such abstract knowledge as science or traditional philosophy, with a view to expressing a more primordial contact with the world—a contact which is presupposed but ill understood by abstract reflection. In a sense, Merleau-Ponty gives us a paradigm for the application of such phenomenological method to art, since, for him, it is art which is most successful in giving expression to man's fundamental contact with being. Unfortunately, Merleau-Ponty never wrote any large systematic work upon the subject, and to grasp his thought as a single theory of art involves reference to most of his large works, and numerous essays besides. Existing discussions of Merleau-Ponty's aesthetics[1] have suffered from the shortcoming of considering the earlier and later phases of his thought, in isolation from one another. In this discussion I shall attempt to synthesize an overall view that at the same time elucidates some of Merleau-Ponty's cryptic terminology. This task of interpretation and clarification is made easier by the fact that Merleau-Ponty's aesthetics do converge upon a specific theme: 'It is the expressive operation begun in the least perception, which amplifies into painting and art.[2]

Accordingly, in section 1 of this chapter I shall briefly outline Merleau-Ponty's theory of perception, and then, in the second section, proceed to describe how perception 'amplifies' into artistic

This chapter was originally published under the same title in the *British Journal of Aesthetics*, vol. 22, no. 2 (1982).

[1] Namely Marjorie Grene, 'Merleau-Ponty and Sartre's Aesthetic Dialogue', *British Journal of Phenomenology*, vol. 1, no. 2 (1970), 69–72; Stephen Levine, 'Merleau-Ponty's Philosophy of Art', *Man and World*, no. 2 (1969), 438–52; Eugene Kaelin, *An Existentialist Aesthetic* (University of Wisconsin Press, 1966), chs. vii–xi.

[2] Maurice Merleau-Ponty, *The Prose of the World* (Heinemann, London, 1974), 83.

creation. In section III I shall elaborate Merleau-Ponty's understanding of the significance of the artwork, and will, in conclusion, briefly relate his theory to other phenomenological approaches to art, with a view to highlighting some of their deficiencies.

I

The central theme of all Merleau-Ponty's philosophy is the primacy of embodiment. Our fundamental contact with things arises from a 'practical synthesis'—from handling them, looking at them, using them, etc. Traditional philosophy, in contrast, takes consciousness as its starting-point, and constructs the 'external' world from the sense data or 'atoms' of sensation that are presented to the pure perceiving subject. For Merleau-Ponty, however, the body and its operations are that which makes any consciousness possible. For example, it would be difficult to explain in terms of traditional philosophy why judgements about depth ever come about. There is no intrinsic reason, say, why one element in a landscape should appear farther away than another; there is, however, as Merleau-Ponty puts it, a 'motive'.[3] Judgements about depth can only come about in so far as it has been revealed beforehand as the ground or arena which our body inhabits and operates in.

On these terms, our fundamental knowledge of the world comes through our body's exploration of it. Consciousness is not a purely mental phenomenon, but a function of the integrated operation of all the senses. We find in perception not atoms of sensation or pure sense data, but nodes of 'meaning' which emerge as a foreground (through their proximity to the body and its interests), against the background depth of the whole perceptual field. A brick, for example, will define itself by its colour, texture, shape, size, position, and intended use in relation to other objects and phenomena in the field. Even if our attention, say, is focused upon the colour alone, we will still find a meaning that emerges from its harmony or opposition to other colours and light levels in the field, and indeed from the texture, shape, and weight of the object whose colour it is.

For Merleau-Ponty, then, perception is an encounter with 'meanings'. Things impress themselves upon the body not as 'logical constructions' or 'substances with attributes' but as tangible, dynamic,

[3] Maurice Merleau-Ponty, *The Phenomenology of Perception* (Routledge & Kegan Paul, London, 1974), 48.

intersensory presences or 'emblems' of a certain style of being. As Merleau-Ponty puts it: 'I perceive in a total way with my whole being: I grasp a unique structure of the thing, a unique way of being, which speaks to all my senses at once.'[4]

Our knowledge of the world is thus founded upon the body's relating and habituating itself to things. Such encounters will leave behind them not so much mental 'pictures' or memory-images as 'carnal formulae'—structures constituted from all the sensory and affective life of the subject. The acquisition of language, of course, facilitates this sedimentation, and enables 'carnal formulae' to be projected in thought or imagination even when the things or situations that originally gave rise to them are not present. This means that all our perceptions are 'subtended by an "international arc" which projects round about us our past, our future, our human setting, our physical, ideological or moral situation, or rather which results in our being situated in all these respects'.[5]

It is now time to gather up two important points from this brief outline of Merleau-Ponty's theory of perception. First, we remember that the body articulates the world into meanings by grasping it through the integrated operation of the senses, and relating what is thus grasped to its past and future life. In this sense, perception is creative, the body does not find meaning pre-existent in the world, but calls such meaning into existence, through its own activity. Second, such activity is, for the most part, pre-reflective; the body operates amongst, and upon, things, persons, and situations without being explicitly and directly aware that it is doing so. There are moments, however, when we do stand from the flux of life, and ask, 'What's really going on here?' This attitude, of course, finds its most systematic articulation in philosophy. The problem with such reflective thought is that it has great difficulty in expressing the intersensory and historical complexity of our being in the world, and tends therefore towards over-simplification. Ryle and Heidegger, for example, have both argued, in different ways, that philosophical understanding has been distorted by conceiving the world in terms of abstract models derived from the secondary realm of mechanics and technology. This is also Merleau-Ponty's position. Although our fundamental contact with the world is not

---

[4] Maurice Merleau-Ponty, 'The Film and the New Psychology', in *Sense and Non-Sense* (Northwestern University Press, Evanston, Ill., 1964), 50.
[5] *The Phenomenology of Perception*, 136.

a conceptless chaos, its structure and cohesion is not of the same order as that of abstract thought. An object given in perception is encountered first as a meaning-for-us, an intersensory style of being, rather than a 'mental' construction from sense-data. It is grasped in the context of complex relationships in the immediate perceptual field, and in terms of its significance in our past, and for our future life. To use Merleau-Ponty's terminology, any 'meaning' which becomes 'visible' or 'speaks' to us, in perception, does so only in so far as it is defined against an 'invisible' or 'silent' background of perceptual, reflective, and historical relationships.

Given, then, this notion of the creativity of perception, and its invisible–silent foundations, we are in a position to proceed to Merleau-Ponty's theory of art.

II

It will be remembered that, in Merleau-Ponty's term, our perception of things or of their interrelations leaves 'carnal formulae' ingrained upon our body. In handling objects or palpating them with the eye etc., our body habituates itself to the 'style' of being that characterizes the things or situations it encounters. Merleau-Ponty is hence led to distinguish between primary expression, which brings new perceptual meanings into existence, and secondary expression, where meaning is derived from already familiar 'carnal formulae'. For example, if we see a woman walking towards us, it may be that this is 'just' a woman—we pass her by without thinking anything about it. Our body is accustomed to such experience, and regulates its behaviour accordingly. However, it may be that the woman strikes us as particularly beautiful or mysterious—her way of varying the 'accent' of feminine being is one which does not square with our usual expectation of it. On these terms, our carnal formula of feminity is called into question and enriched; the silence of our practical engagement with the world is ruptured by a situation which demands that more should be said about it. Now it may be, of course, that this new meaning to feminity, this instance of 'primary expression', is one which simply flares up for a moment then is sedimented into our 'intentional arc', ready to inform future perceptions. However, there are some occasions when perception encounters a meaning or meanings which cannot be grasped immediately—the aura of 'something still to be said' lingers and becomes unbearable. We feel the need to preserve them, or articulate them further. Here, of course, is the take-off point for artistic creation. The artist is a person who sees the world in terms of such further possibilities. It is unfortunate that Merleau-Ponty uses the term 'equivalences' to describe the artist's response, since it is clear that what the artist's vision picks out are those deviations from perceptual norms (or the possibility thereof) which can find a fuller articulation in his work. His 'equivalences' are, to use a term which Merleau-Ponty borrows from Malraux, 'coherent deformations'.

Now, why should the artist be especially prone to seeking out the deviation rather than the norm in perception? Is it just a case of his being rather more 'inspired' than the ordinary person? As one might expect, for Merleau-Ponty the answer to this question is to be found in embodiment rather than in realms of the spirit. The artist is a person whose approach to life has been significantly defined by a relationship to a medium such as painting or writing. He has learnt an affinity between his body and the handling of a specific medium that enables his body to take a fuller grasp on the meanings he encounters in perception. This discovery may have been a natural outcome of early ability in relation to the medium, or it may come about through a crisis in life or a series of extraordinary situations that awaken him to a lack of fullness in his existence. Whatever the origin, once the artist has lent himself to a medium, his perception thereafter will be influenced by its demands. As Gombrich says in relation to one branch of the arts, 'painting is an activity, and the artist will therefore tend to see what he paints rather than to paint what he sees'.[6]

Why should this relationship to a medium be so important when there is, after all, a strong creative element in perception itself? Well, Merleau-Ponty notes that perception 'stylizes'. Each person is a unique individual, and though we can expect different subjects to share a common phenomenal field and similar carnal formulae (through the fact that we are all embodied), each person will have his own style of relating his body to the field. He will place his own valuations on phenomena—some will be the object of interested attention, others will be passed over. These gestures of

---

[6] Ernst Gombrich, *Art and Illusion* (Phaidon, London, 1971), 73.

emphasis or understatement are the basis of style in perception. Now, in the artist, such style is even more pronounced. In re-creating or exploring these original responses through the handling of a medium, the artist not only responds to, but, in a sense, relearns the situation(s) which gave rise to his equivalences. Consider again the example of a woman passing by:

If I am . . . a painter, what will be transmitted to the canvas will no longer be only a vital or sensual value. There will be in the painting not just 'a woman' or 'unhappy woman' or 'a hatmaker'. There will also be the emblem of a way of inhabiting the world, of handling it, and of interpreting it by a face as by clothing, by ability of gesture as by inertia of body—in short, the emblem of a certain relationship to being.[7]

In other words, working in a medium enables the body to continue the creative stylizing process begun in the artist's perception itself, in order to concentrate the 'scattered' meanings found there, and make them exist in a unified concrete form. It brings his own perceptual style to a point of consummation.

Given, then, the importance of continuity of style from perception to handling of medium, we must not forget the ground which makes this possible. At every moment the artist's respones will be informed by that 'international arc' already alluded to. He has learned techniques, discussed art, looked at other people's works, and perhaps finds that the system of 'equivalences' which gave rise to other works by him has become immanent in his present creation or points towards certain modifications. From all this we see that each brushstroke or stanza or whatever is underpinned by an enormous complexity. As Merleau-Ponty says of Cézanne: 'The rules of anatomy and design are present in each stroke of his brush just as the rules of the game underlie each stroke in a game of tennis.'[8]

Now, the very possibility of the artist's style evolving in the light of influence from other works, or 'rules of design', depends on works of art being publicly accessible, not merely 'equivalences' in the artist's mind. In working out his 'equivalences' in a medium, the artist is not translating a ready-made thought but rather adding to it. In the process of creation we find hoverings, reworkings, estimations

[7] Maurice Merleau-Ponty, 'Indirect Language and the Voices of Silence', in *Phenomenology, Language, and Sociology*, ed. John O'Neill (Heinemann, London, 1974), 51.
[8] 'Cézanne's Doubt', in *Sense and Non-Sense*, 17.

of the effect of individual signs upon the developing whole. The work-in-progress takes its stylistic clue from perception and extends it until the qualitative configuration of marks or words or whatever announces that the perception is complete. To simply reduce art-works to the artist's mental states or intentions etc. is to reduce them to insignificance. It is the process of physical re-creation in a medium that takes the creativity of perception to completion. We could not, in fact, as Merleau-Ponty puts it, understand how a 'mind' could paint. Hence, the conclusion that 'A novel, a poem, picture or musical work are individuals, that is, beings in which the expression is indistinguishable from the thing expressed'.[9]

To those who have done their aesthetics in the Analytic tradition, the rejection of the art-as-mental-states thesis may seem a battle long won. Why tread this ground again? There are a number of reasons. First, Eugene Kaelin[10] has argued that if we forget the art-as-mental-states thesis, it is to Croce's aesthetics that Merleau-Ponty's theory can best be compared. However, the enormous polarization manifest in their respective attitudes towards the onto-logical status of the artwork is so irrevocably fundamental as to make further comparisons of less than academic interest. There is a second, related, point here. Some of the most influential phenome-nological philosophies tend to reduce the human subject to a mere network of intentional acts, and interpret the artwork itself in terms of mental states. Sartre has been seen as occupying this posi-tion,[11] and, more significantly, Ingarden—who argues that the artwork is primarily the artist's intention, with its physical embodi-ment a mere 'existential substrate'.[12] In his stress on the physicality of artistic creation, Merleau-Ponty differentiates himself from this tradition in a way that at the same time goes beyond the piecemeal analysis of Gallie's 'journeyman aesthetician' in the Analytic tradi-tion. We find a depth account of the origin of the work of art that places it in the broader context of human existence. This analysis has, as I shall argue in the following section, an important contri-bution to make to our understanding of the significance of the art-work; and to our understanding of art as a transcultural

[9] *The Phenomenology of Perception*, 151.
[10] Kaelin, *An Existentialist Aesthetic*, chs. vii–xi.
[11] e.g. Margaret Macdonald, 'Arguments used in Criticism of the Arts', in *Aesthetics and Language*, ed. William Elton (Basil Blackwell, Oxford, 1970).
[12] See e.g. Roman Ingarden, 'Artistic and Aesthetic Value', in *Aesthetics*, ed. Harold Osborne (Oxford University Press, Oxford, 1972).

phenomenon. It is with a consideration of the latter point that I shall round off this section.

Merleau-Ponty speaks of 'a unity of human style which transcends spatial and temporal differences to bring the gestures of all painters together in a single effort, a single accumulative history—a single art or culture'.[13] The reasons for this are twofold. First, all human gestures or perceptions are comparable in that they have meaning, i.e. refer beyond themselves, and are statements within the same syntax—embodiment. Given the importance of bodily gesture in the creation of art, it is not surprising that we find, for example, so much similarity between paintings from different cultures since they all have a common ground—the body's physical articulation of meanings discovered in perception. It is sometimes pointed out, of course, that 'art' is a concept peculiar to Western culture. However, if we follow Merleau-Ponty's clues we are led to search beneath the diverse social functions of artworks to find a distinct ontological category—namely artefacts which consummate the stylizing process begun in perception itself. Though the term 'art' arose (and rather late at that) in the context of a specific culture, there was a unique kind of existent already waiting beneath the web of social and cultural usages, for the dignity of being picked out by a distinct name.

Now, in its character as a public embodiment of individual experience, the artwork has social consequences. It is a source of possible influences on other works; it creates new possibilities of meanings, and is integrated into the perceptual style of those who encounter it. Even a work which is first found unintelligible will, if it has any worth, eventually create its own public.

Hence we see that painting, indeed art in general, is conceived by Merleau-Ponty as an institution inaugurated from the simple ground of perception. It occurs when tendencies given in an individual's perception interact with a certain social context—specifically, the tradition that has arisen in relation to a medium. As Hegel observes, 'even if the talent and genius of the artist has in it a natural element, yet this element essentially requires development by thought, reflection on the mode of its productivity, and practice and skill in producing'.[14]

---

[13] *The Prose of the World*, 81.

[14] G. F. W. Hegel, *Aesthetics*, trans. T. M. Knox (Oxford University Press, Oxford, 1975), 27.

These productive skills are, of course, acquired by acquaintance with a tradition, and it is this, I think, which places Merleau-Ponty's aesthetics in a proper context—namely as a prefiguring of that confluence of Hegel and Heidegger brought about in Hans-George Gadamer's 'philosophical hermeneutics'.

III

Any serous theory of art must answer at least two related and fundamental questions. First, how do we differentiate works of art from other human artefacts; and second, why do we find the art-work so especially rich in meaning? Merleau-Ponty offers answers to both these questions; indeed, such answers constitute the very heart of his aesthetic theory. It is to this I now turn.

A first point to note is that on Merleau-Ponty's terms the work of art is separated from the bulk of human artefacts by having semantic qualities—formal configurations which refer, in some sense, beyond themselves. This is true even of abstract art or music, in that the former refers to the 'allusive logic' of visual reality itself—or, as it were, the perceptual 'flesh' beneath the visual skin; and the latter sets out 'certain outlines of Being—its ebb and flow, its growth, its upheavals, its turbulence'.[15]

This semantic quality, of course, is not in itself enough to define the work of art, since it is a feature common to any sign-system or language. It will be remembered, however, from Section 1 of this chapter, that our fundamental and pre-reflective contact with the world is 'silent'. Language, as formulated in the traditional intellectual disciplines, gives it only an incomplete or distorted expression through being unable to grasp the depth of 'invisible' relationships that underlie and define 'visibilia' (i.e. those meanings encountered in perception). The artwork, however, is better equipped to give voice to this silent domain.

To bring this out, let us contrast the way we apprehend meanings in the traditional disciplines with the way we apprehend them in the novel or poem. To begin with, the fundamental business of, say, the philosophical, scientific, or historical text, is analytic. It seeks to reduce some specific phenomenon or range of phenomena

---

[15] Maurice Merleau-Ponty, 'Eye and Mind', in Osborne (ed.), *Aesthetics*, 57.

to a statement of objective laws or relations which are immanent in them. In other words, it draws us into an essentially cognitive engagement, an abstract mode of understanding which seeks to grasp the 'invisible' foundations of the phenomenon or phenomena investigated. Now, of course, any poet or novelist may be moved by such abstract ideas, but his specific presentation of them in a medium seeks to engage our whole being rather than cognition alone. To use a sign-system analytically, as in the traditional intellectual disciplines, or indicatively, as in the propositions of ordinary language, involves a bare and essentially cognitive operation with signs. There are occasions, though, when we use signs in a much richer way, in a way that seeks to construct or reconstruct some aspect of the world in all its sensuous immediacy—in other words, as it might be encountered in perception itself. This is the realm of the imagination, and for Merleau-Ponty the work of art is essentially an imaginary or imaginatively reconstructed situation presented in a publicly accessible form.

There is a clear, but for the most part unacknowledged, debt here to Ingarden, and, even more importantly, Sartre. However, Merleau-Ponty's account makes significant advances on both, and, in so doing, gives us an explanation of why we find the art-object so especially meaningful. To illustrate this, let us briefly consider Satre's theory of the artwork, and specifically his example of the painter. On Sartre's terms the artist begins with a mental image of his subject, and, in painting it, 'simply' constructs 'a material analogue of such a kind that everyone can grasp the image, provided he looks at the analogue'.[16] This is, quite simply, a more sophisticated presentation of the argument that has bedevilled the philosophy of art since Book X of Plato's Republic: namely that the physical work of art is ontologically 'inferior' to the state of mind from which it emanates. For Sartre, the work of art exists in order to refer us back directly to some image in the mind of the artist. This account, however, cannot explain the peculiar richness of meaning that we find in works of art. Specifically, it fails to grasp the important changes that take place in the transition from 'inspiration' to execution and end-product, in the process of artistic creation. In section II of this chapter I presented Merleau-Ponty's plausible account of how the act of making an artwork

[16] J.-P. Sartre, *The Psychology of Imagination* (Methuen, London, 1972), 220.

significantly extends and articulates the ideas or 'equivalences' which are its starting-point. This process has a further crucial consequence which I shall now outline in some detail.

Merleau-Ponty tells us that the novelist 'takes up his dwelling in a character's behaviour and gives the reader only a suggestion of it, its nervous and peremptory trace in the surroundings'.[17] In other words, the basis of the artist's expression is 'tacit' or 'indirect'. He uses his medium to present some aspect of the world in its sensuous immediacy, but because this involves a particular style of handling the medium, what appears in the work will be indelibly stamped by what style. Hence, some aspects of the subject-matter will be emphasized and made figural, whilst other aspects will be omitted or underplayed. The work of art gives us an interpretation or evaluation of its subject-matter, and will depend as much on what the artist omits in the process of creation as on what we find in the end-product.

The work of art, then, does not aspire to reproduce perception but rather to give a sensuous interpretation of it; one which, through the artist's style, 'carves out relief in things' or 'distends' the world into 'fuller meaning'.[18] This seems rather a strong claim. Are we to take Merleau-Ponty as saying that the artwork is 'visible' or 'meaningful' in a stronger sense than perception itself. Our answer here must be in the affirmative, for the following reasons. Everyday perception gives us constant encounters with 'visibilia', but the demands of life are such that we do not have time to take note of the various 'invisible' relations which define these situations. This, however, is precisely where the artist's indirect expression comes into its own. Merleau-Ponty tells us, for example, that 'No one has gone further than Proust in fixing the relations between the visible and invisible, in describing an idea that is not the contrary of the sensible, but is in fact its lining and depth'.[19] The thinking behind this remark is as follows. Proust does not simply indicate or describe a series of characters and events—rather, he weaves his narrative from a sensuous presentation of only those events which essentially link and bind the characters in their common situation. We find their crucial decisions and mistakes, the moments of insight, the chance occurrences

[17] 'Indirect Language and the Voices of Silence', 73.   [18] Ibid. 75.

[19] Maurice Merleau-Ponty, *The Visible and the Invisible* (Northwestern University Press, Evanston, Ill., 1968), 149.

which prove pivotal in the course of their relationships. In other words, the author builds the 'visible' meaning—the ostensible story or plot—from a scaffolding of what he takes to be the most important 'invisible' relationships in the situation. The choices he makes here will be a function of his own moral, political, or aesthetic values, and these more abstract ideas of course will appear in 'transparency' behind the sensuous surface of the narrative, as its 'lining and depth'.

Merleau-Ponty offers us a similar analysis of the visual arts. We are told, of painting, for example, that 'it gives visible existence to what profane vision believes to be invisible'.[20] In this cryptic observation Merleau-Ponty is pointing out that as embodied subjects we are surrounded by a rich variegated texture of visual being, of which discrete objects are merely the punctuations or caesurae. We see or imagine something as, say, a mountain without taking note of the fact that what makes it visible as a mountain is a differentiated play of greens and browns, in juxtaposition to various other textures and shapes. Everyday vision 'forgets its premises', but this is precisely what the painter captures. He makes the mountain 'visible' in such a way that we cannot help but notice the invisible perceptual relationships that define it. Indeed, in so far as the artist has constituted his sensuous image from just 'these' 'inivisible', and just 'these' combinations of brushstrokes and colours, we are placed in a new relationship to him as well as to his subject-matter. Hence the work of art expresses the artist's personal relation to a shared world, and is, therefore, of interest both in its own right and in its implications for other lives. The meaning and richness of the work will be inexhaustible simply by virtue of our historicity. As the patterns and meaning of personal and collective existence take on new meaning, so will our understanding of particular works of art and their creators.

In Merleau-Ponty's theory, then, we find that the artwork is defined and given its rich meaning by virtue of occupying a unique half-way position between perception and reflection. Unlike ordinary language and abstract thought, it has a sensuous immediacy that comes close to that of our fundamental perceptual contact with the world. Unlike perception itself, however, it preserves and

---

[20] 'Eye and Mind', 62.

articulates the most crucial 'invisible' scaffolding of the specific situation it is expressing.

One could perhaps summarize Merleau-Ponty's conception of art in terms of a distinction between showing and saying. Art shows what traditional philosophy tries to say. It is not insignificant in this respect that Merleau-Ponty (like Heidegger before him) was led in his later philosophy to a quasi-poetic vocabulary in order to express man's fundamental relation to Being.

IV

I have sketched out what I take to be the fundamental features of Merleau-Ponty's theory of art. It is a theory not without shortcomings and I shall indicate some of these at the end of this chapter.

However, even in its broadest outlines, Merleau-Ponty offers a theory which already marks a significant advance on some phenomenological approaches to art. Its improvement upon Sartre's has already been noted. I shall now relate it briefly to the thought of two key figures in the German tradition of phenomenology.

In the writings of Gadamer on art,[21] we find (as with Sartre) an inclination to favour what the artwork is perceived 'as', i.e. the salient meaning, at the expense of the relationship between meaning and the 'invisible' scaffolding which makes it possible. Whilst, like Merleau-Ponty, Gadamer holds that the work of art is in some sense enriched being, the reason for this is that the artist gives us the 'essence' of the subject-matter. In such work, the 'original' which is represented 'emerges into truth' and enjoys an 'increase of being'. Unfortunately, this account presents some difficulties. For example, in what sense does the artist give us the essence of his subject-matter? What would differentiate this 'emergence' into truth from truth in the context, say, of philosophy or science? Indeed why should it constitute an 'increase of being' for the 'original'. Matters become especially problematic when we remember that many artworks are realizations of imaginary conceptions which take actual situations or originals in life only as their clue, or starting-point. In Merleau-Ponty's account, we find that the 'originals' which prompt artistic creation are not simply objects or

---

[21] H. G. Gadamer, *Truth and Method* (Sheed and Ward, London, 1975), 99–119.

situations, but carnal responses to them. These are articulated in terms of a medium, unlike reflective thought, that gives a sensuous and more complete expression to meanings encountered in perception. It is in this sense that the artwork is 'enriched being'. What Gadamer's approach fails to grasp is the nature of what is emerging in the artwork and where it is emerging from. The unique richness of the work cannot be accounted for simply in terms of the presentation of a subject-matter's essence—the abstract methods of philosophy are quite adequate to such a task.

Heidegger's philosophy of art can be criticized from roughly the same direction. We are told, for example, that 'All art, as the letting happen of the advent of the truth of beings, is as such, in essence, poetry. The essence of art, on which both the art work and artist depend, is the setting-itself-into-work of truth.'[22] Here we find again the notion of the artist expressing the 'truth' or essence of his subject-matter. However, 'essence' in Heidegger's sense is much more a relation to that pre-reflective contact between man and Being which looms so important in Merleau-Ponty's thought. For Heidegger it is Being which figures more significantly in this relationship by summoning man into language. Thereafter man expresses Being in two specific modes of language: first, the inauthentic, which forces Being into abstract, technologically originated concepts, and second, the authentic, which is language close to the primal source of things and which allows them to appear before consciousness as they are 'in truth'. Art (and poetry especially) is an instance of the latter.

Unfortunately, whilst Heidegger is prepared to admit that in the artwork 'createdness is expressly created into the created being, so that it stands out from it',[23] he does not think through the implications of this in relation to his main thesis that art allows things to appear as they 'truly' are. Merleau-Ponty's theory of art, in contrast, affords a very reasonable primacy to style—that 'distention' which draws the world out of focus into 'fuller meaning'. Though the artwork has certain objective semantic qualities, it is the artist's articulation of these through his own personal style which gives us a sensuous and unique image of the perceptual world, with its scaffolding made tangible. In other words, what the artist is expressing

---

[22] Martin Heidegger, 'The Origin of the Work of Art', in *Martin Heidegger: Basic Writings* ed. D. F. Krell (Routledge & Kegan Paul, London, 1978), 184.
[23] Ibid. 181.

is not simply the essence of objects or situations as they are 'in themselves', but the way a certain style of Being impresses itself upon his flesh and finds a new mode of visibility. Hence Merleau-Ponty makes us aware of the artwork's significance as an expression of the artist's individual embodiment. Heidegger's account, in contrast, unfairly subordinates the artist's own expression to the demands of the 'truth' of his subject-matter.

This is really symptomatic of a wider malaise. In much modern phenomenology (and, indeed, modern philosophy as a whole) there is a universal stress on language and, at one remove, ideology, as being the fundamental link between man and the world. This, however, leaves open the question of how language and ideologies are themselves possible. Merleau-Ponty's philosophy gives us the opportunity to think this problem through. We find that language, ideology, and art are founded upon a more fundamental link between man and world—namely embodiment. With all its sensuous means, it is art which gives this dimension its fullest expression.

I have argued, then, that Merleau-Ponty's theory of art constitutes a significant philosophical advance. It has, however, several important areas of incompleteness. At the root of these is the fact that his definition of art is ontological: in other words, he identifies it with a specific class of existents, namely stylized artefacts—such things as paintings, sculptures, novels, and poems. This approach both allows in too much and excludes too much. For example, whilst paintings and poems are modes of stylizing a visual medium or language respectively, we would surely not allow that all paintings or poems *ipso facto* are works of art. Some stylized articulations of a medium engage us profoundly but others do not, in so far as they simply repeat established stylistic tendencies and methods. What Merleau-Ponty needs to stress, therefore, is that, whilst a specific ontological class of existents forms the domain of art, it is only a significant subclass of these which engage us in terms of positive critical and aesthetic responses. Our full definition of art, in other words, must be founded on *evaluative* criteria as well as descriptive ones.

This general exclusion of evaluative issues comes to a head in one quite severe problem. As we have seen, Merleau-Ponty stresses the fact that art has its origins in our primordial historicity *as embodied beings*. However, he seems to suppose that the dimension of *empirical* historicity (i.e. the individual's relation to the particular socio-historical circumstances of his or her existence) has no direct bearing on the production and reception of art *qua* art. This is false. For, whilst style is rooted in the difference between human beings at the level of embodiment, the articulation of this difference, and our reading of it, draws from, and plays off against, the techniques, traditions, and ideologies in terms of which different human beings are located. This means that the content and significance of a particular style is a function of an individual's relation to specific socio-historical circumstances as well as to more constant factors in experience. What Merleau-Ponty lacks, therefore, is an adequate account of how empirical history mediates the primordial historicity of our embodiment. This means, in effect, an understanding of the structure and role of *critical awareness*. To this omission must be added a related worry. The burden of Merleau-Ponty's theory falls upon the nature of the art-object. He has almost nothing to say about the question of our *aesthetic* responses to it. Yet if art is to be something more than the social or institutional functions which it serves, or anything more than an indirect mode of philosophizing, then we must be able to link it to some logically distinctive and existentially privileged mode of experience.

The task which faces us, then, is to go beyond Merleau-Ponty by clarifying the relations between art, critical awareness, and aesthetic experience. As a starting-point for this task. I turn to the philosophy of Kant. In *The Critique of Judgement* (1790) he offers a particularly well-balanced account of the relation between the factors just mentioned.

3

Beyond Formalism

Kant's Theory of Art

Kant's theory of art has been neglected to an extraordinary degree. In this chapter I shall rectify the situation by arguing that Kant's theory reaches far beyond the constraints placed on his work by the familiar label of 'formalist'.

To show this, I will adopt the following strategy. In Section I I will outline the salient features of Clive Bell's and Clement Greenberg's approaches to art, as examples of both formalism's strategies and its problems. I will then indicate the basis of Kant's general aesthetic theory, arguing that it suggests a way beyond the limitations of formalism. In section II I shall explore this possibility in depth, by means of a detailed exposition of Kant's theory of art. In section III I will make a few critical revisions to the theory; and shall conclude that, unlike the formalist approaches of Bell and Fry, Kant's theory defines art without severing its connections to life.

I

The basis of Clive Bell's aesthetic formalism is his attempt to define art in terms of 'significant form'—which he defines as 'relations and arrangements of lines and colours'.[1] This, it should be noted, does not of itself disqualify representational works from counting as art. As Bell remarks, 'a realistic form may be as

This is an extended and revised version of a paper of the same title which was presented at the International Colloquium on 'Form', held in Ljubljana, 11–12 Oct. 1990. I am grateful to participants in that Colloquium for their useful comments. I am also grateful for comments received in discussion with my graduate students on the 'Art in the Context of Philosophy' course, at the University of St Andrews. This chapter was published under the same title in the Slovenian journal *Filozofski Vestnik*, vol. xii, no. 1 (1991).

[1] Clive Bell, *Art* (Chatto and Windus, London, 1931), 68.

significant, in its place as part of the design, as an abstract. But if a representative form has value, it is as form, not as representation. The representative element in a work of art may or may not be harmful; always it is irrelevant.'[2] Bell goes on to claim that the only sort of knowledge required for the appreciation of art is a sense of form and colour and, to a lesser degree, a knowledge of three-dimensional space. We must also, of course, be aesthetically sensitive. Again, in Bell's words,

. . . to appreciate a work of art we need bring with us nothing from life, no knowledge of its ideas and affairs, no familiarity with its emotions. Art transports us from the world of man's activity to a world of aesthetic exaltation. For a moment we are shut off from human interests; our anticipations and memories are arrested; we are lifted above the stream of life.[3]

On these terms, then, the experience of significant form provokes aesthetic emotion—an emotion wherein we are distanced from the concerns of practical existence. A work only counts as art to the degree that it can arouse such an emotion in us.

Now, the apparent strength of Bell's theory is its seeming capacity to establish art's distinctness from all other human activities and experiences. It is, indeed, this affirmation of the autonomy of art which is responsible for aesthetic formalism's profound influence on twentieth-century theory and practice in the arts. Bell's approach, however, is seriously flawed in a number of respects. One area of difficulty is as follows. Every visual object *qua* visual object has a formal aspect—in other words, it can be viewed as a configuration of line, shape, and colour. But why is it that .we do not view every such object in these terms? Why is it that some configurations of form arouse aesthetic emotion, but others do not? One presumes that Bell would say 'because only some objects (i.e. artworks) have *significant* form'. But again we must ask what is it that makes such forms significant? Bell's only answer would be 'because they have the capacity to arouse aesthetic emotion'. This, of course, makes the argument into a logically vicious circle. Bell cannot, in other words, provide us with adequate criteria for distinguishing significant artistic form from insignificant non-artistic form.

At the heart of Bell's problem here is the fact that he argues art's autonomy at the price of a far too rigid distinction between

---

² Ibid. 72.   ³ Ibid.

art and life. With the formalist theory of Clement Greenberg somewhat different considerations come into play. Greenberg argues
that 'Quality, aesthetic value, originates in inspiration, vision,
"content", not in form. Yet form not only opens the way to inspiration; it can also act as a means to it; and technical preoccupations, when searching enough and compelling enough, can generate
or discover "content".'[4] Now, as I interpret him, Greenberg's
approach here holds that the aesthetic value of a work resides not
simply in the formal configuration as such, but in the way in which
the configuration exemplifies the artist's having had some original
ideas about the employment of his or her medium. However, in a
recent symposium Greenberg has also emphasized the central role
of 'taste' in the experience of art. By taste he means 'unanalysable'
acts of 'aesthetic intuition'. Yet, at the same time he also holds
that 'Value judgements constitute the substance of aesthetic experience', and that 'taste at its best, in its fullest sense, likes whatever
is good'.[5] On the one hand, then, Greenberg wants to link aesthetic value to complex appraisal of the formal configuration's
relation to broader developments within the medium, and on the
other hand he wants to say that judgements of aesthetic value are
unanalysable acts of intuition. These two claims are clearly in
conflict. Greenberg does, indeed, go one step beyond Bell in allowing that aesthetic judgements are logically complex, involving historical factors; but like Bell he is bewitched by the psychology of
such judgements. He sees them as private experiences, wholly dis-
connected from the continuum of life. This is the great problem of
all aesthetic formalism in its attempt to comprehend art.
To explain why form is aesthetically significant, we must
account for the aesthetic judgement as a logical complex
involving the interplay of perceptual and, in the broadest sense,
socio-historical factors. But, at the same time, we must be able to
relate this to the psychology of the experience: its capacity to
distance us from the demands of everyday practical existence.
Aesthetic formalists such as Bell at one extreme, and Greenberg at
the other, fail to make this connection in any adequate way. They
dramatically over-emphasize the gap between art and life. Kant's
theory of art offers a way of bridging this gap. Before addressing

---

[4] Clement Greenberg, 'Necessity of Formalism', *Art International* (Oct. 1972),
106.
[5] Clement Greenberg, 'Art Criticism', *Partisan Review*, vol. xlvii, no. 1 (1981), 36.

it, however, I must first say something about his own version of aesthetic formalism.

The very essence of Kant's position can be grasped in terms of a few basic points (which I shall outline in a different order from that adopted in the *Critique of Judgement*). The first centres on the claim that pure aesthetic judgements have the 'form of finality' but are 'apart' from any definite 'end' or concept.[6] By this Kant means that the aesthetic judgement is simply and solely directed to the relation between parts and whole in phenomenal configurations, i.e. ones which are immediately present to the senses. Now, an object's relation to the senses can also give rise to pleasure in two other ways. First, when the pleasure is determined by what kind of thing the object is. We might enjoy the look of an object or animal, for example, because they seem to be perfect specimens of their kind; we might enjoy the look of a tool because it promises an efficient performance. In these cases our pleasure arises from the conformity of a particular item to some external 'end' or standard. Kant describes this as our pleasure in the 'good'. In other cases, our pleasure in the way an item relates to the senses is determined by a purely causal relation. For example, our enjoyment of one particular colour or flavour rather than another is based solely on personal preference—on what one's eyes or taste-buds happen to like coming in contact with.

The pure aesthetic judgement, in contrast, is determined neither by conformity to a concept or end nor by mere causal impact on the senses. We may, for example, simply enjoy the relation of balancing shapes and colours in some formal configuration for its own sake. This means that, in order to enjoy an object's formal relations, it is not presupposed that we know what kind of thing the object is, nor even whether it is real or not. Kant thus describes the pure aesthetic judgement as being 'apart from any concept' and 'disinterested'—in a way that judgements of the good and the agreeable are not. But if this is so, how is it possible for us to enjoy the disinterested play of the cognitive faculties upon the aesthetic object? Kant's answer is that our perceptual interaction with such an object is one that brings the understanding and imagina-

[6] Kant's main discussions of this are in the First, Second, and Third Movements of the Analytic of the Beautiful, in *The Critique of Judgement*. All further citations from Kant in this chapter refer to *The Critique of Judgement*, trans. J. C. Meredith (Clarendon Press, Oxford, 1973).

tion—broadly speaking, our capacities to comprehend and to attend and recall—into a harmonious, mutually complementary relationship. The bringing of these capacities into such a relation is of extreme significance. For, according to Kant, it is the understanding and imagination whose joint function makes all communication possible. Hence, when the formal richness of a perceived configuration stimulates these capacities into heightened co-operation, it is, thereby, enhancing our general cognitive hold upon the world. It furthers our 'sense of life'. This is why the formal configuration appears to have structure and purposiveness over and above that which is determined by the kind of thing it is.

Now, I have discussed the merits and demerits of Kant's general theory of the aesthetic at length elsewhere.[7] Putting it concisely, he is right in the essentials if not in the details of his theory. However, for present purposes it is crucial to say something now about the theory's scope. First, what Kant is describing are the logical and phenomenological outlines of a very fundamental experience. But he is describing the experience in its simplest and purest state—giving us, as it were, the prototype. This is, in part, why his account gives so much emphasis to nature. Artefacts, and human and animal forms, are things which appeal directly to our practical and instinctual needs, whereas purely natural forms tend not to. It is nature, therefore, which is most amenable to the pure aesthetic judgement. Given this, however, we must not suppose that aesthetic experience arises exclusively from our intercourse with nature. In this respect, Kant offers examples of artefacts of a decorative kind—such as wallpaper—whose function is such that their artefactual status is entirely overlooked. We engage with them as purely formal configurations.

And this at last brings us to the work of art. Kant's treatment of this topic is kept separate from his main aesthetic theory because the demands which art makes on us cannot be reduced to those of the pure aesthetic judgement. Kant is aware of this, and after the main exposition of his Analytics of the Beautiful and the Sublime, he gives art systematic treatment in a way that brings out both the kinship and difference between the pure aesthetic judgement and the aesthetic experience of art.

---

[7] In my *The Kantian Sublime: From Morality to Art* (Clarendon Press, Oxford, 1989). See esp. chs. 3 and 6.

Before addressing that, however, I shall conclude this section with a brief comparison between Bell and Greenberg on the one hand, and Kant on the other. First, Kant does, I think, do justice to the pervasiveness of the aesthetic by tracing its root to the enjoyment of formal configurations as such, and, most notably, those of nature. Greenberg, in contrast, has nothing to say about nature; and Bell's dismissive remarks concerning it seem to unwarrantably reduce all enjoyment of nature to that which Kant terms the 'agreeable'. It should also be noted that not only is Kant's theory more comprehensive in scope, it is also more comprehensive in structure. By linking pure aesthetic judgements to the harmony of understanding and imagination, Kant is able to explain both why we find such judgements pleasurable and why this pleasure is of such existential significance. This latter point is precisely what highlights the common weakness which I noted earlier in relation to Bell and Greenberg. The latter thinkers fail to tie the cognitive complexity of the aesthetic judgement to its elevating psychological effects. After all, why should the enjoyment of form 'transport' us from everyday life (Bell); why should it be felt as 'intuitive' and 'unanalysable' (Greenberg)? Kant's answer is that as the outcome of an achieved harmony between the two capacities which are the basis of all cognition and communication, aesthetic pleasure further stimulates these functions; it enhances our sense of life. Ironically enough, through its distance from the pleasures of everyday existence, the aesthetic both lifts us above and relates us back to that life. Let us now investigate the special conditions which, for Kant, govern art's role in this process.

II

I shall expound Kant's theory of art by presenting his arguments in substantially the same order as they appear in §§43–50 of *The Critique of Judgement*.

Kant's first major claim is that fine art is a distinctive and privileged mode of artifice which is intrinsically 'final'—an end in itself. It is to be contrasted with handicraft which (although there are ambiguous cases, such as watchmaking) is only attractive 'by means of what it results in (e.g. "the pay")'.[8] Fine art must also be

---

[8] Kant, 164.

contrasted with two modes of artifice which are commonly regarded as art. The first of these is 'mechanical art', which seeks 'to actualize a possible object to the cognition of which it is adequate'.[9] What Kant probably has in mind here are representations which are created solely with a view to conveying factual information, and which make no demands on us beyond that. The other mode of artifice commonly regarded as art is rather more difficult to comprehend. Kant suggests that when art is intended to arouse pleasure it is called 'aesthetic'. Fine art is the major example of this, but there is also another mode, which Kant terms 'agreeable art'. This applies 'where the end of the art is that the pleasure should accompany the representations considered as mere sensations'.[10] As examples of this, Kant cites such things as the 'entertaining narrative' and 'play of every kind which is attended with no further interest than that of making the time pass by unheeded'.[11] Kant's characterization of this as 'agreeable art' is rather unhelpful since he has earlier made it clear that the agreeable is linked to the causal impact of stimuli upon the subject's sensibilities. Clearly such a relation is not involved here. However, Kant's point is that some representations, in effect, function like this. All we ask of them is that they amuse or entertain. We are dealing with, in other words, kitsch—though Kant himself, of course, does not use this term.

In §45, Kant takes his first major step in the definition of fine art proper. We are told that 'A product of fine art must be recognized to be art and not nature. Nevertheless the finality in its form must appear just as free from the constraint of arbitrary rules as if it were a product of mere nature.'[12] Kant's point here is not that art must represent nature, but rather that artistic representation must appear free from contrivance and 'laboured effect'. It must have the quality of—let us call it—*naturalness*. On these terms, the work of fine art is recognized as the product of artifice, but, in so far as it conceals the rules and techniques which governed its production and thence appears natural, it will be more amenable to aesthetic appreciation.

This first major point is of extreme significance in terms of defining art *qua* object. For the naturalness of the fine art object means that it will appear different from products of mechanical

---

[9] Kant, 165.   [10] Kant, 165.   [11] Kant, 166.   [12] Kant, 166–7.

and agreeable art. One presumes (though Kant does not remark upon it) that works in these latter categories are produced, by and large, according to familiar rules and formulas, and that these rules will be manifest in their appearance.

Having defined, then, what is distinctive about fine art at the level of reception—our engagement with the artwork *qua* phenomenal object—Kant procedes in §46 to trace the origins of this, at the level of the artist's creative subjectivity. Fine art, we are told, is the product of 'genius'. By 'genius' Kant does not mean something ineffable and extraordinary, but rather natural talent—that element in the creative process which cannot be acquired by simply learning the technical rules of artistic production, and which, conversely, cannot be adequately explained by the artist to others in terms of such rules. Indeed, it is originality which is genius's 'primary property', in the sense of being a necessary condition. It cannot, however, be a sufficient condition, since, as Kant rightly points out, there can also be 'original nonsense'. The originality of the fine artwork, therefore, must be 'exemplary'. It must serve as a model to stimulate the creativity of other artists.

In §47, Kant clarifies and deepens several of the points made above. First, genius is the province of fine art alone. This is shown by means of a contrast. In Kant's words:

. . . all the steps that Newton had to take from the first elements of geometry to his greatest and most profound discoveries were such as he could make intuitively evident and plain to follow, not only for himself but for everyone else. On the other hand no *Homer* or *Weiland* can show how his ideas, so rich at once in fancy and in thought, enter and assemble themselvs in his brain, for the good reason that he does not know himself, and so cannot teach others.[13]

Hence the conclusion that 'In matters of science, therefore, the greatest inventor differs only in degree from the most laborious imitator and apprentice, whereas he differs specifically from one endowed by nature for fine art'.[14] Kant's point, then, is that, since all the steps in the formulation of a scientific theory can be sufficiently explained, whereas those in the creation of a work of fine art cannot, we must infer, accordingly, that scientific creativity is of a different order from that of art.

Now Kant is, I think, right in his conclusion, but somewhat

[13] Kant, 170. [14] Kant, 170.

misguided in his argument—which pushes in a different direction. For the fact that the construction of a scientific theory is sufficiently explicable in terms of the following of logico-mathematic rules, whereas for art there are no analogical rules, simply indicates that scientific theories and artworks are different kinds of artefacts. To posit a difference at the level of subjective creativity as well requires a supplementary argument, which I shall provide in section II of this discussion.

Kant's other main point in §47 is an elaboration of his previous claim that the originality of the fine artwork must enable it to serve as a model of others. This is not simply a case of such works being imitated. Rather they are 'followed', in a kind of creative dialogue. As Kant puts it, 'The artist's ideas rouse like ideas on the part of his pupil, presuming nature to have visited him with a like proportion of the mental powers.'[15] However, this being said, Kant insists again that originality is not a sufficient condition of fine art. Again in his words, 'there is . . . no fine art in which something mechanical, capable of being at once comprehended and followed in obedience to rules, and consequently something *academic* does not constitute the essential condition of art'.[16]

Now, it might be thought that in making this stipulation Kant is simply asserting the prevailing late eighteenth-century ideology of neo-classicism, against the wilder innovations of the *Sturm und Drang* tendency. That this may be a part of Kant's meaning is shown by the fact that, in the course of his earlier contrast between scientific and artistic creativity, he notes, that despite not being grounded in genius, science admits of continuing progress, whereas 'genius reaches a point at which art must make a halt, as there is a limit imposed on it which it cannot transcend. This limit has in all probability been long since attained.'[17] In these remarks, Kant is possibly exemplifying the neo-classicist view that the highest standards of creativity were attained in classical antiquity. However, even if in his discussion of originality Kant is indeed giving neo-classicism its due, there is certainly more to his position than just that. For, if an original work is, as Kant holds, to be exemplary, and able to stimulate creativity in others, then it will only do so in so far as there is some common ground between

---

[15] Kant, 171.   [16] Kant, 171.   [17] Kant, 170.

artist and pupil. Technical issues and the academic system of rules provide such a shared starting-point for dialogue.

I am arguing, then, that in making originality *and* academic rule-following into necessary conditions of fine art, Kant is both making obeisance to contemporary values and setting forth a position with claim to more general validity. The awkward relation to these two strategies reaches a crisis point in §48, which is entitled '*The relation of genius to taste*'. Here Kant makes the crucial claim that 'A beauty of nature is a *beautiful thing*; beauty of art is a *beautiful representation* of a thing'.[18] In order to enjoy the beauty of nature we do not have to know what kind of thing the object which sustains the beautiful form is. The enjoyment of artistic beauty, however, is rather different. Here there are two mediating factors. The first is as follows: 'If . . . the object is presented as a product of art, and is as such to be declared beautiful, then . . . a concept of what the thing is intended to be must first of all be laid at its basis.'[19] Kant's point here is that if we are to judge a work of art to be beautiful *qua* art, then we must be able to recognize it as, say, a picture of a landscape, or a poem about love, or a sonata in a minor key, or whatever. However, as well as being able to recognize the work's format and subject-matter, Kant stipulates the mediation of a further condition, as follows: 'since the agreement of the manifold in a thing with a inner-character belonging to it as its end constitutes the perfection of the thing, it follows that in estimating the beauty of art the perfection of the thing must also be taken into account'.[20]

Kant's argument here is ambiguous. By 'perfection of the thing' he could mean either that of the kind of subject-matter being represented—for example, the perfection of the landscape itself, or ideal love itself—or he could mean the perfect or ideal standard of achievement for artworks addressing that kind of subject-matter—for example, such works as Claude Lorraine's landscapes or Shakespeare's Sonnets. Actually, there is evidence that he means *both*. For, in an important passage, Kant now formally defines what he means by the 'beautiful representation of an object'. It is

the form of the presentation of a concept, and the means by which the latter is universally communicated. To give this form, however, to the product of fine art, taste merely is required. By this the artist having practised

---

[18] Kant, 172.   [19] Kant, 173.   [20] Kant, 173.

and corrected his taste by a variety of examples from nature or art, controls his work and, after many, and often laborious, attempts to satisfy taste, finds the form which commends itself to him.[21]

This is a strange passage. For in it Kant stresses how the artist must draw selectively upon examples from both nature and art. But surely this is not a question of taste—as Kant explicitly suggests. It is rather the striving for perfection, a feature which enables art to transform what is ugly in nature. Significantly, Kant goes on to describe the process involved here in the following terms. The achievement of the beautiful artistic form, the *artistic* function of taste, 'is not, as it were, a matter of inspiration, or of a free swing of the mental powers, but rather of a slow and even painful process of improvement, directed to making the form adequate to his thought without prejudice to the freedom in the play of those powers'.[22]

This yields an apparent contradiction. In §46 Kant traces the achievement of naturalness in art to the effect of genius. Yet here he ascribes it to the effect of patient and systematic study. It may, of course, be that Kant is simply wanting to give the neo-classicist aesthetic of perfection its due, but, again, there is a case for saying that he is also trying to make a more universal claim. In this respect, we must remember that, for Kant, naturalness is a property of the art-object, and genius is a property of the creative subject. To get from the latter to the former in such a way that the art-object will be exemplary demands that the artist has not only assimilated the most perfect products of nature and tradition, but is also able to embody these in original artefacts. Taste in art, in other words, is the process whereby genius is refined by mastery of perfection. It is the ability to achieve the quality of naturalness in an artefact.

What Kant has been doing so far, then, is moving from the naturalness of the artwork's appearance, to a detailed analysis of the demands which this imposes on the creator. What he has not yet done is to show in any depth what enables the reception of the work of art to be regarded as aesthetic. He addresses this task in earnest in §49.

The key concept here is that of the 'aesthetic idea'. Kant formally defines it as 'that representation of the imagination which

---

[21] Kant, 174.   [22] Kant, 174.

induces much thought, yet without the possibility of any definite thought whatever, i.e. concept, being adequate to it'.[23]
Further on he offers a much richer description of it:

. . . the aesthetic idea is a representation of the imagination, annexed to a given concept, with which, in the free employment of the imagination, such a multiplicity of partial representations are bound up, that no expression indicating a definite concept can be found for it—one which on that account allows a concept to be supplemented in thought by much that is indefinable in words, and the feeling of which quickens the cognitive faculties . . .'[24]

On these terms, then, an aesthetic idea is a concept whose embodiment in an image or sensible form serves to energize that concept by allowing it to be taken up and imaginatively developed by the receiver. This does not simply mean that the aesthetic idea evokes a trivial play of associations. In its highest function, imagination can 'remodel experience' in two ways. First, by addressing fictional subjects, or, in the case of material which does occur in experience, by making that material present to the senses 'with a completeness of which nature affords no parallel'.[25] The upshot of this remodelling is that we are no longer tied to familiar empirical laws of association. Artistic form does not simply present the world, it represents it, so that it is known and responded to in a new way.

Now, it is artistic form's capacity to take familiar material and to overwhelm our customary understanding of it that is, as I read Kant, the basis of its aesthetic character. The pure aesthetic judgement—addressed to nature—places understanding and imagination in a generally harmonious relation. The diversity of a formal configuration—its imaginative richness—offers different ways of perceptually exploring, i.e. unifying it. In the work of art, a particular way of unifying—the artist's presentation of his or her material—opens up a diverse play of imagination. Art, in other words, invites a more focused form of aesthetic judgement. Its narrower scope, however, is, as we have seen, by no means a disadvantage.

To summarize, then, Kant argues that fine art consists of artefacts which have the quality of naturalness, a quality which is both a function of a unique mode of creativity—namely genius—and the capacity to refine such talent through the mastery of artistic and

---

[23] Kant, 175–6.   [24] Kant, 179.   [25] Kant, 177.

natural perfection, i.e. taste. The artefacts which embody this relation are sources of aesthetic ideas. They instantiate concepts in a
way which stimulates the imagination in creative directions. Given
the theory, I shall now offer a critical review of it.

III

A first point to note is the usefulness of Kant's general outline of
fine art. He clearly identifies it as a mode of artifice in whose exercise and in whose finished product both producer and consumer
find enjoyment for its own sake. Kant is, therefore, identifying art
with *unalienated labour*, a mode of artifice wherein the creator
achieves self-recognition and through which his or her audience
can share the artist's view of things. Kant is also right to separate
this from 'mechanical' and 'agreeable' art, which simply relate
information, or provide mere distractions from everyday life.

These distinctions are given their force by Kant's detailed analysis of fine art. His notion of naturalness is central here, but
requires very careful appraisal. Clearly there are works wherein the
artist has mastered tradition, but which do not declare themselves
as derivative or academic. However, this 'absence of laboured
effect' cannot have quite the fundamental role which Kant assigns
to it. Within the category of fine art itself we need criteria of both
good and bad works. Naturalness is one such criterion. To insist
that all works *qua* fine art must have this quality would be to
restrict the class of fine artworks to an unacceptable degree. For
surely we need to be able to talk of good art, bad art, and non-art.
Kant's approach, however, would leave us with the distinction
between art and non-art as such.

Given this, we should look for the real basis of distinguishing
between fine artworks and other artefacts, in the direction of
Kant's other key notions starting with genius. The primary property of genius, we will recall, is originality. We must, however, also
remember that Kant does not mean originality *per se*, for, as he
puts it, there can be original nonsense. Hence, the quality of originality in art essentially involves the mastery of perfection in terms
of both natural form and the tradition of the medium. Originality,
in other words, must be tasteful. Now, Kant's claims here cannot
be accepted quite as they stand. For one thing, the concept of orig-

inality is itself complex. It has two opposite poles. On the one hand, there is its use in the sense of innovation, literally the invention of new things; on the other hand, there is the case where an item refines some existing genre to an exceptional degree of sophistication. A single work can, of course, combine elements of both these. Delacroix's *Death of Sardanapalus*, for example, is radically innovative in one sense *vis-à-vis* its handling of violent subject-matter, yet in another sense it can be seen as a sophisticated refinement of *Rubeniste* painterliness. Kant's failure to define originality in terms of both innovation and refinement and the overlaps between the two is again symtpomatic of the tension between proposing a general theory of art and ratifying a particular neo-classical ideology. In particular, his stress on originality's link to taste means that he is in effect privileging originality in the sense of refinement, at the expense of originality in the sense of innovation. This affirmation of the neo-classical ideology is unacceptable; for there can clearly be art which is original in the innovatory sense, but is neither original nonsense nor a mere refinement of tradition. The greatest achievements of *Sturm und Drang*, such as Goethe's early novels, are excellent examples of this.

Now, if we insist that originality be understood in this more complex sense, what is of general validity in Kant's theory of art begins to stand in clearer relief. The original artwork—the work of *fine* art—is one which breaks with traditional rules of production, or which refines them to an unexpected degree, or which combines elements of both these. Whichever case applies, the key point is that what defines art is not simply an artefact's possessing an appropriate form (a topic which I will address in a moment), but also the form's relation to other works—and that means, in effect, its historical situation.

Now, whilst being a necessary condition of fine art, originality cannot be a sufficient condition. For clearly other kinds of artefact can be original in the senses just describeed. We must, therefore, look for further conditions which, in conjunction with originality, can serve to demarcate fine art from all other modes of artifice. The first of these is to be found in the notion of the 'aesthetic idea'. This (we will recall) is a sensible or imaginative manifold which presents a concept or symbolic content in such a way as to engage the imagination in a non-arbitrary and explorative play. In such an engagement, the symbolic content is taken up in a way that 'remodels' experience. This is where the link with originality proves crucial. For the 'entertaining narratives' of 'agreeable' art can also involve the sensible presentation of symbolic content, as is the case in television 'soap operas'. But here experience is not remodelled. We are simply lifted into a world that is an alternative to our own. It furnishes us with a route to voyeuristic escapism. If, however, the sensible or imaginative manifold generates its symbolic content in an original way, this arrests our normal relation to things. We view the content in a way which opens out new ways of assimilating it, and, indeed, which places us in a sharing and empathic relation to the creator.

We thus reach a final fascinating point, which is a function of the relation between originality and the aesthetic idea. In this respect, it will be recalled that in section II I argued that Kant's attempt to separate art and science on the basis of genius is not wholly successful. The fact that all the steps in the creation of a scientific theory can be sufficiently explained, and taught but those involved in the creation of fine art cannot, means only that we are dealing with different kinds of artefact—and not different kinds of creativity at the subjective level. To establish this latter claim requires an additional argument. One might provide it briefly as follows. Scientific theories are founded on principles of inference, deduction, and measurable quanta. This means that, in principle, a scientific theory could be devised by someone other than the person or persons who did in fact formulate it. The identity of the work of fine art *qua* original aesthetic idea, in contrast, logically presupposes the existence of just that person or persons who is responsible for its production. The creativity involved in art draws directly on the creator's personal orientation towards history (in the broadest sense) and upon what is distinctive about that person's view of the world, and his or her capacity to handle material. In science and other modes of technological production, the identity of the creator is contingent *vis-à-vis* the objective meaning of the end-product. In the work of art, in contrast, the piece's objective meaning—its general human significance—flows decisively from the particularity of its origins and articulation. Kant, of course, did not explicitly propose this argument. It is, however, not only consistent with his position but is, in effect, also pointed towards by his contrast between scientific and artistic creativity.

IV

In Section I of this chapter I argued that, in its most general terms, Kant's general aesthetic theory is more comprehensive in both scope and structure than those of Bell and Greenberg. Kant's theory of art consolidates this superiority to an extraordinary degree. He offers general criteria whereby fine art can be clearly distinguished from other modes of artifice and the aesthetics of nature. But, much more than this, he clarifies and explains something of art's existential *depth*. This achievement is grounded on his analysis of genius and the aesthetic idea, which, with the modifications proposed in section III, do justice to fine art at the level of its object, the psychology of its reception, and the artist's creativity. Of especial significance is Kant's willingness to stress that what defines fine art is not just the possession of an appropriate kind of form, but the fact that this appropriateness is actively determined by the work's relation to rules and standards established by other works. This relational context is the very flesh of artistic form. It is through this emphasis that Kant's approach is able to overcome the tensions and restrictiveness of Bell and Greenberg's formalism. He overcomes the unwarranted gap between art and life by making social and psychological dimensions a part of art's full definition. We are thus led far beyond aesthetic formalism. More significant still for the purpose of this study, we also find some remedy for the shortcomings of Merleau-Ponty's account of the artwork— namely his failure to give adequate emphasis to the artwork's relational context and its aesthetic significance. In the next chapter I will investigate these issues in somewhat greater depth. The focus of discussion will be the complex issue of art and the aesthetic's relation to politics, and, in particular, Walter Benjamin's account of it.

4

The Producer as Artist

From Benjamin to Critical Aesthetics and Postmodernism

In recent times, Walter Benjamin has come to enjoy an almost canonical status amongst artists, critics, and social theorists of art. Rather than participate in the canonization, I shall critically address a few of the many issues raised by one of Benjamin's most influential essays, 'The Author as Producer'.[1] That this text is so influential is due, I think, to two things. First, whilst addressed specifically to literature, it might appear to bring about some kind of general reconciliation between political commitment and art's claim to autonomy; and, second, it shares the postmodern scepticism about the worth of specialized forms of knowledge and production, and, indeed, about the viability of such ideas as 'creative personality' and aesthetic experience. In this chapter I shall both expound and criticize Benjamin's text with these problems in mind and will consider its relevance to the visual arts, as well as to literature. The basis of my approach will be a Critical Aesthetics derived from Adorno and Kant, and one which is grounded on a historicist notion of aesthetic experience. I will hope to show that this approach not only improves on Benjamin, but can also serve as a working example of postmodern philosophy construed in a positive sense.

I

First, the way in which Benjamin uses the notion of the 'political tendency' or 'commitment' in art is in the sense of 'what will be of

[1] For a discussion of aesthetic disinterestedness in specific relation to art, see pt. 3 of my 'Alienation and Disalienation in Abstract Art', in A. Harrison (ed.), *Philosophy and the Visual Arts* (Reidel, Dordrecht, 1987).

use to the proletariat in the class struggle'. He suggests that the usual understanding of this notion is 'perfunctory' and involves two assertions that are difficult to reconcile—on the one hand, art must be 'politically correct', and, on the other hand, it must be of high quality. Benjamin claims that the relation between these two assertions must be understood in the proper light, and to this end he proposes an alternative formulation of the problem. 'One can declare that a work which exhibits the right tendency need show no further quality. Or one can decree that a work which exhibits the right tendency must, of necessity, show every other quality as well.'[2] Benjamin commits himself to the second of these alternatives, and proposes to demonstrate its validity by showing that 'the tendency of a work of literature can be politically correct only if it is also correct in the literary sense'.[3] He is going to show, in other words, that for art to be politically correct it must also possess a correct artistic tendency which comprises the 'quality' of the work.

Benjamin's approach to this is 'dialectical'. He wishes to consider the artwork 'inserted into the context of living social relations' and this means, of course, in the context of the 'productive relations' which characterize the society in which the work is produced. However, where Benjamin differentiates himself from other Marxist commentators is the way he interprets this approach. Instead of asking 'what is a work's position *vis-à-vis* the production relations of its time [he will ask] what is its position within them'.[4] This means, in effect, that before asking which class interests in society a work serves to represent, we must first clarify the work's contribution to techniques of artistic production in that society. Benjamin explores this issue through extensive discussion of a number of examples. I will depart from the order and emphasis of his presentation so as to make the major points of his argument stand in clearer relief, and so as to highlight the relevance of his discussion to the visual arts.

First, Benjamin offers us the example of the 'New Objectivity' movement in German photography and literature of the late 1920s and early 1930s. This tendency is regressive in both an artistic and a political sense because, whilst it addresses material of revolutionary significance, its technical treatment of this material simply involves the refinement of existing—that is to say bourgeois—tech-

---

[2] Walter Benjamin, *Understanding Brecht* (New Left Books, London, 1977), 86.
[3] Ibid.   [4] Ibid. 87.

niques of specialized artistic production. The result of this is that
New Objectivity's photography 'has succeeded in turning abject
poverty itself, by handling it in a modish technically perfect way,
into an object of enjoyment'.[5] Likewise, the literature of New
Objectivity 'has turned the *struggle against misery* into an object of
consumption . . . The characteristic feature of this literature is the
way it transforms political struggle so that it ceases to be a compelling motive for decision and becomes an object of comfortable
contemplation.'[6] At the heart of this, and other regressive tendencies, lies the 'myth' of 'creative personality' and the desire to
achieve 'masterpieces' that perfect the 'finish' demanded by bourgeois artistic techniques.

The first major step in Benjamin's argument, then, is that if
a work simply achieves technical excellence within established, specialist bourgeois, modes of production, it will nullify any potentially revolutionary material by transforming it into an object of
aesthetic contemplation. What, then, is the alternative? It is useful
in this respect to consider the example of Dadaism. Benjamin suggests that

> The revolutionary strength of Dadaism lay in testing art for its authen-
> ticity. You made still-lifes out of tickets, spools of cotton, cigarette stubs,
> and pictorial elements. You put a frame round the whole thing. And in
> this way you said to the public: look, your picture frame destroys time;
> the smallest authentic fragment of everyday life says more than painting.[7]

In Dadaism, in other words, the claims of painting as a bourgeois
specialism are subverted by breaking the conventional barriers of
the medium. Likewise, John Heartfield's photomontage with its
conjunction of image and text shakes up the medium in such a
way as to allow even a book-jacket to become a 'political weapon'.
The second major step in Benjamin's argument, then, is that if art
is to have a politically correct tendency it must be technically innovative in a way that subverts the specialist categories of bourgeois
art production. As Benjamin puts it, 'intellectual production cannot
become politically useful until the separate spheres of competence
to which, according to the bourgeois view, the process of intellectual production owes its order, have been surmounted; more precisely the barriers of competence must be broken down by each of

[5] Benjamin, *Understanding Brecht*, 95.   [6] Ibid. 96–7.
[7] Ibid. 94.

the productive forces they were created to separate, acting in concert'.[8] On these terms, then, the artist must not simply 'supply an apparatus of production'; he or she must change that apparatus in a way that subverts specialization. By so doing, the artist will be brought closer to producers working in other media, and will begin to break down the producer–consumer divide which lies at the heart of the bourgeois concept of art itself. Indeed, the author or artist must understand him or herself as being in essence a producer and in this way achieve identification and solidarity with the proletariat.

I have presented, then, what I take to be Benjamin's major arguments in 'The Author as Producer'. The question now arises as to whether these arguments are plausible. A first point to note is that whilst at the start of his text Benjamin seems to be about to reconcile the possibility of political commitment in art with its claims to autonomy, he does not, in the final analysis, achieve this. This is because he arbitrarily identifies the tendency which constitutes artistic correctness and quality not with technical innovation as such, but with innovation that disrupts bourgeois specialization—and thus helps the proletariat in the class struggle. Art is politically correct only when it is artistically correct, and it is only artistically correct when it is politically correct in a quite particular way. This is not exactly a logically vicious circle, but it certainly destroys any lingering claims that art might have to autonomy. We require politically correct technical means as well as content.

This position is even narrower than one might at first think. To see why this is so we must question Benjamin's criterion of what constitutes politically correct technical means. It is interesting in this respect that much postmodern art, such as the novels of Kathy Acker or the paintings of Anselm Kiefer or Jorge Immendorf, does break down traditional barriers between visual and written media, and thus subverts our sense of rigidly separate modes of production. Indeed, even before this, one of the most fundamental impulses in Pop Art—as evidenced in the work of Robert Rauschenberg or 'Happenings'—is to break down the barriers between art and life itself. However, this disruption of specialized modes of production does not seem to be giving much help to the proletariat in the class struggle, in so far as the market economy

---

[8] Ibid. 95.

thrives upon work of this sort. Indeed, with the rise of postmodern art, the art market has actually undergone unparalleled expansion. Postmodern works give one more variety, and thence value for one's money. To some degree this expansion may be explained by the fact that postmodern art—with its emphasis on figuration, fantasy, and incongruous eclecticism, panders to the taste of the ruling élites. But even radical tendencies have been caught up in this. The Saatchi Collection, for example, has a sizeable holding of work by the feminist photographer Cindy Sherman; indeed, the Tate Gallery has recently acquired material by another feminist artist (Mary Kelly) which subverts the distinction between written text and visual image in the most uncompromising way. The taste of the moment, in other words, likes the removal of barriers between media. There is a veritable culture of deconstruction which unites the radical sensibility with the more chic art buyers amongst the ruling élites. These conditions suggest, of course, that the subversion of specialist practices is not (as Benjamin implies) a sufficient condition of efficacity in the class struggle. We must look, rather, for innovation that is even more specific—and this means, in effect, more narrowly dictated by political concerns. Perhaps our criterion of it would simply be 'something like Brecht'. This, I would suggest, is, in fact, the sentiment at the heart of Benjamin's entire paper.

Let me now address a second problem raised by 'The Author as Producer'. This arises from the fact that the existence of specialist art categories is not just bound up with the bourgeois regulation of society—it is also the basis of conventions which enable art to be generally legible. The proletariat—and even much of the revolutionary intelligentsia—can only read art in terms of categories provided by the ruling class; hence the barrier-breaking technical innovations tend to be misunderstood or dismissed as obscurantist. Now, it may be that Benjamin's emphasis on the different art media co-operating in the task of subverting specialization is meant to bypass this difficulty. For example, the conjunction of images with subversive texts could 'explain' the changes that are taking place in the nature of the image, or it could indeed by the vehicle of subversion—as in the case of Barbara Kruger's overlaying of patriarchally significant photo-images with Letraset. However, even when such innovations are more generally legible, another problem arises. In the latter part of his paper Benjamin emphasizes that in producing the requisite technical innovations the artist must become a 'teacher'—not in the sense of producing propaganda, but in the sense of placing an improved apparatus of production at the disposal of other artists. But Benjamin's pedagogic metaphor is perhaps too revealing. When artists self-consciously take on the role of barrier-breakers, the tendency surely is to preach. Other producers and the audience feel that they are being patronized. This, of course, is the whole problem of the avant-garde. Its 'practices of negation' (to use T. J. Clark's term) may lead it to identify with the proletariat, but this identification does not work the other way. To the proletariat the writer or artist appears as a privileged being who dispenses imperatives or arcane meanings from the heights of superior knowledge. He or she looks, in other words, very much like (in Benjamin's terms) an *author*.

There is another, even more fundamental difficulty in this area. To understand it, we must first note the fact that whilst what counts as aesthetically valuable varies according to different cultures, there is an interesting phenomenon which cuts across these divides. One finds it, for example, in both the Renaissance and our own time, and in numerous African and Oriental cultures both past and present. It consists in an admiration for artefacts which are well made, or unusual instances of their kind. Our attention focuses here not simply on function, but on the relation between function and the qualities of being well made or unusual. Now, whilst Benjamin is clearly aware of this phenomenon, he completely underestimates its pervasiveness. Indeed (in Western culture at least), this contemplative attitude towards artefacts is accentuated and entrenched by conventions pertaining to the format and (where relevant) the packaging of artworks, and the context in which they are encountered.

It is this phenomenon of accentuation which explains the ability of the contemplative attitude to assimilate even the most radical works. The fate of Dadaism proves particularly instructive here. Far from showing (as Benjamin suggests) that the 'slightest' portion of everyday life says more than painting, it has been the fate of even such subversive objectives as Duchamp's 'ready-mades' to be set aside as objects of contemplation. Rather than subverting the very conventions which make 'quality' paintings or sculpture possible, Dadaist works have now been established as extreme versions of such conventions. They are interpreted as directing us towards aspects of reality whose aesthetic potential has not hitherto been realized. That Dadaism and its legacy would meet such a fate was promised as soon as it adopted a format which could be made intelligible in terms of such notions as the picture or free-standing sculpture, or of hybrids of the two. To circumscribe visual material within a picture-frame or to mount it on a plinth or in a gallery space serves of itself to set that material apart from the immediate interests of everyday life. It gives 'finish' to the work and invites us to appreciate the qualities of its material and of the artist's ingenuity in configuring it in this particular way. Ironically, this is even true of artists such as the Art–Language group or Victor Burgin, who have been influenced to some degree by Benjamin's writing. In the case of Art–Language's *Portrait of V. I. Lenin in the style of Jackson Pollock* or Burgin's *Gradiva* series, whatever profound messages about medium and reference may be contained, these are 'lost' in the pleasure of trying to see the image of Lenin, or in the pleasure of recognizing the creator's cleverness in actually being able to establish such relations between image and text. Indeed, even with so subversive an artist as Joseph Beuys, any dimension of insecurity—of tension between the work and our cherished values—is limited by the fact that the work is placed securely in a gallery, i.e. in a space for contemplation. The gallery context provides a position of safety from which even the most disturbing or iconoclastic images can be enjoyed in a kind of low-key spectacle of the sublime.

Similar considerations apply in the cases of literature and music. In works such as John Dos Passos's novel *U.S.A.* or André Gide's *Journals*, the breaking of barriers between 'literature' and reportage or autobiography is contained by features pertaining to the format of the medium itself. Such works are printed by 'name' publishing houses, and in covers whose very design connotes 'high-level quality art product'. The packaging here orientates us towards a quite specific way of reading the work itself. In music, this tendency is even more pronounced. Brecht and Weill's *Threepenny Opera* rarely features in programmes at the Hammersmith Palais. It is much more likely to be encountered in the *Royal* Opera House. Records of it are packaged in sleeves depicting or connoting the sleazy glamour and decadence of Berlin in the 1920s. It is 'serious' music—an exotic part of an ongoing 'great tradition'. A great deal of popular music has now, of course, also been drawn into the contemplative net. For a moment in the 1970s it looked as though the anarchic destructiveness of punk rock (and especially the Sex Pistols' version of it) had found both a musical format and way of packaging records which would defy assimilation by canons of 'respectable' pop culture. But no. Not only has the music itself been assimilataed within the mainstream of pop style and business, but, indeed, even the graphic design of punk LP sleeves for some time enjoyed a broader vogue in commercial packaging.

Benjamin's problems, then, come down to this. He wants art of an innovative, barrier-breaking sort which will lead to political motivation rather than aesthetic contemplation, but the very nature of established and avant-garde art formats and contexts of encounter seems to work against this. One superficially promising way round the problem would be to argue that art of this sort is viable if it is part of a programme which seeks to transform the material conditions under which artworks are themselves received. However, at the present time a revolutionary transformation of the dealer and gallery or publishing and performance systems seems very remote—except in the form of 'alternative spaces' for viewing, or 'self-help' publishing organized by oppositional artists themselves. But, again, even if a wholesale transformation on these lines could be carried out, little, I suspect, would really be changed. As soon as a work is encountered in any context which displays it *as* an object-to-be-viewed (and—or read, or heard), our attention will focus on it in terms of its aesthetic quality. This, I would suggest, is also the case where artists adopt the familiar strategy of situating or performing their work on the factory floor or canteen, or in the community centre. For even if such works are directly relevant to these contexts, this will not, of itself, energize the political dimension. A bad work will be found boring no matter how relevant it may seem in theoretical terms; a good work will receive attention (pertaining to its quality or unusualness) which will go beyond immediately relevant political considerations.

Now, in conversation with the author, Charles Harrison has suggested that the foregoing critique of Benjamin is not wholly adequate. It neglects the fact that Benjamin's paper was written specifically in the context of the rise of Fascism. Hence his analysis should not be extrapolated in general terms, in so far as it embodies a strategic response to quite specific historical conditions.

Against this, however, it must be noted that in 'The Author as
Producer' Benjamin is implicitly assigning a more general
significance to his position. This is shown by the praise he gives
to the way in which newspapers in the Soviet Union dissolve the
barrier between reader and writer. The clear implication is that
art of the barrier-breaking sort is not just a strategic response to
Fascism, but rather exemplifies the patterns of production in a
progressive socialist society. Of course, his Soviet example now
seems, to say the least, ill-advised in historical terms. However, at
a theoretical level, his position *vis-à-vis* Marxism as such is
wholly consistent. For the ultimate goal of a socialist society must
be the elimination of alienation—and this entails the abolition of
the division of labour in processes of production. At present, this
division remains fundamental to production, even in a 'postindustrial' society. Indeed, the system of 'wage-slavery' and the
rigid demarcation of work and leisure also remain. Hence, even
under present historical conditions Benjamin's barrier-breaking
artwork still has the potential significance which he assigns to it,
and the continuing influence of his paper bears witness to the
fact. Indeed, if one is a Marxist, such an artwork embodies an
imperative which is both artistic and ethical. For since it is, in
effect, an image of productive relations in a socialist society, the
creation of such works is demanded if only to focus and reaffirm
(in at least partially concrete terms) the ultimate political goal.
The difficulty with this, however, is not only in the areas which I
have already indicated. Rather, it gives the barrier-breaking work
the same kind of rigid authoritarian role that until recently was
held by socialist realism in the Eastern Bloc. Its logical role in a
Marxist theory of art is to embody a testament of utopian purity
that the socialist faithful must bear witness to. But, of course, history moves on. The situation changes. Hence, what one must
demand of politically progressive art is not reaffirmation of some
abstract goal which seems increasingly unlikely in both theoretical
and practical terms. *Rather one must ask art to profess the possibility of change itself.*

The criticisms made here and throughout this section now point
us in the direction of an alternative treatment of the relation
between artistic autonomy and politics. It involves, on the one
hand, retaining Benjamin's basic insight of there being some connection between artistic quality and technical innovation; and, on

the other hand, relating this connection to a theoretically adequate historicist notion of aesthetic experience.

II

As a first step in this task, it is worth addressing the aesthetic theory of Theodor Adorno. According to him, late-capitalist–state-capitalist society is a wholly administered one. In such a society, concrete material things and the human subject's modes of cognition are dominated and reduced by the demands of instrumental technocratic reason and the exchange value of commodities. Specifically, that which is individual and/or dynamic finds itself bludgeoned by patterns of stereotypical classification. As Adorno puts it, 'the concrete *qua* particular serves only the trivial purpose of identifying some commodity, of buying and keeping it. The marrow of experience has been sucked out of the concrete.'[9]

It is against this background of a reified society that the artwork must be viewed. However, whilst such a work internalizes the historical conditions under which it was produced, it does not simply reflect these. We find, rather, that creative embodiment in an artistic medium sublimates these conditions in such a way that the artwork takes on an antagonistic relation to the society in which it was produced. Integral to this process of sublimation is the fact that art has a manifest illusionistic or apparitional quality, due to the fact that, whilst being a material thing, the artwork—through its semantic qualities—is much more than a mere thing. Adorno tells us, for example, that artworks 'are an empirical appearance free of the burden of empirical being in general . . . [and] However clearly they may have been actualized as durable products, owing for example to their material, they nevertheless have something momentary and sudden that is imparted to them by their act-like nature.'[10] This active illusionist or apparitional quality places the artwork in a relation of determinate negation to the repressive society in which it was produced. As Adorno puts it,

. . . apparition defies the ruling principle of reality, which is the principle that all things can be exchanged for other things. By contrast, the appearing

[9] T. W. Adorno, *Aesthetic Theory* (Routledge & Kegan Paul, London, 1984), 46.
[10] Ibid. 120.

or apparition is not exchangeable because it is neither a torpid particular being, replaceable by other particular beings, nor an empty universal, sub-suming and levelling specific being in terms of some common characteristic. Whereas in the real world all particulars are fungible [i.e. exchangeable], art protests against fungibility by holding up images of what reality itself might be like if it were emancipated from the patterns of identification imposed upon it.[11]

Another level of determinate negation is set up by the fact that the artwork follows relatively autonomous laws of form and technique. Again, in Adorno's words,

The formative categories of art are not simply different in kind from those outside. They actively seek to impart what is peculiar to themselves to the outside world. In the latter the prevailing forms are those that characterize the domination of nature, whereas in art, forms are being controlled and regimented out of a sense of freedom. By repressing the agent of repression, art undoes some of the domination inflicted on nature. Control over artistic forms and over how they are related to materials exposes the arbitrariness of real domination which is otherwise hidden by an illusion of inevitability.[12]

Now, this outline of Adorno's theory is crude, but it does at least highlight the main trajectory of his thoughts on the relation between art and politics. Put succinctly, his claim is that if art's sensuous and semantic media are pursued according to laws of form and technique alone, then the resulting artwork will stand in a relation of determinate negation to repressive society: that is, it will issue in artefacts whose very mode of being indicts a reified and dominated social order, and suggests the possibility of an alternative existence. On these terms, in other words, it is pre-cisely art's pursuit of aesthetic autonomy which invests it with socio-political explosiveness. We do not need to give it some overt political content. Indeed, an artwork which is orientated towards ramming home some specific political message will simply repro-duce and consolidate the coercive mentality of a repressive society. Its oppositional significance will be merely formal. It is, of course, this latter realization which gives Adorno's theory common ground with that of Benjamin. Where the two differ most funda-mentally is in relation to art's autonomy—its status as a special-

---

[11] Adorno, *Aesthetic Theory*, 122–3.   [12] Ibid. 199.

ized practice. Benjamin regards such specialization as a reinforce-
ment of bourgeois values and society, whereas, as we have just
seen, for Adorno it is the very insistence and autonomy of artistic
specialization which renders it antagonistic to the means–end func-
tionalist rationality of repressive bourgeois society. If Adorno is
right, then artistic autonomy and authentic political significance
are not just complementary, they are inseparable. His theory,
however, raises many difficulties of its own. I shall focus on just a
few of these.

First, throughout his aesthetic theory Adorno himself highlights
a fundamental tension in our experience of art. It consists in the
fact that since artistic form negates repressive society and gives
voice to the individual's suffering, it is, thereby, affirmatory—a
form of consolation and reconciliation. Hence, whilst the artwork
contains the promise of a better order of things, this must be measured against the affirmatory here-and-now consolation it offers.
Affirmation of this sort, of course, will tend to provide an inclination for quiescence rather than an imperative for oppositional
political consciousness. Now, despite noting art's affirmatory function, Adorno for the most part gives much greater emphasis to its
oppositional significance. He sees modern art, indeed, as a last bas-
tion of resistance against the conformity of an administered society. This is unduly optimistic, given (as noted in section II) the
ability of society to absorb even the most rabidly avant-garde
works. One might say, then, that, having resolved the affirmatory
and oppositional moments of art, Adorno fails to deal adequately
with the present domination of the latter by the former, and,
indeed, also fails to explain how art's escapist affirmation itself
might be energized into oppositional consciousness.

There is a possible way round this difficulty, in so far as Adorno
constantly stresses that artworks are complexes whose meanings
are not absolutely fixed. They will vary, rather, according to the
different historical conditions under which they are received. This
suggests that a proper historico-critical awareness might be the
activational element which would enable art's determinate nega-
tions to be oppositional as well as affirmatory. It is, however,
difficult to follow this insight up, within the immediate framework
of Adorno's theory. For it is central to his overall philosophical
position that the relation between human cognition and the objective world is only partially congruent. We seek to impose identities

upon the world, but the world can never be exhaustively trapped within our classificatory nets. There is always a resistant core of particularity—of the 'non-identical', as Adorno terms it. Now, in order to express this resistance without doing violence to it, Adorno is led to adopt an oblique and unsystematic style of philosophical investigation, which shuns outright definition of key terms. In consequence, what Adorno means by such notions as 'aesthetic form' and 'truth-constant' remains disturbingly generalized. Now, whilst this approach may have some philosophical justification, it paralyses the immediate utility of Adorno's theory. His massive theoretical structure simply fails to engage with many of the problems it addresses, at a concrete enough level. Given the luxury of a large-scale study, it might well be possible to recast a great deal of Adorno's aesthetics into a more directly workable form. For present purposes, however, I shall be content to follow the most general trajectories of his argument—namely the claims that art's oppositional significance is a function of the relation between aesthetic form and a broader context, and that critical understanding has a privileged role to play in energizing this oppositional significance.

III

Let me first readdress the terms 'producer' and 'artist'. In relation to the former, one might say that in a society characterized by the division of labour, the vast majority of productive techniques involve the taking of a means to an end in accordance with definite rules. The criterion of such rule-following is efficiency—the achievement of a maximum output of produce from a minimum input of raw materials and labour time. Now, to produce in this commonplace sense is to engage in rational activity, but only in a very restricted way. There is little or no room for self-recognition or individuality in the productive process itself. Of course, in such production there must of necessity be constant technical innovations, but again this is closely tied to criteria of efficiency, and is hardly ever determined by the individual producer in the direct context of the productive process. It is, rather, the province of an anonymous class of 'experts'. Indeed, when such innovation takes place, it seems merely to happen mysteriously as part of the 'natural' course of production. We do not think of such innovation as created by concrete individuals. It simply occurs.

However (as we saw in my discussion of Kant's theory of art), there is a crucial class of exceptions to this pattern of production and innovation. In certain cases, whilst it is necessary that the producer must have a controlled grasp of existing techniques of production, there is scope for deviation from these in the process of production. Indeed, a producer of this sort may create an artefact which possesses features which were not envisaged at the outset of its creation. There is room for originality, spontaneity, and imagination, which goes beyond what has been established by existing techniques. Do we not, therefore, need a name for this kind of producer? The fact is, of course, that we already have one—namely 'artist'. The creation of art, in other words, is not simply production, and the artist is not simply a producer. The term 'art' denotes rather a domain where production ceases to immediately disappear into the practical consumption patterns of everyday life. Indeed, its consumption takes the form of us recognizing aspects of the way in which the work was produced. Its original qualities arrest our attention and thereby display the work as having its origins in the creative artifice of a specific individual or social ensemble. It is interesting in this respect that Benjamin asserts that such notions as 'creative personality' and 'masterpiece' are now 'myths'. But this would be true only if human beings were mind alone—passive tablets whose actions simply reflected the imprint left upon them by the socio-historical. Of course, we are not like this—we are, rather, embodied beings; and this means that no matter how much our behaviour is determined by cultural and ideological norms, there is always an irreducible residue of individuality in our outlook on the world. Those who merely produce are orientated towards behaviour that is rational but socially over-determined. Those who create art, in contrast, edge towards the residue of individuality and a relatively free expression of their rational being.

Given this distinction between producer and artist, an interesting way of reappropriating the notion of aesthetic experience is opened up. For a long time many people (including Benjamin) have assumed that the aesthetic is fundamentally a psychological state—a 'disinterested' or 'contemplative' 'feeling' which we sometimes enjoy in relation to art and nature. However, whilst there can be an important dimension of such feeling in aesthetic experience, it is not this psychological dimension which defines such experience. The aesthetic, for example, may make us feel contemplative, or elated, or whatever, but so can the positing and solution of problems in philosophy or politics. To define aesthetic experience, therefore, we must concentrate on its logical features: on the kind of objective qualities which give rise to such experience, and on the nature of the interest we take in them. Now, whatever else may be involved, aesthetic pleasure arises from our cognition of *elements of structure amongst phenomenal qualities* in nature and art. As we saw in Chapter 3, critics such as Clive Bell assume that the qualities in question here are formal in the extreme—such things, for example, as harmonies of line and colour. This, however, is only the *infrastructural* level of aesthetic form. In addition we must take account of *superstructural* qualities. By these, I mean features which pertain more to the 'content' of the work. Suppose, for example, we respond to the violently disfigured limbs in a painting by Francis Bacon, or to the seemingly tactile palpability of apples in a Cézanne still life. Now, at one level our response may take the form of a continuation of our everyday attitude to things. The violence of the disfigured limbs in Bacon's painting may simply make us feel uneasy, and Cézanne's apples make us want to touch them. However, since we also know that these are elements in a painting, we can also (and are perhaps more likely to) judge them in terms of their contribution to its compositional unity. Indeed, what is of special interest is the way infrastructural qualities—such as delicately cross-hatched lines or transitions of tone—make the superstructural qualities emerge from them.

Now, under normal circumstances, our appreciation of structure in things logically presupposes references to some end or network of values external to the thing itself. For example, we may like the look of a machine because its structure promises optimal performance—that is, we judge the particular structure in relation to its more general function or significance. In the case of enjoying an artwork's or natural formation's formal cohesion as such, no such reference to an external context is necessarily presupposed. We are concerned, rather, with how the item hangs together as a particular.

In fact that aesthetic pleasure focuses on particularity is of much deeper significance. It will be recalled, from Chapters 2 and 3, that Merleau-Ponty and Kant both ground art's distinctiveness in the fact that it is a form of meaning which is at once rational and sensuous. It has semantic qualities, but these cannot—as with ordinary or technical forms of language—be adequately paraphrased. We can only gather up the artwork's meaning by direct sensory or imaginative intercourse with it. Its referential qualities are necessarily tied to its particular sensuous embodiment. On these terms, to enjoy an aesthetic object is to have our capacities for rational comprehension and sensory–imaginative receptivity engaged in a mutually complementary and profoundly harmonious synthesis. The world comes into focus in a way which draws on the unified structure of our embodied being, rather than on our rational and sensible dimensions in isolation, or in a mere means–end relationship.

The major point to gather from these remarks is that what is fundamental to aesthetic pleasure is not its psychological quality—its 'contemplative' or 'disinterested' 'feel'. Such terms are only justified in so far as they are interpreted as *logical* characteristics. One might, for example, describe such pleasure as 'contemplative' because it logically presupposes direct acquaintance with a sensible particular in a perceptionally well-integrated way. Again, one might describe aesthetic pleasure as 'disinterested' because it is a mode of enjoyment which does not logically presuppose direct references to some more general context or function. (I shall elaborate some further aspects of disinterestedness's relation to art in the next chapter.)

Interpreted as logical characteristics, then, contemplativeness and disinterestedness define aesthetic pleasure as a logically distinctive mode of enjoyment. This logical autonomy, however, is no more than that. For the particular conditions—both personal and historical—under which our capacity for aesthetic pleasure is exercised mediate it to a profound degree. In the case of the modern Western sensibility, for example, a harmonious cohesion of form is often not enough to aesthetically engage us in any deep sense. Familiarity tends to deaden our capacity to respond to the aesthetic configuration. We require, therefore, a dimension of originality in such appearances: structures which in some respect—however small—we have not seen the like of before. We require, in other words, an addition to our knowledge of the world, an aesthetic *experience*, an appraisal of merit, rather than just an aesthetic pleasure.

To thoroughly historicize aesthetic experience, therefore, we must now consider how it links up with the distinction between production and art outlined earlier. A first question in this respect is that of how it is possible for us to judge some combination of infrastructural and superstructural qualities as being of high quality. This may seem 'intuitive'—a case of the work's properties simply 'looking right', but whilst our criterion of rightness may have this psychological feel, it logically presupposes acquaintance with a comparative context, i.e. a background history of previous encounters—both satisfactory and unsatisfactory—with aesthetic situations. There is a subjective and an objective dimension to this. In subjective terms, an artwork may please us because we personally have not had much experience of this way of articulating form before. However, this may testify only to our inexperience. Viewed in a detailed comparative context of other artworks, the work may well count objectively as an unusual or unprecedented development of the medium. Now, if an artwork were simply to reproduce existing styles and patterns of unity and (where relevant) socially 'acceptable' content, then it would have to be judged objectively as mundane and commonplace. We would tend to regard it as mere production rather than art. It is only when the work to some degree imaginatively departs from existing techniques and principles of composition and/or ideologies of form and content that our aesthetic enjoyment is energized into an aesthetic experience of art. Again, there are two aspects to this. On the one hand, the work may be radically innovative and constitute a rupture with tradition. On the other hand, it may refine a traditional genre or style to an unprecedented degree of sophistication. What both these features have in common is the achievement of originality.

Now, to admit that originality is a criterion of aesthetic experience in art is to acknowledge that aesthetic experience is at heart historically mediated. To enjoy the work's aesthetic merit logically presupposes—whether we are explicitly aware of the fact or not—that the work has been appraised in relation to a background context of personal or collective historical existence. If, indeed, it is this collective background (i.e. a sound knowledge of the medium's techniques and traditions) which informs our enjoyment, then our judgement of aesthetic merit can lay some claim to objectivity. It becomes an instance of rational discourse in so far as it can be justified by arguments based on comparisons and contrasts with other works. Now, let us suppose that we enjoy an aesthetic experience in relation to an artwork, and let us suppose also that we are committed to the historicist criterion of such experience which I have outlined above. If we wish to explain why we take such pleasure in this particular work, a programme of research is opened out before us. We must ask how the originality of the work is made possible. What conventions—technical and ideological—does it refine or break; to what degree does it do this; why did innovation of this sort take place at just this moment rather than before; how did the previous conventions become established; what broader societal interests did they serve? These sorts of question become all the more pressing when the dimension of originality involve politically significant material.

Consider, for example, Picasso's *Guernica*. Why does this work have the kind of aesthetic impact which it does? To explain this, one is led to ask some fundamental questions about Socialist Realism and Surrealism. The former tendency is packed—one might even say saturated—with political meaning, yet it is precisely this saturation which renders any dimension of artistic innovation inert. By so doing it negates the one feature which could have energized the political content so as to make Socialist Realism into something more than propaganda. Surrealism, in contrast, moves in the opposite direction. Here we find the revolutionary intention of destroying bourgeois canons of collective visual rationality. But this destruction ends up by subverting canons of collective visual rationality as such. The image is pushed too far in the direction of the individual's private fantasy. Picasso, in contrast, combines the tendencies to realism and surrealism in a way that intelligibly situates us in the disturbing zone between the two. His image works because it brings together and thereby transforms two tendencies which had already begun to ossify into cultural conservatism. Why this ossification had taken place can, in turn, he explained by reference to the broader socio-historical conditions which sustain these tendencies. I do not, however, propose to investigate this question further. It is enough for us to note that in explaining the aesthetic effects of *Guernica* we are led in this direction.

Another two examples—from the world of film—are also instructive here. These are *Wall Street* (1987), and *The Long Good Friday* (1979)—directed by John Mackenzie from a screenplay by Barrie O'Keefe. *Wall Street* is a big Hollywood film, with big Hollywood stars, and was rewarded with a big box-office success, and Academy awards. Aesthetically speaking, it is a small film.

The plot and stereotyped characterization converge upon a single theme—the ugliness and dehumanizing effects of Wall Street share-brokering. This theme is rammed home constantly and reaches its climax in a courtroom scene where one of the central protagonists defends the virtue of . . . greed. Now, *Wall Street* panders to liberal anxieties about the unacceptable aspects of capitalism. However, whilst the film projects this comfortable oppositional stance, it at the same time utilizes and affirms precisely those 'lowest common denominator' techniques of insistent persuasion and stereotype which are amongst the worst aspects of market 'culture'.

The Long Good Friday, in contrast, makes political points without this dimension of contradiction. It sets out to be, and succeeds in being, an exemplary gangster film. It is not formally innovative, but rather utilizes conventional narrative techniques with a high degree of refinement and sophistication, in terms of both plot and characterization. However, what makes the film so remarkable is that the narrative lucidly emerges from a quite determinate set of socio-economic relations and political tensions. In the plot's resolution, these are shown to be far more potent than the vanities, ambitions, and powers of even London's leading gang boss. The film's structural pivot, in other words, is the familiar Marxist notion that the socio-economic infrastructure of capitalist society is decisive and disfiguring in respect of the destiny of the agents within it. This political 'message' is, however, not oppressively stated and reiterated at every possible opportunity. Rather, it is gradually made visible as a matrix which guides and impels the narrative to its tragic outcome. The political idea appears—to use Merleau-Ponty's phrase—as the 'lining and depth' of the narrative, and makes its point all the more persuasively in so far as actions and events constellate around it with *aesthetic* necessity, rather than one which simply manifests an authoritarian insistence that 'this is how things are in the world'. What makes this fact itself of political significance is that it shows how art can be politically effective without succumbing to crude market methods of 'selling a message'. Doubtless *The Long Good Friday* was made to make money, but its superb integration of the political and the aesthetic in the unexpected context of an exemplary gangster film shows that artistic and commercial success need not involve 'selling out'.

These considerations now enable us to place Benjamin's worries about the relation between political art and aesthetic effect in a proper perspective. Benjamin's fear, we will remember, is that the aesthetic contemplation of a work prevents it from becoming a vehicle for 'compelling' political decision. This, I would suggest, is true only if we construe aesthetic experience psychologistically as a private state or feeling. In contrast to this I have argued that a hostoricist notion of such experience presents matters in a rather different light. For we know that the 'comfortable' contemplation of an artwork is not simply 'intuitive' or 'unanalysable'; we can rather explain how it works, and to do so sensitizes us to historical issues and (if we are searching enough) to cultural politics. Indeed, in the case of art with an overt political content, the dimension of aesthetic effect is a necessary one if the work is going to strike us as anything more than propaganda. The problem with propaganda is that it is something to be seen through—either in the sense of recognizing it as 'mere propaganda', or in the sense of being forced to go beyond the work by taking up the political stance which it thrusts towards us. To experience political meaning as a necessary feature in the original aesthetic unity of an artwork, in contrast, is to encounter that meaning at an equalizing distance. We are not simply being preached at by a superior being who knows what is good for us. Rather, we see the political content as something which contributes to the distinctive vision of this particular artist or creative ensemble. It is important enough to help define who and what the artist or ensemble is. If, therefore, it can figure in the artist's self-definition, it can also figure in ours. We are, in other words, invited to share the artist's political values. They are not rammed down our throats. Aesthetic experience can allow us, therefore, a freedom to make political decisions which propaganda cannot; and decisions made freely, of course, are always the most compelling.

Similar considerations hold in the case of art which does not have any explicitly political content. For art's visionary power is not a private communion with the particular recipient. Historicized in the way described above, the aesthetic experience centres on a distinctive vision of the world which has been achieved through a struggle with tradition and ideology. If the work sublimates this struggle, rather than pressing it directly and violently upon us, then it takes on the character of an invitation. The work respects the existential space of its recipients, and clarifies aspects of their own struggle with the world. Indeed, it is this very dimension of respect for the recipient which enables the work to be all the more readily and deeply assimilated within his or her experience. Artistic vision and recipient, in other words, are linked in a kind of liberating empathy. Interestingly, in a reply to his critics, Habermas has recently declared that

> If aesthetic experience is incorporated into the context of individual life-histories, if it is utilized to illuminate a situation and to throw light on individual life-problems—if it at all communicates its impulses to a collective form of life—then art enters into a language game which is no longer that of aesthetic criticism, but belongs, rather, to everyday communicative practice. It then no longer affects only our evaluative language . . . rather, it reaches into our cognitive interpretations and normative expectations and transforms the totality in which these moments are related to each other.[13]

I would suggest that the empathy flowing from historicized aesthetic experience is precisely the medium wherein the aesthetic can be integrated within the totality of a life, whilst retaining its own distinctive character and its positive moral and political energy. This will be discussed more fully in the next chapter.

I am arguing, then, that there is no magic formula for political art. Art is only politically effective when it is *good*; and for its merit to be fully realized we must engage in a Critical Aesthetics grounded on a historicist notion of aesthetic experience rather than on its psychological dressing. If this propensity is cultivated, aesthetic experience then figures not as the culmination of our engagement with the artwork, but rather as the starting-point. It falls upon the consumer to generate political meaning from clues— intended or unintentional—which the artist provides. This, I would suggest, is the only way in which the artist–consumer divide can be crossed whilst at the same time preserving the aesthetic, political, and, indeed, moral integrity of both parties.

The ideologically pure at heart, of course, will not be much satisfied with an answer of this sort. They will demand political significance in a much more crude and direct sense than the one just outlined. This demand is not just authoritarian; it is, in the final analysis, contradictory. For if direct political effects are so vital to an agent, then it is incumbent on that agent to give up art.

---

[13] Habermas in Richard Bernstein (ed.), *Habermas and Modernity* (Polity Press, Cambridge, 1985), 202.

In almost all historical circumstances, political effects are achieved most effectively by direct political action. If the artist, however, is still insistent on creating political art, he or she must ask why. Where does this need for art spring from? The answer is, of course, aesthetic pleasure—the satisfaction of externalizing oneself in a medium where one's rational and sensible—imaginative capacities are optimally integrated. But if this is the case, to use art as a mere vehicle for political action or meaning is to split these rational and sensible aspects apart—to place them in a merely contingent relation. The sensible base becomes a mere means for emphasizing some political imperative. This is actually worse than it sounds. For it internalizes and validates the crude techniques of means–end rationality which lie at the heart of capitalist production. Of course, it might be objected that there is no harm in turning the methods of capitalism against itself. But that is not the case here. For if the oppositional artist really wishes to use capitalist methods, then efficiency and maximum effect must be the keynote. This means . . . give up art, become an activist. Thus, in the very final analysis, the crude demand for political art issues in art's dialectical suicide.

IV

I would like, finally, to relate the theoretical position adopted in this paper to somewhat broader debates. First, my use of the term 'Critical Aesthetics' has several reasons underlying it. It is not just that I wish to stress the logical continuity which exists between the aesthetic experience of art and the practice of criticism. I also want to stress the lineage and kinship of my position. This goes beyond a mere utilization of insights from Benjamin and Adorno. For the account of art as a form of production which cannot be reduced to the following of rules is informally derived from that theory of genius in Kant's *Critique of Judgement* which I discussed at length in Chapter 3. Indeed, the kind of research programme which I see the particular aesthetic experience as inaugurating involves a focusing and extension of the question which is fundamental to Kant's Critical philosophy as a whole, namely, 'How is experience possible?' Kant's best answers to this question consist (in effect) of an attempt to articulate those features which are logically presupposed by any experience. I have endeavoured to offer such an articulation in relation to the particular case of aesthetic experience. More specifically, we have seen, here, the importance of originality or rule-breaking—i.e. features which logically presuppose historical awareness on the audience's part in order to be recognized. Hence, in order to understand the particular aesthetic experience of art, we are led first to a philosophy of that experience, then to historical issues implicit in it, and finally to cultural politics. By keeping attuned to Kant's fundamental Critical question, in other words, we grasp those broader connections which are entailed by his theory of genius but which he himself failed to make.

Now, Kant's Critical method is widely seen as an important factor in the rise of Modernism. He establishes a basic framework wherein different forms of human experience, such as the philosophical, the aesthetic, and the ethical, can be displayed as autonomous disciplines—each logically irreducible to the others. This separation enables the various disciplines to be pursued more efficiently, and promises unlimited progress with the ultimate possibility of universal human emancipation.

The project of Modernism, however, has now been called into question. As noted in the Preface to this work, we live in a 'postmodern' epoch whose main characteristics are a thoroughgoing mixing up of categories and a scepticism towards the idea of progress. We hear much talk, for example, of 'post-philosophy' and 'discourse'—intellectual apparatuses which are not specifically criticism, philosophy, history, or politics, but which combine these in an undifferentiable complex. Now, given the fact that the economic and social basis of society has undergone radical transformation since the late 1950s, it is only to be expected that cultural production will to some degree reflect this transformation. Discourse theorists, however, see their products as significant far beyond this. They see their work as marking out epochal limits—all in all the 'end' of philosophy, history, and social theory, or whatever—the entry into a post-metaphysical age. This approach, however, is self-contradictory. For any attempt to talk of ends, limits, or the impossibility of limits, presupposes precisely the logocentric–metaphysical system which it calls into question.

Especially instructive here is the notion of 'rigour'—a term used as extensively and insistently by poststructuralists and their apologists. As I argued in Chapter 1, rigour implies consistency, struc-

ture, and a whole framework of logical distinctions, and converges
ultimately upon well-defined notions of meaning and presence.
(Even the most hysterical and anarchic texts of Baudrillard, for
example, hinge upon discernible structures of claim and overstate-
ment.) In fact, without rigour and consistency no communicative
act whatsoever would be possible. Now, to admit the claims of
rigour and consistency is to admit the claims of rational criteria for
the validation or refutation of discourses. Given this, the postmodern era does not amount to quite the epochal break which it might
at first seem. We are dealing not with the breakdown of canons of
rational thought as such, but rather with hugely complex new patterns of production, distribution, and interaction amongst them. A
strategy wherein this process of continuity and change might be
articulated is as follows.

   Kant's modernism provides a useful framework for articulating
the relative autonomy of different forms of human experience, but
we must go beyond him in the direction of Jürgen Habermas's version of Critical theory[14] by acknowledging that such forms are not
each enclosed in an existential vacuum. Forms of experience such
as the aesthetic, the historical, and political are logically distinctive
but in practical terms can also modify and be of relevance to the
formation of one another. By mapping out these logical
autonomies and the way they enmesh with one another in practical
existence, we can come to some sort of terms with the complexity
of postmodern reality, and thus retain some grounds for belief in
progress. This means, in effect, that philosophy must take on a
definite role. As well as concerning itself with the description and
analysis of what is distinctive about various forms of experience, it
must also be a means of synthesis—an attempt to recuperate such
experiences within the context of the concrete human situation. In
effect, this means that philosophy must be prepared to learn from
disciplines such as social theory. This will make it postmodern in a

---

[14] I have in mind here Habermas's well-known paper 'Modernity—An
Incomplete Project', in Hal Foster (ed.), *Postmodern Culture* (Pluto Press, London,
1985). Habermas suggests there that Modernity should be continued as a project
seeking to reintegrate differentiated experiences within the unity of the lifeworld.
He is not, however, very illuminating about what form such reintegration might
take. Indeed, whilst the possibility of such reintegrative task gives some grounds for
a belief in progress and consensus, Habermas's vision of a totality of consensus is, I
think, totally at odds with the present economic and intellectual directions in which
society is moving. Progress is a reasonable hope—but *absolute* progress is not.

positive sense. Such a philosophy will legitimize specialist practices but only in so far as, at the same time, it also clarifies their debts, implications, and responsibilities in relation to other areas of knowledge and existence. The Critical Aesthetics which has been advocated in this chapter is a viable example of this approach. It articulates the relative autonomy and distinctiveness of art and the aesthetic experience whilst reintegrating them with other fundamental aspects of our embodied historical experience. In so doing, it affirms the changing conditions under which we experience the world, *but it does not surrender to them.* As a further example of how this approach might be applied, I shall now consider another case of art's connection to broader existential issues, namely the relation between violence and painting.

5

Violence in Painting

That he with energy and art
Can picture evil and its sequel
Prives the beauty of his heart.
(Baudelaire on Daumier, in *Fleurs du Mal*,
trans. Alan Conder, No. LXI)

The representation of violence is a source of enduring pleasure and
fascination in our culture. Why is this? A familiar answer is one
which characterizes the approach of many feminist art historians.
This view seeks to link pleasurable responses to violence in painting to the way male sexuality is 'constructed' in a patriarchal society. The violent work is found pleasurable because it reflects, and
thereby consolidates, male fantasies of virility, power, and control.
It feeds, in other words, upon socially negative attitudes—especially towards women—which are deeply embedded in patriarchal
ideology. Unfortunately, the current debate about violence in painting seems to be conducted entirely in terms of this gendercentric
approach. This places the female viewer of an impossible position.
For, if she should respond positively to a violent image, then, from
the gendercentric viewpoint, she is implicitly identifying with the
conditions of her own kind's oppression. The gendercentric
approach is, however, radically incomplete, in so far as it takes no
account of the way in which responses to violence in painting can
be restructured and redirected by properties and effects arising
from both the medium itself, and the semantic conventions in
terms of which it is read. The gendercentric view, in other words,
fails to engage with the ontological and semantic specificity of the
medium itself. If, however, full due is given to this specificity, the
question of our response to violence in painting becomes, accordingly, much more complex. In this chapter, therefore, I shall, in

This chapter was published under the same title in the *Journal of Philosophy and
the Visual Arts*, no. 1 (1988).

section I, outline the three major categories of violent painting, and will, in turn, elaborate three factors which can mediate our reading of violence in such works. In section II I will then consider the question of what cognitive competences are logically presupposed in order for such categories and mediating factors to be brought into play. With these considerations in mind, I will, in section III, finally be able to offer a detailed explanation of some of the different kinds of positive response which we enjoy in relation to violent painting and the relation of these to aesthetic experience.

I

Let me first briefly outline the three major categories of painting which might be described as violent. The most obvious kind are those figurative works (such as Artemisia Gentileschi's *Judith and Holofernes*, Capodimonte, Naples) which depict violent events, or the immediate aftermath of such events. The second category consists in those figurative or semi-figurative works (such as Jackson Pollock's *Man With a Dagger*, Tate Gallery) which distort or disfigure some recognizable subject-matter to a wildly exaggerated degree. The final category can apply to either figurative or wholly abstract works. It consists of those cases—for example, Jackson Pollock's *Number 3: Tiger* (Hirschhorn Museum, Washington) which embody and manifest violent painterly means—such as hyper-vivid colouring, nervous and agitated handling, broken brushstrokes, and heavy impastos. Now, it is of course possible for some works to involve several or even all three categories (Pollock's *Man With a Dagger*, for example, might be seen in this light), but even if a work falls under only one of the categories, there is at least a prima facie case for describing it as violent. However, our willingness to describe a work in these terms must also take account of the fact that our reading of violence in painting is often mediated by three crucial factors. I shall now outline these in some detail.

The first factor to be considered is that of *narrative-function* (using this term in a very broad sense). In Pollaiuolo's *Martyrdom of St Sebastian* (National Gallery, London), for example, we do not simply find an act of violence depicted. Rather, this particular act embodies a recurrent and recognizable signifying motif. It nominally suggests that the Christian believer can transcend his or her finitude by accepting all earthly suffering—even unto death—in the expectation of ultimate redemption. The act of violence, in other words, signifies an imperative. It is to be recognized not in its own right—as a murder—but as a vehicle for some theological-moral message. Consider also Emile Node's *Head* (National Gallery of Modern Art, Edinburgh). Here the exaggerated distortion of the central motif and the reduction to basic shape and colour serves a narrative function beyond the demands of mere formal unity. It takes up an insistent stand against the traditions and values of Eurocentric academic art, by seeking a more 'primitive' and thence more direct communication between artist and viewer. The putative violence of the technical and formal means, in other words, should not be seen in just those terms—as an act of pure aggression. It signifies, rather, a particular insistent rejection and reformulation of the rigidified relation between painter and viewer. I am arguing, then, that a dimension of violence in terms of the subject-matter or medium of painting often serves a broader narrative function bound up with the affirmation of prevailing sets of moral or cultural values, or with the rejection of such values.

Let me now consider a second way in which our response to violence in painting might be modified. This is bound up with its *expressive function*. Consider, for example, Goya's *The Executions of the Third of May* (Prado, Madrid). In a work such as this, the artist is not presenting violence as an object of enjoyment in its own right, nor is he making it the vehicle of a partisan narrative about the rights and wrongs of the Peninsular war. Goya presents us, rather, with a vision of the sheer callousness and barbarity of the execution. The image is manifestly addressed to our tragic sense of life, and to feelings of pity for the victims, and outrage at the continuing barbarity of the human species. We might also consider here David's *Death of Marat* (Royal Museum, Brussels). At one level this is clearly a monumentalization and celebration of French revolutionary idealism. At the same time, however, the work solicits our awareness at a more universal level of feeling. The ultimate isolation and inescapable destiny of the finite embodied being are both set forth in the starkest and most uncompromising terms. I would suggest, then, that in some works the violent dimension is articulated not for its own sake, but in a way that invites a specific range of affective responses from the viewer.

The final modifying feature which I shall consider is *aesthetic function*. Pollaiuolo's *Martyrdom of St Sebastian*, for example, interprets the violent event as much in terms of its utility as a compositional device as it does in terms of its religious narrative function. This means that the violence is wholly subsumed within the demands of formal pictorial unity. We may even feel that the St Sebastian motif is simply an excuse for Pollaiuolo to produce a visually interesting composition. A rather more complex and profound work in this broad category is Delacroix's *Death of Sardanapalus* (Louvre, Paris). Here the violent subject-matter and its episodic distributions provide material which could easily disrupt the formal unity of the work. However, Delacroix integrates this material within a sophisticated composition wherein the episodic violence is organized in relation to firm diagonals, and finds a psychological point of convergence in Sardanapalus's gaze. I would suggest, then, that in some works our reading of violence is orientated towards its formal and aesthetic function. (This aesthetic level of significance can, indeed, reach beyond issues of formal unity alone—as I shall argue in section III of this chapter.)

Now, it should be clear that the three factors which I have here described as modifying our reading of violence are not mutually exclusive. They can coexist in the same work, and, indeed, it will sometimes be very difficult to separate them. The works by Goya and David, for example, might be characterized as complex expressions of moral indignation, i.e. as involving both normative and affective responses in an inseparable combination. This actually shows the complexity of the whole relation between violence and painting. Sometimes we will feel that a work quite clearly satisfies one or more of the three criteria by which it might be described as violent. Other works, however, might seem more ambiguous. Likewise, we might feel that in some paintings (such as Pollaiuolo's *Martyrdom of St Sebastian*) the violence is so modified by other functions that it would be misleading to describe it as violent at all. But, again, in other works the role of the mediating functions might seem highly ambiguous, or even completely overridden by the violent aspects. To determine, therefore, whether a painting can be described as violent, and whether (or to what degree) it is modified by other functions, involves some complex cognitive discriminations on the viewer's part. I turn now to the question of what competences are logically presupposed in order to make such discriminations.

II

If we are to recognize that painting x is a depiction of some violent act, this logically presupposes only that we have learned the basic code of pictorial representation itself, i.e. that we can recognize what kind of thing the picture is 'of'. However, to call a painting violent on the basis of its disfiguring of form or its roughness of handling, or indeed to see it in terms of mediated violence, presupposes another competence besides. For in order to recognize these aspects, we must not only have assimilated the basic code of pictorial representation, we must also have assimilated different ways in which the resemblance between paintings and violent acts can be instantiated.

Let me illustrate this. Suppose that by, some fluke, there is a culture wherein all painters represent in exactly the same style: in other words, they depict what can be recognized as different kinds of subject-matter but the *way* in which they depict is entirely uniform. Now, in such a culture there could indeed be depictions of violent scenes. But there could not be 'violent' disfigurations of form or handling, or the narrative, expressive, and aesthetic mediation of violence, because we can only describe works in terms such as these when there is a discrepancy between different individual styles of manipulating paint. We characterize a work as violently handled, for example, because it differs and contrasts with the handling we find in other works. We say that this act of violence is mediated by its narrative function, because it is clear that (on the basis of a contrast with other works) the violence is being manipulated in the direction of a message rather than simply presented in its own right. On these terms, then, to recognize a painting as violent or to recognize the way in which the violence is modified, logically presupposes both a basic literacy in the code of pictorial representation as such and the capacity to recognize different styles and conventions in terms of which this code can be articulated. In practice, this latter condition means that we must have a comparative knowledge of painting, i.e. a familiarity with many different instances of the medium.

It is, however, important to note that 'comparative knowledge' here is not synonymous with highly specialized iconographical art-historical knowledge. It should be construed rather as a much more basic competence. In childhood, for example, we learn to read pictures as being 'of' things. Indeed, through our broader immersion in cultural life we acquire the ability to read pictures as narratives—especially, of course, in terms of familiar moral and religious messages. Likewise, we learn to associate certain shapes, colours, and qualities of paint with certain kinds of emotion. On these terms, then, we acquire what might be called a proto-icono-graphic literacy in relation to painting, on the basis of a familiarity with both the code of pictorial representation as such, and with the broad cultural conventions which surround it. It is, I would suggest, at this level of the proto-iconographic—i.e. at the level of *immediate* legibility—that painting finds its major audience, and takes on its general cultural significance. Art historians, of course, may be able to read the work in terms of much more complex and less immediately apparent levels of signification, but this level of literacy does not determine the conditions of painting's general cultural reception. (Art, in other words, is not created for the purposes of art history.)

The full importance of the proto-iconographic level of literacy only becomes clear if we now consider some features which are not logically presupposed in order to recognize violence or the mediation of violence in painting. These features consist in a physical acquaintance with the artist, knowledge of the context in which a work was produced, and knowledge of biographical details of his or her life. (By biographical details here I mean both events in the artist's life, and those elusive impulses which are sometimes called the 'artist's intentions'.) The reason why these features are only contingently involved in our readings of violence and its various mediations is because when a painting is finished, it becomes physically independent of its creator and, indeed, of the immediate causal context of production. This destiny, of course, is known by the artist at the very outset. If he or she is to find an audience for a work, then it must not only follow the basic code of pictorial representation, but must also use generally familiar formal, narrative, and expressive conventions which enable it to be read in a more closely focused way.

Now, of course, from the viewpoint of art history as a discipline we are not only concerned with comparing and contrasting paintings. We want also to be able to explain the causal origins of the picture—why the artist produced it, what sort of audience he or she intended it for, and how it discloses the artist's broader relation to prevailing ideologies and societal conditions. In terms of art-historical understanding, in other words, a knowledge of the artist's biography, and the work's context of production, is indispensable. However, from the viewpoint of painting's general cultural reception, i.e. its life as a proto-iconographic mode of distinctively visual communication, such details are wholly secondary.

Suppose, for example, that an artist paints a work in the knowledge that it contains a reference which will only be recognized if the viewer has access to biographical data. This means that the work is now directly tied to the physical existence of its creator, or (at least) to the traces of the creator's existence beyond the painting itself. What makes this so self-defeating is not only the fact that it is at odds with pictorial representation's status as an immediately 'legible' proto-iconographic mode of visual communication, but also the fact that such private meaning will tend to be overlooked by the viewer. The audience will orientate itself instead towards those levels of signification which do not require distracting researches into the artist's life or historical circumstances in order to become intelligible. That there are such levels is shown by the very fact that, in creating a painting, an artist—whether he or she intends it or not—is taking up a position in relation to the tradition and history of the medium. The artist will employ technical, formal, and narrative motifs, which have general historical and cultural connotations, and which a viewer will read on the basis of his or her own knowledge of the medium and cultural experience. Even, in other words, if the intended private reference remains unrecognized, the work's contrast with and similarity to other works will enable it to be read aesthetically or expressively or even, perhaps, in terms of alternative narratives which are dependent on the culture which artist and viewer share, rather than upon what the artist consciously intends.

I have argued, then, that we describe a painting as violent, or as involving the mediation of violence, on the basis of a knowledge of pictorial representation as a code and by comparison and contrast with other paintings. We do not require any biographical details of the artist's life or the work's context of production. The reason why I have given these latter points such emphasis is because they are crucial to the understanding of a number of our responses to violence in painting—and most especially to the aesthetic ones. It is to the question of viewer-response that I now turn.

III

I want to begin with those cases where a violent picture is experienced fundamentally in terms of its violence as such. That it is experienced in these terms may hinge upon three facts: (*a*) the absence or minimalization of mediating factors in the work itself; (*b*) an inability on the viewer's part to recognize the presence of mediating factors; or (*c*) a sheer indifference to mediating factors (i.e. the viewer is interested *only* in the violence). Let us suppose, then, that for one of these three reasons a viewer is able to respond directly to the violence of the painting. How do we explain the fact that his or her response can be pleasurable? One way of accounting for it would be to take the approach noted in the introductory section to this chapter—namely that the violence reflects and consolidates male fantasies of power and control. Now, in relation to many male (and some female) viewers this will constitute an adequate basis for explaining the pleasurable response. It is, however, by no means exhaustive. For the fact that the viewer is here engaging with a violent painting rather than a real scene of violence can restructure the response in a significant way.

Consider, for example, the following situation. We witness an act of violence from a position in which we ourselves are not in any danger. Now, although the event may be fascinating, and although we may be powerless to intervene, most people will feel that they ought to take some action—even if only that of expressing disapproval. Simply to contemplate real violence normally leads to bouts of conscience and guilt at our inability to intervene. To contemplate violence in painting, however, brings no such psychological pressure. For the distance between what is real and what is here known to be imaginary serves to eliminate the moral constraints which conscience places upon our response to violence. There is, indeed, another dimension of elimination to be considered. Again, let us suppose that we witness some actual event of violence. Here the build-up to the event, its development and outcome, and its aftermath, are all entirely independent of us. We are unable to intervene. If, in contrast, we contemplate violence in a painting, we are dealing with one single moment from an imaginary event. Indeed, even if the work depicts some event which actually took place, or is a work which is violent in terms of disfiguring its content or in terms of handling, then because the painting is physically discontinuous from the depicted event (in the former case) and from the state of mind of the creator (in both cases), we can in such examples respond imaginatively to the painting without being constrained by reality. We can construct the build-up, development, and aftermath to the depicted violence or the violence of the painting itself at will—using the work only as a vehicle or focus for our own fantasies of control and power. On these terms, then, whereas the contemplation of violence in real life is inhibited by a sense of conscience and a sense of the independent reality of the events taking place, in painting these constraints are removed. The viewer can achieve a complete appropriation of the violence in terms of his or her personal fantasies and interests.

Now, this structuring of the response may again simply embody patriarchal attitudes to sexuality. But it need not be analysable solely in these terms. Many individual men and women crave power and control over others in contexts and for reasons other than sexual ones. Indeed, it does not take a repressed or incipient megalomaniac to fantasize about what it would be like to exercise power and control freed from moral, institutional, and physical constraints. The desire to transgress such limits at will, is, I would suggest, one of the major sources upon which our positive response to violence in painting draws. Now, against this, the gendercentrist might reply that whilst such fantasies as these may not involve an overtly sexual dimension, the fact that they exist at all is ultimately a reflection of patriarchal ideology. However, in retort to this one might say, that even if—in a matriarchal society—the violent aspects of male sexuality were eliminated, what would not be eliminated is the finitude of the individual embodied being and of the species itself. Indeed, if our world-view is materialist, a sense of finitude—with all its anxieties, challenges, and desperation, must be paramount. It is here, I would suggest, that we must look for the ultimate origin of that desire for violent transgression upon which painting sometimes draws.

Let me now consider our response to violence when it is mediated by narrative, expressive, or aesthetic functions. To read violence in terms of the first two functions can involve intellectual or affective responses which are, logically speaking, of the same short which we experience in the continuum of everyday life. We recognize, for example, the moral message of the work, and respond to it—either negatively or positively—in much the same way as we would respond to an ordinary moral statement, situation, or argument. Or again, we may find ourselves moved by the plight of the victim of violence in the picture, in much the same way as we might be moved by an encounter with such suffering in real life. In these cases, in other words, we read the violence fundamentally in terms of its relevance to, or contact with, the interests and values of everyday life. In the case of violence's aesthetic function in painting, however, matters are rather different. Here the violence and any of its narrative and expressive meanings are judged fundamentally in terms of their contribution to the painting's formal unity. It is in this sense that our appreciation of the violence and its significance is disinterested. There is, indeed, a further (more subjectively orientated) level of aesthetic significance here. If, for example, a work is highly original, we may find that its formal organization of the violence and its narrative and expressive functions serve to delineate a highly individual yet shareable vision of the world. This, I would suggest, is one of the most profound—perhaps *the* most profound—and valuable experiences which we can enjoy in relation to art.

To illustrate this in more detail, I shall consider Delacroix's *Death of Sardanapalus*. If, as art historians, we are familiar with the play by Byron which furnished the idea for the painting, we may read the work in terms of Sardanapalus's melancholia. On his death, the Despot is required by custom—willing or not—to put his slaves to death. This specialist knowledge, however, will not characterize the more general cultural reception of the work. For what the painting invokes at the proto-iconographic level of immediate appearance is a vision of barbarity and tragedy. The relations of brute force and cruelty on which Despotic power (however noble the Despot) is ultimately founded are laid bare in the most uncompromising terms. Now, aesthetically to empathize or identify with an artistic vision is not simply in some sense to agree with the narrative presented by the particular painting under consideration. It is also to delight in the visual means whereby the narrative has been realized. Delacroix's painting is colouristic, opulent, and formally sophisticated, and thereby runs the risk of merely presenting violence as a glamorous spectacle. But it can be argued that the work does not fall into this trap. The artist wins his narrative even though his visual means are so risky in relation to it. Indeed, it is precisely this dimension of risk which gives the *Sardanapalus* its verve, panache, and existential depth. Delacroix is not simply making a statement about Despotic barbarity, he is setting this notion forth in an original sensuous configuration. We find a distinctive and complementary balancing of rational understanding with sensuous embodiment—the two features which are fundamental to the human condition itself. The viewer may, therefore, feel able to identify with this risky and stylish way of articulating Despotic power. Now, those who prefer their moral truths uncluttered, of course, will not be able to identify with the work at all. But it is this very dimension of ambiguity in the *Sardanapalus* which gives a further reason for empathizing with its style of articulating violence. For, since the viewer is here invited to wrestle with the issue of whether the work celebrates violence or should be seen rather as a tragic revelation of it, this means that his or her own interpretative autonomy is respected. The viewer is engaged, in other words, at the level of exercising free, active choice, as opposed to merely passive receptivity.

I am arguing, then, that if the narrative, expressive, and formal aspects of a 'work' cohere in a strikingly original way, the work can present a style of engaging with the visual world that leads us to identify and empathize with it. The question now arises as to why this mode of empathy should be regarded as aesthetic. Do we not, for example, empathize with people in everyday life, i.e. identify with their opinions and values, their way of holding these, the total image they project to the world—all in all, their sheer style of being? It is, of course, true that we empathize in this way. However, there is a crucial logical difference between this and the aesthetic empathy we enjoy in relation to art. For to empathize with a person's style in the ordinary course of things presupposes that we are directly acquainted with that person or have at least fairly detailed biographical knowledge about them. We have, in other words, an interest in the real existence of that person. To empathize with the personal style of engaging with the world which is embodied in an artwork, however, is disinterested in an additional sense to that already noted. This consists in the fact that it does not presuppose any acquaintance with the artist or any knowledge of biographical details concerning his or her life. For, as I showed earlier, to read the narrative, expressive, and aesthetic functions of a painting, and to recognize its originality, presupposes only comparative knowledge. This comparative knowledge, in conjunction with our basic fluency in the code of pictorial representation, enables us both to read the painting in terms of its basic signifying functions and to discriminate unusual and striking articulations of the code, namely those paintings which in comparison with other works present a distinctive style of engaging with the world. On these terms, to empathize with an artwork is not to seek any mystical communion with the artist's life, or soul, or intentions; it is rather to identify with the painting's own special way of deviating from established norms and clichés of narrative, expressive, and formal signification.

This interpretation of aesthetic empathy raises several questions. First, even if such empathy does not logically presuppose any knowledge of or interest in the real existence of the artist, it is, nevertheless, true that we often do have such knowledge. How, then, does this affect our response? In this respect it should be noted that secondary details about the artist's source material can often enhance our empathy with a work. If, for example, we know that the Byron text which is the source for Delacroix's *Sardanapalus* does not contain any description of the massacre, but that the artist has, rather, harmoniously supplemented the ideas provided by the source text with scenes of carnage derived from engravings of Etruscan reliefs, then this can make us enjoy the originality of *Sardanapalus*, the painting, all the more. But, equally so, such knowledge might take us in the opposite direction. We might become preoccupied with iconographical analyses, and, in consequence, treat the painting as an object of historical discourse alone. I am arguing, then, that biographical or genealogical details can enhance our aesthetic empathy, but that, equally, they can detract from it. Logically speaking, in other words, biographical issues are entirely contingent in relation to aesthetic empathy.

There is, however, another, rather more serious question. It is simply this. Even if we admit that everyday empathy presupposes acquaintance or detailed knowledge of the person with whom we are identifying, but that to empathize with paintings we need know nothing about the person who created the work, what really hangs on this difference? I would suggest that, in fact, quite a lot hangs on it. When we empathize with a person in ordinary life our empathy is generally tied to the actual existence of that person. We may like their style—the way they look or speak; the views they hold, the way they express them; the totality of values which seem to inform their outlook on the world. But, of course, all might be what it seems to be. On the basis of deeper acquaintance or acquired knowledge, we may decide that the person in question is just projecting an image. We may decide that at heart they are insincere; or that they hold the views of which we had not previously been aware, and which (in their unacceptability) outweigh all the features with which we can identify. Indeed, we must also remember that the other person's individual style of being is ultimately theirs. If we are acquainted with them or know a great deal of information about them, the sheer presence or force of their personality may lead us away from empathy. Instead of a felt identity with, and sharing of, their style, we may be pushed in the direction of blind admiration, and ultimately mere hero or heroine worship. Or we may find that their style becomes so intimate and dear to us that our identifying with them is not a sharing, but rather a total absorption in the other's style of being. In the case of empathy experienced in relation to other persons as such, in other words, our sharing of their style is subject to various psychological pressures which may tend to inhibit or modify the experience.

One might contrast this with our empathy with style in painting. In the case of Delacroix's *Sardanapalus*, for example, the artist has not just provided us with a report of his own private interests and attitudes in relation to violence. Rather he has worked those out in accordance with the formal, expressive, and narrative demands of a medium informed by a tradition, and aimed at a much broader audience than that of other artists or (indeed) art historians. The artist's own intentions, feelings, and attitudes, in other words, are not merely translated into paint. The 'message' is not located in some opaque zone of subjectivity 'behind' the medium; it is rather embodied and mediated within that semantically and syntactically charged, and (in the best art) *deviant* surface which we call this particular painting, and in its relation to other paintings. By inscribing his or her feelings and attitudes within a publicly legible medium, those private feelings etc. are transformed. The artist, as it were, meets him or herself and the viewer half-way. He or she offers *a possibility of viewing the world. Delacroix the person* may have been reactionary, élitist, a dreamer, even a vicarious sado-masochist of sorts; but because in *Sardanapalus the painting* his private sense of violence is inscribed in, and modified by, the publicly accessible medium, the image is thereby detached from the matrix of personal obsessions in which it finds its causal origins. The style of engaging with and understanding the world which the painting offers is an individual one, but because our reading of it is not constrained by necessary reference to the actual presence of the artist himself, we are able to identify with it without the psychological pressures which I have described.

Now, it might be wondered why, in an essay on violence and painting, I have addressed so much attention to the question of aesthetic empathy. It is, after all, only one of a variety of responses. In this respect, it should first be noted that there is certainly no intrinsic connection between violence in art and the experience of aesthetic empathy. Whether we empathize with a violent work or not will be a function of the relation between the originality of its style and our own individual set of values. Indeed, many—perhaps most—of the works we identify with will have no dimension of violence at all. However, this being said, it is clear that violence does have an important contingent role in relation to aesthetic empathy. For the paintings which stake most claim to such a response are surely those in which problems and crises fundamental to our status as rational but sensuous and finite beings are wrestled with and clarified. The nature and function of violence in human life is, of course, one of the most fundamental of such problems. (I shall return to this issue in the discussion of Burke, in Chapter 6.)

The second reason why I have devoted so much attention to aesthetic empathy is to balance out the gendercentric approach. Gendercentrism tends to reduce the problem of violence in painting to the crudest moral simplicities. If the 'work is violent (and especially if it involves violence towards women), then to enjoy the work is to enjoy it on the oppressive basis of sexuality in a patriarchal society. To suppose that this is a sufficient explanation of the enjoyment of violent painting is, however, not only an insult to the intelligence of many male and female viewers, it is to degrade painting itself. For it is only the mediocre work which orientates itself exclusively to the setting forth of violence. In the best creations, violence is re-presented; that is to say, we do not enjoy the violence as such, but rather the way an individual fellow being has here coped with it and shown it for what it is. To empathize with such a vision is, in effect, to acknowledge that we need not be passive in the face of violence. Indeed, it is to *know* that some other human being has shown how a stand might be taken, and that we can stand with them.

I shall conclude this chapter by explaining an omission. It is the one which is implied by my concentrating on the relation between violence and painting alone, rather than on the relation between violence and other modes of visual representation such as photography and film. The reason for this omission is that these latter modes of representation will require a substantially different analysis from the one appropriate to painting. This is because painting and photography (and the arts derived from the latter) have a fundamentally different ontological structure, which will, in consequence, tend to produce different cognitive and psychological effects. In the Introduction to this book I discussed the general significance of the impact of mechanically reproduced images on experience. In particular I noted how, in relation to art, the ubiquity of reproductions enhances our awareness of the special status of the original. This, of course, has a bearing on the present context of discussion. In the case of painting, for example, it is rare that we respond to it just in terms of its violence of content or treatment. We know that paintings are not simply mechanical reproductions of reality. They are images which interpret the world. Hence we are predisposed to regard them as complexes of narrative, expressive, and aesthetic signification, which set forth a particular style of viewing the world. The photographic arts, in contrast, are fundamentally mechanical reproductions of various aspects of visual reality.[1] In recent years, of course, a great deal of work has been done to show that the camera is not an innocent eye. Its images can be staged, manipulated, and even, to some degree, fabricated. But the fact that so much theoretical work has

---

[1] For some characteristically extreme animadversions on this theme, see ch. 9 of Roger Scruton's *The Aesthetic Understanding* (Carcanet New Press, Manchester, 1983). The question of film, of course, is rather more complex, depending on how one theorizes its relation to dramatic composition. Scruton presents a forceful argument on this topic in chs. 9 and 10 of the work just cited. For an insight into the gendercentric approach to film, a useful paper is Laura Mulvey's 'Visual Pleasure and Narrative Cinema', in *Screen*, vol. 16, no. 3 (1975).

been required in order to clarify this fact is itself of great significance. It shows that we are strongly inclined to read photographs at the level of their basic code alone, as mechanical copies of the visual. This in turn means that we tend not to look for any broader and more complex levels of signification. Hence, if we encounter a photograph of some violent scene, we will tend to respond to the violence as such. This at least is the present state of our culture's literacy in relation to the reading of photographs. But, of course, this may change. In Chapter 8, for example, we shall see how J.-F. Lyotard links photography to the sublime on the basis of its technoscientific aura.

We now reach a key transitional point. In this study so far I have shown that, whilst our experience of art and the aesthetic is founded on embodiment, it is thoroughly historicized. For configurations to engage us they must be out of the ordinary in some respect. Now, in my Introduction I argued that the postmodern sensibility is orientated towards affective jolts and that originality in art is a key means to this. The chapters in this first part of my study now show that this involves rather more than some glorified consumer pleasure. Rather, the dimension of originality is at the heart of aesthetic experience itself. It energizes aesthetic form in a way that generates empathic responses which reintegrate the individual with the lifeworld. This aspect of the postmodern sensibility, then, is of positive significance.

The question now arises as to whether the other dimension of shock orientation outlined in my Introduction—namely a susceptibility to the sublime—is also of positive significance. The chapters in Part Two will address this question.

Part Two

6

The Existential Sublime

From Burke's Aesthetics to the Socio-Political

In the Introduction to this book, I briefly described a class of aesthetic experiences which involve an ambiguous kind of pleasure which hinges on negative as well as positive elements. These pleasures have come to be known under a common rubric—the *sublime*. For a long time the sublime has been out of fashion, but (as I also noted in my Introduction) it has become widely debated again in relation to the question of postmodern sensibility. We must, however, note a basic problem. The great theorists of the sublime—Burke and Kant—both offer global but very different explanations of the experience. Could it be, then, that they are actually talking about two different but related sorts of experience? The answer is, of course, yes. Kant's theory (which I shall discuss at length in subsequent chapters)[1] is fundamentally addressed to the aesthetics of our rational response to sheer overwhelming excess of size or power. Burke's theory, in contrast, is orientated towards the aesthetics of those situations where excessive or less spectacular items are felt as painful or threatening. In this chapter, I will address myself to Burke, and the ramifications of his treatment of this latter sort of response.

In section I, accordingly, I will outline the logical structure of Burke's theory of the sublime at length, and will offer a critical review of it. In section II I will first rectify the major problem faced by Burke's theory. This rectificational strategy will take the form of a clarification of the sublime's logical status as a form of

This chapter has appeared under the same title in *Tradition and Innovation: Proceedings of the XII World Congress of Aesthetics*, ed. Richard Woodfield (Nottingham Polytechnic Press, Nottingham, 1990).
[1] See also chs. 6 and 7 of my *The Kantian Sublime: From Morality to Art* (Clarendon Press, Oxford, 1989).

disinterested aesthetic experience. I shall then proceed—with the aid of key insights from Burke—to explain its phenomenological structure by reference to patterns of experience in the modern and postmodern epochs. In section III I shall conclude by discussing the contemporary moral and socio-political implications of my rectified version of Burke's theory.

I

In Part One, section II of his *A Philosophical Inquiry into the Origin of Our Ideas of the Sublime and the Beautiful*, Burke sets the scene for the argument which he regards as fundamental to his entire theory. We are told that pleasure and pain are (logically) independent of one another. That is to say, pleasure is not simply the absence or diminution of pain, and vice versa. The reasoning behind this is as follows. Most of the time, we are in a state of 'indifference' (or 'tranquillity') where neither pleasure nor pain preponderate. Given this, it is clearly possible (as Burke shows through several examples) to move from a state of indifference to a state of pleasure without the mediation of pain, and vice versa. These unmediated states are termed by Burke 'positive pleasure' and 'positive pain', respectively. Having established this logical independence, Burke now makes his crucial move.

Whilst the diminution or removal of pain and danger does not yield a positive pleasure, yet it has 'something in it far from distressing or disagreeable in its nature'.[2] To pick out this agreeable state arising from the diminution of pain and danger, Burke introduces the technical term 'delight'.

With this point in mind, we can now consider the next major stage in the argument, which occurs in Part One, sections VI and vii. As Burke's exposition is extremely unwieldy, I shall paraphrase its substance in terms of four points. (1) Terrible things, descriptions of them, or phenomena associated with them, can excite ideas of pain and danger in us, thereby causing Terror or some

---

[2] Edmund Burke, *A Philosophical Inquiry into the Origin of Our Ideas of the Sublime and the Beautiful*, ed. John Boulton (Routledge & Kegan Paul, London, 1958), 35.

similar passion. (2) Terror and its kindred passions are the most powerful of all, because they pertain ultimately to our instinct for self-preservation. (3) Anything which can cause Terror or the like is a potential source of the sublime passion. (4) This passion arises when the Terrible things which excite ideas of pain or danger in us are moderated, or beheld at a distance. In such cases, our state of terror is likewise moderated, and becomes, thereby, delightful.

Now, it is surprising that commentators have not remarked upon the puzzling status of point (2). Burke places some emphasis on it, yet it seems superfluous to the logical progression of this argument. The reason for Burke's emphasis is, I think, to be found in point (4). He wants to ground the enjoyable nature of the sublime passion in terms of 'delight', the sensation arising from moderated pain or danger. Now, whilst this achieves the desired contrast with beauty (which is a 'positive pleasure') at the subjective level, it might be thought the sublime passion is of less worth or significance precisely because it involves the mediation of pain and danger. However, by stressing that the most powerful passions arise from our sense of mortality and the instinct for self-preservation, and by showing that the sublime is intrinsically connected with them, Burke is able to invest the sublime passion with an intensity and, as it were, existential magnitude that more than compensates for its lack of positivity. He ensures, in other words, that the separation of the sublime and the beautiful in terms of the contrast between delight and positive pleasure will not be taken as evidence of the sublime's axiological inferiority. Indeed (as we shall see in section II, below) Burke's linkage of the sublime to psychologically intense feelings bound up with our sense of mortality actually proves to be one of his keenest insights.

Now, having separated the beautiful and the sublime at the subjective level, Burke then declares that he will go on, in Part Two, to consider the contrasting objective qualities that 'cause' those passions characteristic of sublimity and beauty. Given this intention, it seems puzzling that the opening two sections of Part Two should be entitled 'Of the Passion Caused by the Sublime' and 'Terror' respectively. To see why Burke is not yet done with the subjective dimension, we must look ahead to two points made in Part Four. First, Burke suggests that vast objects, darkness, and the like cause vibrations of the ocular parts which 'approach near to the nature of what causes pain and consequently must produce an

idea of the sublime'.[3] Second, 'The only difference between pain
and terror is, that things which cause pain operate on the mind by
the intervention of the body; whereas things that cause terror, generally affect the bodily organs by the operation of the mind suggesting the danger.'[4]

Now, we will remember that, in Part One, Burke construes the
sublime passion as a moderation of the terror consequent upon
ideas of pain and danger. In the first of the above passages, however, he makes it clear that actual pain (as long as it does not
reach the threshold of conscious discomfort) can also issue in sublime passion. Physiologically speaking, it is on a part with moderated terror. The difference between the two consists only in the
fact that the objects which give rise to moderated pain do so by
direct causal impact upon the body; whereas those which give rise
to moderated terror presuppose the mediation of judgement.

With these points in mind, let us now return to the problematic
opening of Part Two. First, the section entitled 'Of the Passion
Caused by the Sublime'. We are told, here, that

The passion caused by the great sublime in nature, when those causes
operate most powerfully, is astonishment; and astonishment is that state of
the soul in which all its notions are suspended, with some degree of horror. In this case the mind is so entirely filled with its object, that it cannot
entertain any other, nor in consequence reason on that object.[5]

Here the sublime passion arises solely through the object's impact
upon the senses. For example (though Burke does not actually provide one here), a mountain range, in itself, is not threatening and
cannot, therefore, give rise to terror. However, its very size so fills
up the senses that it creates that form of pre-conscious ocular pain
which (as we have just seen) Burke regards as a cause of sublime
passion. Let us now see how this compares with what Burke has to
say concerning 'Terror'.

No passion so effectually robs the mind of all its powers of acting and
reasoning. For fear being an apprehension of pain or death, it operates in
a manner that resembles actual pain. Whatever therefore is terrible, with
regard to sight, is sublime too, whether this cause of terror, be endued

[3] Ibid. 137.   [4] Burke, *A Philosophical Inquiry*, 132.
[5] Ibid. 57.

with greatness of dimensions or not; for it is impossible to look on anything as trifling, or contemptible, that may be dangerous.[6]

Here Burke emphasizes the physiological affinity that enables both
pain and terror to be moderated into the sublime passion.
However, the cause of the passion is here additionally traced to
things which, irrespective of their size, are judged as dangerous or
threatening in themselves. What Burke is in fact doing, then, in the
first two sections of Part Two is not simply redescribing the phenomenology of the sublime passion, but, rather, clumsily showing
that it arises from two different ways[7] of being affected by
objects—namely through their direct overwhelming impact on the
senses, or through the mediation of ideas of pain and danger.[8]

Having, then, extended his account of the grounds on which we
find things sublime, Burke now occupies himself, in the rest of Part
Two, with outlining those qualities which things must possess in
order to occasion such delight. Amongst the qualities he lists are
Obscurity, Power, Privation, Vastness, Infinity, and so on, and so
forth. The details of his account need not detain us here; rather, we
must now consider a final step which Burke takes in order to complete his theory. This is to be found in Part Four of the *Inquiry*,
where we are offered an account of the efficient causes of sublime
delight. It is interesting in this respect that Addison[9] declares us
'unable' to conduct analyses of the pleasures of imagination in
terms of such causes. However, in going beyond Addison, Burke is
actually doing more than just that. He is also, in effect, attempting
to fill a gap opened up in his theory of the sublime by the unexpected arguments (noted earlier) which we find at the begin-
ning of Part Two. The gap consists in the following. Burke regards
the sublime passion as a delight (i.e. negative pleasure) arising from

---

[6] Ibid.

[7] Burke's clumsiness in presenting his contrast is due, I think, to architectonic
considerations, i.e. both a reluctance to broach the physiological theory too much in
advance of its more thorough and systematic exposition in Part Four, and, indeed, a
reluctance to emphasize any element which might seem to disrupt the unity of his
theory. This reticence has led at least one of Burke's recent commentators, namely
Nathan Rotenstreich (in his paper 'Sublimity and Terror', *Idealistic Studies*, vol. 2,
pt. 3 (1972), 238–51), into mistakenly supposing that, for Burke, 'there is no aesthetic response related to delight, unless there is the mediation of an idea' (p. 239).

[8] It should not, of course, be thought that these two categories are mutually
exclusive.

[9] Joseph Addison, *Collected Works*, vol. iii, ed. H. Bohn (Bell and Sons, London,
1890), 401.

the moderation of terror. Given this, however, why should the pre-conscious pain which arises from our perception of overwhelming objects also count as delight? Do we not, rather, simply have a case of weak positive pain, as such? If so, how is our delight in such objects to be explained? It is, in part, to answer this that Burke introduces his physiological account of efficient causes.

The argument is constructed as follows. A state of inactivity has a generally debilitating effect on the body.[10] In consequence, the maintenance of good health requires exercise through labour, which is 'a surmounting of difficulties, an exertion of the contracting power of the muscles, and as such resembles pain which consists in tension or contraction in everything but degree'.[11] Burke's point, then, is that, in effect, labour is a mild sort of pain that has an invigorating influence on the body. He then makes his crucial move. Just as labour is necessary, in order to keep the 'grosser' parts of the body healthy, so likewise is stimulation required for the 'finer' parts upon which the mental powers act. Indeed, it is on those very occasions when we experience moderated terror or pre-conscious pain that the finer parts receive such healthy stimulation. Hence we are told that

. . . if the pain or terror are so modified as not to be actually noxious; if the pain is not carried to violence, and the terror is not conversant about the present destruction of the person, as these emotions clear the parts of a troublesome encumberance, they are capable of producing delight; not pleasure, but a sort of delightful horror; a sort of tranquillity tinged with terror . . .[12]

This passage is crucial. Previously, Burke has consistently given the impression that in the delightful experience of moderated terror, it is the fact that the terror is moderated which is the source of delight. However, he is now suggesting that moderated terror—like the pre-conscious pain which arises from perceptually overwhelming objects—is also efficacious in stimulating the finer parts, thus diminishing the possible dangers which inactivity poses to the system. Burke concludes accordingly that the sublime passions which arise from pre-conscious pain and moderated terror are 'to be accounted for on the same principles'.[13]

---

[10] In this view Burke is following du Bos.
[11] Burke, *A Philosophical Inquiry*, 135.   [12] Ibid. 136.   [13] Ibid.

Now, the difficulties raised by Burke's theory are numerous. Let us first consider one which can easily be rectified. It pertains specifically to the pre-conscious pain variant of the sublime. In relation to this we will recall Burke's claim that if an object overwhelms and fills the senses then its direct impact causes the sublime feeling. This direct causal story is, however, in itself implausible. For it would follow from it that even small innocuous objects placed close up to the eye would, by overwhelming our vision, cause the pre-conscious kind of sublime feeling. This problem is, however, easily dealt with, in so far as one can theorize both versions of the sublime on a common judgemental basis; in other words, we can argue that objects will only give rise to sublime delight if we judge them to be perceptually overwhelming, or terrifying, or whatever. This means, in other words, that both variants of the sublime logically presuppose the mediation of ideas.

The major difficulty facing Burke's theory, however, cannot be dealt with so easily. It centres on the causal–physiological argument which he invokes in order to explain the salutary effects of the sublime on our bodily and mental powers. By introducing this physiological argument, Burke may have felt that as well as rendering his theory more original and comprehensive, it could also deal with a very obvious and potentially damaging objection. It is simply this. Although in beholding a terrible object we might not describe our response as sublime unless our terror was appreciably moderated, this in itself is not a sufficient condition for the ascription of sublimity. There are clearly cases where terrible things experienced from a distance can simply occasion weak terror or even mere relief at the fact that we are not presently threatened. We may, in other words, have an initial feeling of terror, but its moderation need not involve sublime delight. Now, by suggesting that moderated terror can have further significance through clearing the finer parts of an 'encumberance', Burke may have felt he was describing an extra feature which would set sublime delight apart from that of mere relief or moderated terror as such. This, however, would be equally problematic. For, in terms of Burke's physiological (as evidence, for example, in the late quoted passage), it is clear that any state of non-'noxious' moderated terror must serve to invigorate the finer parts. Yet, of course, we still want to say that not every moderation of terror counts as delightful in the sublime sense. Similar problems hold in relation to the pre-conscious pain variant of the sublime. For (irrespective of whether we modify it on the judgemental basis suggested a little earlier) Burke's global physiological explanation entails that *any* object which is experienced as perceptually overwhelming must serve to invigorate the finer parts, yet we do not, of course, find every such object sublime. (Indeed, in cases such as these, Burke has the additional difficulty of accounting for why our response should be one of 'delightful horror'. If the painful aspect is pre-conscious and non-'noxious', we would surely feel delight and nothing more.)

I am arguing, then, that whilst Burke's ultimate physiological account is original and comprehensive, it is in a sense too comprehensive, in so far as it entails that any passion arising from the moderation of terror, or the perceptually overwhelming, is sublimely delightful.

II

Having expounded Burke's theory at length and having considered some of the critical issues it raises, the question now arises as to how the theory might be made more viable. This task hinges on the drawing of logical and phenomenological distinctions between mere pain and shock as such, and the aesthetic experience of them. To accomplish this task we must first consider and dismiss one superficially promising approach. Burke—like others before him, and many since—holds that in order to find an object sublime, it is necessary that one engages with its overwhelming or shocking properties from a position of security or safety. There are two reasons, however, why we must question this putative role of safety as a logical pre-condition of the sublime. First, even *if* a safe distance between us and the object were presupposed, it would be insufficient to separate the sublime from those experiences where, from a position of general safety, we experience mild shock as such. Second, the safety clause is not in fact necessarily presupposed in so far as even in situations of extreme danger it is surely possible on occasion to find the object that is threatening one awesome and fascinating—and thence an instance of the sublime. The experience of Poe's Norwegian fisherman whose vessel is trapped in a whirlpool in the story *Descent into the Maelstrom* is a good example of this. I would suggest that the real significance of

Burke's insistence that the sublime can only be experienced from a position of safety is, in effect, to emphasize how distance from the threatening object acts as a kind of psychological framing device— one that suspends our natural attitude to the world. This is not to claim that viewing from a safe distance is a necessary condition for experiencing the sublime; rather it is to assert that when horrifying phenomena are encountered at a distance, the distance between us and the object will tend to facilitate our viewing it as a spectacle for contemplation alone. Distance momentarily invests the object with the character of representation rather than that of real physical existence. In the case of artworks, of course, this distancing factor is built into them metaphorically *qua* media of representation. We can, for example, experience the shudders and shocks of a horror film without running for the exit, because we know that the frightening phenomena are representations rather than realities. Something of this distancing element can even carry over in our response to television reports of actual catastrophe and disaster. For, although we know that the image on the screen has a causal relation to that which it is an image of, it remains, nevertheless, an image. It is a shrunken and framed representation which detaches the event from the broader complex of life in which it originated. The image *qua* image, in other words, can distance us from the full impact of actual horror, even as it reproduces it. If developed, then, Burke's safety clause amounts only to an insight as to how, psychologically speaking, distance from a horrifying event—be the distance actual or (as in the case of representation) metaphorical— will tend to facilitate our responding to that event in terms of the sublime. It will not furnish us with what we are presently searching for—namely sublimity's logical characteristics.

I would suggest, then, an alternative approach. Generally speaking, in human experience, pains and shocks—even mild ones—are things which we try to avoid. When they do occur, they most frequently lead us into actions—specifically ones which are expected to put a safe distance between us and the painful ·or shocking object. Aversion, one might say, is the governing logic of normal pain and shock. However, there are also more unusual occasions when we actively solicit experiences of pain or shock in the belief that by voluntarily subjecting ourselves to them our general capacity for coping with the world will be enhanced. As I noted in the Introduction to this book, Walter Benjamin, for example, notes that 'The more readily consciousness registers . . . shocks, the less likely they are to have a traumatic effect'.[14] Hence, by voluntarily subjecting ourselves to mild pain or shock, we expect to be able to cope all the better with the big involuntary ones when they come along. There are also some other, rather out-of-the-ordinary, contexts where pain and shock can be voluntarily solicited. For example, there are those occasions when we thrust ourselves into some threatening situation, and undergo adversity in order to prevent some other person, who is of concern to us, from suffering. Or, in the case of the masochist, pain and shock may be sought out for sexual gratification. Now, what all these cases of voluntarily solicited pain and shock have in common is the belief that the experience of them is a means to a definite end—be it strength of character, the protection of a valued person, or sexual gratification. If the agent were to experience the pain and shock without such definite beliefs concerning their utility or significance being present, then he or she would simply experience pain or shock as such. In the case of the sublime, however, matters are somewhat different. Such experiences are solicited in the belief that they will be enjoyable, but (unlike the foregoing cases) their enjoyment or bearability does not logically presuppose that the element of pain or shock is mediated by some definite belief as to its broader practical or sexual significance. Rather, we enjoy the dangerous thrills of the sublime for their own sake. They are, in logical terms, disinterested.

To summarize, then, the sublime can be distinguished from pain and shock as such on logical grounds. These are (*a*) that, unlike normal negative experiences of pain and shock, it admits of voluntary solicitation, and (*b*) that, unlike the more unusual voluntarily solicited pains and shocks, its enjoyment does not presuppose the belief that such states will issue in some specific kind of practical or sexual gratification.

Now, these logical criteria of the sublime must be supplemented by an answer to what is the most interesting question of all—namly how is it even possible to enjoy pain and shock for their own sake? We must, in other words, be able to come up with some plausible phenomenological explanation of the sublime. It is

---

[14] Walter Benjamin, *Charles Baudelaire: A Lyric Poet in the Era of High Capitalism*, trans. H. Zohn (Verso, London, 1983), 115.

at this point that Burke's theory (bearing in mind the slight modification I made to it in terms of judgementality in section I) proves extremely fruitful. Burke holds, we will recall, that states of prolonged inactivity are deleterious to our bodily and mental well-being, and that mild pain or shock, in consequence, provide stimulating counter-effects to such inactivity. This insight can be applied by analogy to the broader existential domain.

Let us commence with a simple point. By and large, human beings dislike monotony—be it in terms of work processes, environment, or leisure. They crave, rather, complex and unusual stimuli, side by side with the comforting security of the familiar. Now, in capitalist and state-capitalist societies founded on the division of labour, the monotony of work processes and the urban domestic environment is heightened to an extreme degree. The industrial or office worker's routine, for example, reduces experience to a mere continuum which must be undergone in order to procure the means of subsistence and leisure. The introduction of such things as background music to the workplace may do something to relieve the monotony, but such practices are not universal, and, even when they are employed, familiarity with them will tend to deaden their effects. They will become a part of the routine, hence, in societies founded on the division of labour, the very processes of work will tend to deaden one's sense of things happening—one's very sense of being alive. Now, if the worker is to reaffirm his or her sense of life, the monotony of the work process must be compensated for by a profusion—either extensive or intensive—of sensory stimuli. The accessibility of the extensive dimension, however, is limited for the vast majority of the population, by restricted financial resources and the temporal obligations which are owed to the family unit. It is, therefore, in the dimension of intensive stimuli that existential compensation for the monotony of the work process must be sought. The means of this compensation are the thrills, surprises, and shocks provided by the media—especially television with its sports events, violent gangster programmes, horror films, and sensational news items. These shock-stimuli can be voluntarily solicited and enjoyed for their own sake, i.e. without us necessarily believing that the thrills and shudders which they induce will in some sense be good for us. But the reason why we enjoy them (whether we are explicitly aware of the fact or not) is because they rejuvenate our sense of life in the midst of monotony.

Now, the experience of the sublime clearly involves monotony-relieving jolts of the sort just described. However, it is by no means the only experience of this kind. For any affective responses to that which is bizarre, unexpected—or, all in all, simply out of the ordinary—can have similar effects. The question is, then, does the sublime have any special or privileged role within this general repertoire of affective jolts? I would suggest that it does.

To see why this is so, we must first ask why it is that monotony is so unacceptable to human beings. What is ultimately at stake here? In this respect, it is useful to consider some of the adjectives used to characterize the experience. We describe it, for example, as 'grinding', 'paralysing', 'stifling', or 'suffocating'. All these terms liken monotony to aggression against, or afflictions of the body itself. Metaphorically speaking, monotony destroys the senses—it negates life. Now, whilst this common usage is indeed metaphorical, there is also a widespread current acceptance that it has a basis in medical fact. Monotony inhibits the development of capacities for cognitive discrimination, and induces a state of mind wherein the mind and body prove particularly susceptible to illness. Given these considerations, then, it is clear that monotony's adverse rating in human experience is due to its profound metaphorical and factual associations with bodily decay and the ultimate reality of death itself.

It is at this point that a second insight from Burke proves decisive. It consists of his claim that what gives the sublime its distinctive character is its connection with our sense of mortality. Consider, for example, the following passage.

We delight in seeing things, which so far from doing, our heartiest wishes would be to see redressed. This noble capital, the pride of England and of Europe, I believe no man is so strangely wicked as to desire to see destroyed by a conflagration or an earthquake, though he should be removed himself to the greatest distance from the danger. But suppose such a fatal accident to have happened, what numbers from all parts would crowd to behold the ruins, and amongst them many who would have been content never to have seen London in its glory.[15]

Here Burke's linking of sublimity and mortality is given one of its most striking exemplars. Horrifying events involving death and destruction—be they actual, or mere representations—cast an espe-

[15] Burke, *A Philosophical Inquiry*, 47–8.

cially profound spell on us. We are fascinated, and unable to look away, even though we may want to. This fascination extends far beyond any sense of pity for real or imagined victims of the horror, or any sense of relief at the fact that it is not we who are suffering. For here, a spectacle of mortality—of life under attack or threat—rejuvenates our sensibility. In such an experience, the present moment of consciousness—our very sense of being alive—is intensified into a felt quality, precisely because it is directly underscored by some actual or represented negation of life. Here, we do not simply have an experience which disrupts monotony. Rather we also have one wherein that upon which our aversion to monotony is ultimately founded (namely the negation of life) is, itself, encountered and reacted against to positive effect. In such an experience the horrifying event detaches from its immediate matrix of surrounding actualities and comes to symbolize the dialectic of authentic human finitude. We here vaguely sense and celebrate the fact that moments of lived experience owe their intense and particular felt quality to the fact that they are constantly subtended by the threat and ultimate eventuality of death.

What Burke offers us, then, is the basis of an existential variety of the sublime. In it, some actual or represented negation of life disrupts the normal monotonous tenor of our existence and makes the present moment of consciousness all the more vivid. Such an experience directly embodies that ultimate reaction of life against death of which the various other monotony-relieving affective jolts are, so to speak, merely the metaphorical echoes. Two major qualifications, however, now need to be made. First, whilst I have applied Burke's insight specifically in relation to life in modern and postmodern industrial society, it must not be thought that it applies only to them. One can find traces of the existential sublime in any society where the arduousness and monotony of labour is relieved by such things as, say, suspense-filled tales of battles and heroic deeds, recounted by the fireside at nightfall. However, this being said, it is certainly true that the rise of the existential sublime as a culturally prevalent mode of aesthetic experience is very much bound up with specific historical conditions. It is, for example, no accident that the sublime is first extensively theorized in the eighteenth century. At this point we find an established aristocracy relieved of its feudal obligations, and a rising mercantile class with money and leisure at their disposal. Both these social formations require new stimuli to counteract the *ennui* of their considerable leisure hours. The existential sublime, of course, provides a particularly intensive fund of such stimuli. Again, with the modern deceleration and reversal of proletarian impoverishment and the eventual rise of a postmodern consumer society, the experience of the sublime once more becomes a culturally prevalent tendency— but this time very much as a response to shock stimuli provided by the mass-media. We are thus led to our second qualification; it concerns the very serious and far-reaching moral and socio-political implications of Burke's existential sublime. This topic will form the substance of the final section of this chapter.

III

As we have seen, by its very nature the existential sublime involves an engagement with actual or represented situations where life is (in the broadest sense) negated, but where this negation is enjoyed as a spectacle for contemplation. An experience of this sort logically excludes any dimension of moral or sympathetic concern as the ground of its enjoyment. Now, the moral problem at issue here is well illustrated by Burke's example (already discussed) of how crowds might flock to witness the devastation of London or its aftermath. Responses of this sort—the attraction of fascinated onlookers to scenes of disaster—are, of course, very familiar in modern and postmodern times. But is this disinterested enjoyment of disaster not morally reprehensible to the highest degree? Indeed, do we not rightly describe those who flock to witness such scenes as 'ghoulish'? Matters here, however, must be judged strictly in context. For, although the grounds of our enjoyment of the sublime logically exclude moral concerns, they do not exclude their psychological presence: in other words, whilst enjoying a sublime spectacle we can also feel compassion and concern for those who might be adversely involved in the spectacle. Indeed, whilst the experience of sublimity centres on a reaction of life against death, the aesthetic and metaphysical value of this does not furnish an imperative to seek out and enjoy such experiences unconditionally. Three sets of circumstances in particular would render it morally reprehensible. These are (1) if we instigated or encouraged the instigation of a sublime spectacle knowing full well that it would occasion suffering; (2) if our enjoyment of the spectacle inhibited us or others from offering assistance to the suffering when we or they were in a genuine position to do so; and (3) if the known fact of our enjoyment added to the distress of the suffering, or was found offensive by friends and relatives of the affected parties.

I am suggesting, then, that the existential sublime is not morally reprehensible, in itself, but that there are three sets of circumstances in which it would take on a reprehensible character. There is, however, another problem. For even if the existential sublime is not intrinsically and immediately reprehensible, it could be claimed that its cumulative empirical effects will tend to morally desensitize the observer, or at least help create an adverse societal climate.

Consider the example of warfare. The moral consensus in most societies is that warfare is an evil, and only to be countenanced when the most foundational values and freedoms of the society are directly threatened. However, in Western culture, warfare, its practitioners, and implements, are celebrated and glamorized to a degree that far exceeds their status as elements within some 'last resort'. Contemporary crime films, indeed, have gone far beyond the 'cops and robbers' scenario, to reformulate violence as such as a kind of warfare on an urban scale. Such images of warfare present killing as a case of 'zapping' one's opponent. This discourse is then reduplicated even at the level of computer and video games. Now, of course, any human being with a modicum of intelligence can differentiate between real violence and the representation of violence, but the danger is that, in the minds of some, the effects of the former will be reduced to those of the latter. Killing will be construed as, in essence, just a case of zapping. In response to this line of argument, however, matters must again be viewed strictly in context. For our positive response to violence and representations of it involves a complex of factors—such as fantasies of power and control, and stereotypes of male sexuality. Hence, even if sublimity is implicated in moral desensitization, it is just one amongst other (perhaps more potent) agents. However, whether such desensitization does occur to any significant degree is itself a controversial issue. A selective reading of empirical evidence, for example, might well show that media representations of violence do have a specific range of adverse effects. In particular, a susceptibility to the existential sublime might be implicated in those horrendous crimes where—after the event—the agent is reported to have committed the crime 'just to see what it would be like'. Now, if evidence of this sort is adduced to support the claim that the existential sublime is morally desensitizing, it must be carefully weighed against a combination of three other factors.

First, it may well be that individuals who are so desensitized form only a very small proportion of the criminal fraternity, let alone society at large. Second, the existential sublime is an aesthetic experience which enriches the quality of life for those who enjoy it. Indeed, it is a compensation—and (in principle at least)—a very profound one—for the monotony of existence in industrial and postindustrial societies. This means that sublimity can contribute significantly to that enjoyed fullness of existence which is the goal of any civilized society. Third, in order to cope with the complex problems of finite embodied existence, it is necessary, at some point, to look the negation of life, as it were, squarely in the face. The existential sublime not only embodies this relation, but also, through its enhancement of the present moment of life, is a kind of triumphal coming to terms with it. If an individual did not have this capacity for aesthetic experience, but responded to the negation of life only with fear or aversion, then we might describe that individual as, at best, lacking an important dimension of self-assurance, or, at worst, simply lacking a form of existential courage. The lack of such qualities might well be seen as a factor which would inhibit the development of capacities for moral resolve. On these terms, then, any morally desensitizing effects which the existential sublime might have do not render it *ipso facto* morally reprehensible. Such effects may be very limited in scale, and wholly outweighed by the depth of its positive contribution to fully developed human existence.

The desensitization issue, however, has much broader ramifications of a socio-political kind. An important clue to this is provided by a degradation which the existential sublime itself has suffered in recent times. In the eighteenth and nineteenth centuries, for example, the sublime was an experience which generally could only be had through travel, or through searching out and engaging with an imaginative text or artwork, or through participation in special occasions of collective rite—even if only those of religion or the public execution. In experiential terms, encounters with the existential sublime took on a rather privileged character. In modern and postmodern times, however, the situation has drastically changed. Our access to the sublime is via the push of a button, the depression of a key, or by occupying a psychologically private space in the darkened cinema. The mass-media offer on demand a private consumption of simulacra which occasion those sublime shocks and thrills which once had to be more actively or more discriminatingly sought out, or engaged with in the context of special collective rite.

This ease of access is certainly to some degree a democratization of the sublime, but at the same time it tends to desensitize us to the life-against-death relation which is at the very heart of the experience. For to make the sublime available via the media involves its subordination to both the profit motive and the demands of the specific mode of transmission. In relation to the former, this means that the sublime must not only be standardized in terms of familiar genres—such as the gangster or horror film—but must follow easy formats and structures of audio-visual 'legibility' in order to achieve maximum effects on the widest possible audience. Here, aesthetic effect is, in every sense of the term, administered. Sublimity is watered down or caricatured, and dosed out in quantity as an entertainment, on the basis of the lowest common presentational denominators.

The ontological structure of media transmission themselves further accentuates these desensitizing factors. For, as I pointed out earlier, viewing on a television or cinema screen distances us from the reality of what is represented. Now, whilst this facilitates disinterested enjoyment, it cannot help but also diminish the psychological impact of the represented sublime phenomenon. Mechanically reproduced images are by nature, and through their forms of distribution, both abbreviated and manipulated so as to conform to sanitized consumer standards of morality and audio-visual literacy. It may be that the hyper-sensorama mega-screens of future cinema will achieve simulacra on a superficially perceptual and psychological par with the sublimity of real events, but, even here, the consumer's foreknowledge that these representations are merely simulacra will surely mediate their impact to a significant degree. In particular, our response may well become more orientated towards marvelling at the technological means by which the spectacle is achieved, rather than at the spectacle itself.

All in all, then, ease of access plus excessive exposure to low-grade stimuli, and the distancing effect of media-transmissions,

serve to desensitize us to the life-against-death reaction which is at
the heart of the existential sublime. The experience does not res-
onate with metaphysical significance. Rather it becomes just
another of those out-of-the-ordinary affective jolts which disrupt
the monotony of contemporary existence. It becomes a kind of
simulacrum of the authentic existential sublime—a mere something
whose fundamental significance is an entertainment alone.

Given this analysis, it is clear that whilst the sublime compensates for the monotony of modern and postmodern existence, the
form in which this compensation is largely distributed—via media
formats and formulas—is one that tends to drain it of its vitality
and significance. The compensation is hollow—a mere simulacrum
of real experience. Worse still, its reception is very much a focus of
leisure hours, and will thus tend to reinforce that division of
labour which is at the heart of existential monotony. It may even
act as a substitute gratification for real-life struggle and choice in
so far as the energies of the life-against-death confrontation are
tamed and sanitized and played out in the comfort of one's television room. The existential agent who is addicted to such stimuli is
thus significantly weakened. He or she is nudged in the direction of
socio-political apathy and aesthetic crudity. This difficulty can,
however, be countered. What is demanded is a critical engagement
with different instances of the existential sublime—a willingness to
compare and contrast such experiences with one another, and to
debate their contexts of occurrence and generation. Such an
engagement would involve taking into account the issues discussed
in this chapter, and many of those broached in Chapter 4. As we
saw there, all aesthetic experience is historically mediated and, as
such, is amenable to rationale debate. A debate of this kind is not
one which leaves it object unchanged; rather, it deepens our capacity to appreciate. It enables sensibility to improve itself, and
become orientated towards quality and objectivity (topics which I
will return to in the final section of Chapter 11). If, therefore, the
existential sublime is pursued and understood in the context of
Critical Aesthetics, its contribution to our general quality of life
will be redeemed.

Having, then, addressed Burke's theory of the sublime, I turn
now to Kant's. In formulating his theory, Kant was, in part, delib-
erately responding to Burke, and, indeed, operating on the basis of
an enormously sophisticated philosophical position. His theory is,

accordingly, much more complex and far-ranging. I shall devote the next chapter to a detailed analysis of its structure and significance, before going on to consider its contemporary relevance.

7

Moral Insight and Aesthetic Experience

Kant's Theory of the Sublime

In my book *The Kantian Sublime*[1] I offered an interpretation of Kant's theory of the sublime, and a reconstruction of it in a more viable form. In this chapter I shall refine and strengthen the strategy in a number of ways. The approach will be as follows. In section I I will outline the basic insights and structures of argument in Kant's theory of the sublime as it is presented in *The Critique of Judgement*. In particular, I will clarify an important ambiguity left over from my previous interpretation. In section II I will consider Thomas Weiskel's interpretation of Kant's position. What makes Weiskel's approach so interesting is that rather than simply highlight Kant's strategies, he too attempts to reconstruct them in a more viable form. I shall argue that Weiskel's approach is flawed, and in section III will offer my own reconstruction. This will be based on my position in *The Kantian Sublime*, but the bulk of discussion will be directed towards some recent criticisms of that position, and the particular interests of the present study.

I

Kant defines the sublime stipulatively as 'the name given to whatever is absolutely great'.[2] He continues by noting that 'to be great and to be a magnitude are entirely different concepts'.[3] Kant's

---

This chapter was originally published under the same title in *Pli*, vol. 3, no. 2 (1991).

[1] *The Kantian Sublime: From Morality to Art* (Clarendon Press, Oxford, 1989).

[2] Immanuel Kant, *The Critique of Judgement*, trans. J. C. Meredith (Clarendon Press, Oxford, 1973), 94.   [3] Ibid.

cryptic contrast here comes down to the following. The absolutely great cannot be a question of magnitude, because the greatness of an item's magnitude is always relative to that of other items. No matter how gigantic an item may be, there is always some item in the world whose magnitude will be greater still. Hence, if we are to find that which can truly be described as absolutely great—as sublime—we must look beyond the phenomenal world to that which sustains it, namely the noumenal or supersensible realm, beyond space and time, and the causal framework of nature. It is, literally, immeasurable. It forms a substratum to nature, and, more significant still (for the purposes of this study), it is the seat of that which is most fundamental to human beings, namely that aspect of the self which is free, and able to act on rational principles. This supersensible self is what is ultimately sublime. Kant unfortunately creates needless problems for himself by insisting on this point with such rigidity as to claim that the term 'sublime' cannot be applied to natural objects. Of course, it can—and without jeopardizing his basic point. This is because, whilst only the supersensible may be ultimately worthy of the term 'sublime' used in a purely descriptive sense, the aesthetic experience of the sublime which Kant is addressing in *The Critique of Judgement* is one which hinges on the capacity of certain natural phenomena to evoke an awareness of our supersensible self. In the sublime understood in an aesthetic sense, in other words, the relevant natural phenomena play a necessary role. They are a part of the aesthetic sublime's full meaning. We have, therefore, reasonable entitlement to call them sublime. I will return to this issue elsewhere in this section, and in section III.

The question which now faces us is that of how Kant moves from an encounter with natural phenomena to an awareness of our supersensible self. In affective terms, the experience involved here is a 'mental movement' from pain to pleasure. Kant gives considerable emphasis to this point, but it is by no means decisive. This is because the 'mental movement' is itself grounded on some complex cognitive strategies. These follow Kant's basic division between the *mathematical* and *dynamical* modes of the sublime. I shall consider these modes in turn.

First, the mathematical sublime. This arises when the receptive side of our cognitive faculties (i.e. sensory perception, and imagination) is overwhelmed by the vastness and scale of some natural phenomenon. Kant's discussion of this is enormously complex. His starting-point is the 'aesthetic estimate', by which he means informal estimates of magnitude that proceed 'by the eye alone'.[4] Thereafter his argument moves in two rather different directions which Kant fails to explicitly distinguish between. In *The Kantian Sublime* I labelled these the 'baroque thesis' and 'austere thesis'.[5] For present purposes I will confine myself to an exposition of the latter since it is by far the more philosophically viable. Basically, the argument is as follows. Our sensory and imaginative comprehension of the world is always guided by understanding—our capacity to unify and comprehend with concepts. Now, in his discussion of the mathematical sublime, Kant suggests that this guidance involves not just the capacity to form and apply concepts as such, but also a quite specific kind of concept—in Kant's parlance, an 'idea of reason'. Ideas of reason embody a striving for totality, for absolute comprehension of the object which they are addressed to. In *The Critique of Pure Reason* such ideas are seen as primarily significant as regulative principles in empirical scientific enquiry. In *The Critique of Judgement*, however, Kant assigns them a more global role. There is, as it were, an *experiential* idea of reason. Kant briefly describes its working as follows: 'the idea of the comprehension of any phenomenon whatever, that may be given us, in a whole of intuition, is an idea imposed on us by a law of reason'.[6] Kant's reasoning here is characteristically obscure. The claim seems to be that, given any phenomenal item, reason demands that we comprehend it in terms of a single perception or image, or contained sequence of such perceptions or images. Now, overlooking the questions raised by this claim, its connection to the experience of the sublime can be established as follows. With most phenomenal items we will—as reason demands—be able to comprehend their totality in the sense that none of their major parts or aspects are beyond recall in memory, or projection in imagination. We are, in Kant's terms, able to comprehend them in 'a whole of intuition'. However, the larger the object, the more difficult this task becomes. In a useful passage, Kant outlines what is involved here: 'If the apprehension [of a phenomenon's parts] has reached a point beyond which the representations of sensuous intuition in the case of the

---

[4] Kant, *Critique of Judgement*, 98.

[5] See pt. ii, ch. 4 of *The Kantian Sublime*.

[6] Kant, *Critique of Judgement*, 105.

parts first apprehended begin to disappear from the imagination as this advances to the apprehension of yet others, as much, then, is lost at one end as is gained at the other, and for comprehension we get a maximum which the imagination cannot exceed.'[7]

Vast phenomena, therefore, quickly overwhelm our capacity to comprehend them at the level of perception and imagination. However, a crucial clarification needs to be made, which I did not make in *The Kantian Sublime*. It is this. What is the criterion of a 'part' in the foregoing process? The importance of this question can be illustrated by a simple example. Suppose that we see the Great Pyramid of Cheops at a distance. From this viewpoint it is easy to comprehend it as a totality: its frontal aspect is available to immediate perception, and its hidden aspects can easily be projected from memory, or imagination. This means, of course, that it does not test our cognitive receptivity in the way described by Kant. How, then, could it be found sublime? The answer is, by tacit or explicit reference to human embodiment. Even seen at a distance we know that the pyramid dwarfs us physically. If we tried to comprehend its scale at the level of immediate bodily proximity the task would quickly overwhelm our perceptual and imaginative capacities in just the way described by Kant. Given this, my interpretation of Kant's own position can be more precisely reformulated as follows. Reason demands that we comprehend the phenomenal totality of an item in the sense that none of those major parts or aspects *which are, or which might be, encountered in direct bodily proximity to the item*, are beyond recall in memory, or projection in imagination. I shall return to the significance of this more precise formulation in section III.

From the foregoing points it is easy to see how we arrive at the experience of the sublime. Vast natural objects defeat our powers of perceptual and imaginative comprehension, thus occasioning a feeling of pain. Since, however, this striving for comprehension is instigated by the rational self, the failure of our cognitive faculties at the sensible level serves to present or exemplify the superiority of our supersensible being. Hence, our feeling of pain gives way to one of pleasure. In the experience of the mathematical sublime, in other words, the limits imposed on sensibility reinforce our awareness of what is ultimate and infinite in humans.

---

[7] Ibid. 109.

Kant's treatment of the dynamical sublime is, in some ways, as obscure as his account of the mathematical mode. However, there is only one dominant structure of argument, so his position can be stated much more concisely, as follows. First, Kant suggests that 'the boundless ocean rising with rebellious force, the high waterfall of some mighty river, and the like, make our power of resistance of trifling moment in comparison with their might. But, provided our own position is secure, their aspect is all the more attractive for its fearfulness.'[8] The reason why these fearful phenomena are found attractive is that they evoke an awareness that the human being is more than mere nature. The mighty and potentially destructive phenomenon 'challenges our power (one of nature) to regard as small those things of which we are wont to be solicitous (wordly goods, health, and life), and hence to regard its might . . . as exercising over us and our personality no such rude dominion that we should bow down before it'.[9] The mightly natural phenomenon, in other words, can make us aware that we have a rational and supersensible aspect which is superior to nature. Something like Kant's point here is also made in a famous passage from Pascal. 'Man is only a reed, the weakest thing in nature, but he is a thinking reed . . . if the universe were to crush him, man would still be nobler than his destroyer, because he knows that he dies, and also the advantage that the universe has over him; but the universe knows nothing of this.'[10]

Mary Mothersill has picked up this analogy with Pascal to both his disadvantage and Kant's. She claims that 'Consciousness has its rewards, but there is something ridiculous in preening ourselves on our superiority, as if it were somehow to our credit that whereas we know things about rocks, rocks don't know anything about us'.[11] This observation is, to say the least, shallow. The point of Kant and Pascal's position is that it is self-consciousness which redeems human being, and not only gives it meaning and value but is indeed the very foundation of meaning and value as such. Kant's whole moral philosophy, with its emphasis on morality binding us by virtue of the demands of rationality itself, is a massive affirmation of this.

[8] Ibid. 10–11.   [9] Ibid. 111.
[10] Blaise Pascal, *Pensées*, trans. J. Warrington (Dent, London, 1973), 110.
[11] Mary Mothersill, *Beauty Restored* (Clarendon Press, Oxford, 1984), 236.

Now, even if we cannot accept Kant's moral philosophy, it is at least reasonable to suppose that an encounter with the might of nature in all its fearfulness can lead us to an insight of the kind which he describes. Indeed, one significant aspect of Kant's discussion of the sublime is its existential acuteness—its ability to trace the complex interplay between our awareness of finitude, and our status as rational beings. However, this leads us to the major problem which affects Kant's theory of the sublime as a whole. It is simply this. Kant's arguments indicate how, in the confrontation with nature, we can be led to insights about our existence as rational beings—insights which, in terms of his broader philosophical position, have a fundamentally moral import. But why, then, is the sublime special? What does the experience of it have, that the having of similar ideas in a context outside nature does not? One superficially promising answer is to invoke Kant's claim that the experience of the sublime involves not just the entertainment of a morally significant idea, but a 'mental movement' from pleasure to pain. Unfortunately, this will not do. For he assigns exactly the same psychological structure to the effect of the moral law's determination of the will, i.e. that feeling which Kant calls 'respect'. Indeed, in the course of his discussion of the sublime, he explicitly links the experience of it to the feeling of respect.

Overlooking the internal difficulties of Kant's argument's, then, we are left with the following problematic position overall. He shows how the experience of vast or destructive phenomena (the mathematical and dynamical sublime, respectively) can lead us to existential insights of moral import. However, he does no more than this. The feeling of the sublime is left as a mode of moral feeling which arises from nature. Now, earlier on I suggested that Kant's reluctance to describe natural phenomena as sublime was misplaced. In the aesthetic experience of sublimity, our perceptual and imaginative capacities are tested by the natural phenomenon. It plays a necessary role, and can thence be justifiably described as sublime. What needs to be done, therefore, is to pick up various scattered insights in Kant's exposition, and modify his major arguments so as to allow nature and our sensible receptivity a role equal to that which Kant assigns to rational insight. The sublime, in other words, must be established as a distinctive mode of aesthetic experience, rather than one of moral import alone.

Before addressing this task, however, I shall first address and

reject an alternative reconstructive strategy which has been undertaken in relation to Kant's theory.

II

In his book *The Romantic Sublime*, Thomas Weiskel rightly proposes that in order to be made viable, Kant's approach must be
'purged of its idealist metaphysics',[12] and must also be allowed to
encompass products of artifice—such as the written word—as well
as objects of nature. As a means to this, Weiskel appropriates concepts from linguistics and psychoanalysis. The main linguistic principle consists in Saussure's dichotomy between *signifier* and
signified. The former is, broadly speaking, any material object
which can signify some other object in accordance with a semantic
code. The latter, in contrast, is our concept of specific understanding of that which the signifier refers to, by using this scheme
Weiskel is able to express the object–mind relation involved in
Kant's theory, in a non-Idealist idiom. The major psychoanalytic
principle which Weiskel appends to this involves construing the
sublime moment as 'an economic event in the mind'.[13] This means,
specifically, that it is a reflection of the broader principle that any
loss of energy (i.e. an occurrence of pain and unintelligibility) at
one level must be compensated for by a gain of energy (in the form
of meanings) at another level within a 'constant' field. It is this
principle which enables Weiskel to assimilate Kant's notion of the
sublime as involving a 'mental movement'. Indeed, he even goes as
far as to say that 'If we desert an economic principle—at least the
theoretical possibility of roughly calculating gain or loss—we have
in my judgement no way to keep the sublime closed to "mystical"
explanations'.[14]

With these linguistic and psychoanalytic principles in mind, we
can now consider the way in which Weiskel formulates two varieties of the sublime. The first of these is 'negative' or 'metaphorical' and broadly corresponds to Kant's mathematical mode, it
consists of three phases. In the first of these, some signifier or set
of signifiers—such as words on a page, or the colours and shapes

---

[12] Thomas Weiskel, *The Romantic Sublime: Studies in the Structure and
Psychology of Transcendence* (Johns Hopkins University Press, Baltimore, 1976), 23.
[13] Ibid. 24.   [14] Ibid. 24–5.

of a landscape—stand in a determinate relation to a signified. As Weiskel puts it, 'the flow of the signifiers constitutes a "chain" or syntagmic process whose continuity remains undisturbed'.[15] At this stage, in other words, we simply read the text or landscape in terms of some specific set of signifieds which constitute the meaning of the text of our recognition of the landscape as 'a landscape'. However, in the second phase, our reading is suddenly disrupted. Here,

. . . the feeling is one of on and on, of being lost. The signifiers cannot be grasped or understood, they overwhelm the possibility of meaning in a massive underdetermination that melts all oppositions or distinctions into a perceptual stream; or there is a sensory overload . . . the imagery appropriate to this variety of the sublime is usually characterized by featureless (meaningless) horizontality or extension . . .[16]

In the third phase, however, the principle of economy (noted earlier) comes into operation. In Weiskel's words,

. . . the syntagmic flow must be halted, or at least slowed, and the chain broken up if the discourse is to become meaningful again. This can only be done through the insertion of a substituted term into the chain i.e. through metaphor. The absence of a signified itself assumes the status of a signifier, disposing us to feel that behind this newly significant absence lurks a newly discovered presence, the latent referent, as it were, mediated by the new sign.[17]

On these terms, therefore, we compensate for the absence of an immediate determinate signified by reading its absence as a metaphor for a hidden signified. What this hidden signified is— God, the supersensible, the soul, or whatever—is a function of ideology: in other words, it is determined by the system of beliefs and values which characterizes the encultured individual who is having the experience.

Let me now address some of the problems which this account raises. First, Weiskel's argument faces an internal difficulty in relation to the second phase of the above process. One can certainly make sense of this phase in terms of natural objects in so far as their size or power overwhelms our immediate comprehension: that is, the sheer profusion of signifiers arrests our capacity to grasp them in terms of some immediate signified. This model might also

---

[15] Ibid. 25.   [16] Ibid. 26.   [17] Ibid. 27–8.

apply to certain works of art in so far as they are physically vast. Its application to literature, however, is altogether more problematic. For here, if we are overwhelmed, it is surely not by the profusion of signifiers, but rather by the narrative contents—for example, overwhelming images of power, desolation, endlessness, etc. which the signifiers evoke. This means, in other words, that in literature the dimension of excess occurs at the level of the signified. In fact, the only way that textual signifiers might fail to relate to a determinate signified is if (for whatever reason) we fail to understand the semantic code in which they are inscribed. But this, of course, would be an experience of mere confusion rather than of sublimity.

There is also a rather more general problem which Weiskel's account faces. This consists in the way he takes his theory to be derived from Kant. The basis of this derivation is Weiskel's use of Kant's final definition of the sublime offered in §29 of Book One of the third *Critique*. It reads as follows. The sublime 'is an object (of nature) the *representation of which determines the mind to regard the elevation of nature beyond our reach as equivalent to a presentation of ideas*'.[18] Weiskel interprets this as follows.

In Kant's view the 'representation' of such an object must collapse and this failure yields the intuition of 'unattainability'. But reason's ideas (of the unconditioned, the totality, etc.) are also 'unattainable' since they cannot be imagined or presented in sensible form. Hence the Janus-faced mind is confronted with two dimensions of 'unattainability' and it simply identifies them in what amounts to a metaphorical intuition. The imagination's inability to comprehend or represent the object comes to signify the imagination's relation to the ideas of reason.[19]

It is worth pointing out that, whilst Weiskel here takes himself to be working from Kant's most 'complete' definition, it is, in fact, one of the least satisfactory in Kant's own terms. Not only does he here (in contradiction to the main thrust of his argument) describe the natural object itself as sublime, he also presents his argument in a way that omits the central structural· feature of his overall position. This consists in the claim that it is imagination's inability to meet reason's demand for a presentation of totality which evidences the superiority of our rational being. Now, it is the fact that Kant omits this crucial claim here that leads Weiskel into a

---

[18] Kant, *Critique of Judgement*, 119.   [19] Weiskel, *Romantic Sublime*, 22–3.

fundamental misinterpretation. He suggests (as we have seen) that, for Kant, 'The imagination's inability to comprehend or represent the object comes to signify the imagination's relation to the ideas of reason'. This is true, but Weiskel is mistaken as to the nature of the signifying relation involved here. For imagination's failure to comprehend the vast object in accordance with the demands of reason is an actual example of reason's superiority over imagination. It does not, therefore, involve the 'insertion' of any metaphorical 'latent' meaning; rather, this particular instance of reason's superiority is so vivid and dramatic as to make us indirectly aware of its general significance. To put it in a familiar philosophical idiom, judgements of sublimity exemplify imagination's inadequacy in relation to reason. Now, my grumble against Weiskel here is not simply that he misinterprets Kant, but that he misinterprets him on the one point which is most crucial to reconstructing his theory in a more viable form. For, as I shall show in the next section, judgements of sublimity are founded on a special kind of exemplification wherein the scope of rational cognition is affirmed—albeit not quite in the sense which Kant intends. That Weiskel does misinterpret Kant on this point is due to the fact his mode of reconstruction is organized entirely around the notion of the sublime as a 'mental movement'. However, as I shall argue towards the end of this section, this notion is, in fact, something of a liability.

Before showing this, let me outline the second variety of sublimity which Weiskel putatively derives from Kant. This is called the 'positive' or 'metonymic' mode. Its first phase is the same as that undisturbed 'reading' of text or landscape which characterizes the metaphorical sublime. In the second phase, however, matters are rather different. Here some passage in a text or element in a landscape produces an excess of the *signified*. As Weiskel puts it, 'meaning is overwhelmed by an overdetermination . . . We are reading and suddenly we are caught up in a word (or any signifying argument) which seems to contain so much that there is nothing we cannot "read into" it. What threatens here is stasis, a kind of death by plenitude . . . which destroys the seeking for a signifier . . .'.[20] Here, in other words, the profusion of meanings (i.e. signifieds) is what overwhelms us. In the third phase of this experience, however, 'the mind recovers by displacing its excess of

---

[20] Ibid. 26–7.

signified into a dimension of contiguity which may be spatial or temporal'.[21] Indeed, '. . . the mind begins to "spread its thought", to avert the lingering which could deepen into an obsessive fixation'.[22] On these terms, then, we compensate for the excess of meaning by channelling it into streams of determinate and continuous imagery which (one presumes) express or connote a sense of that excess from which they directly spring. They metonymically signify their own origin. This mode of sublimity—as Weiskel also points out—is especially characteristic of artistic creation.

Now, it is important to note that Weiskel's notion of the metonymic sublime is not meant by him to be analogous with Kant's dynamic mode (although at least one commentator has mistakenly supposed otherwise).[23] It is, rather an extreme case of what Kant would call an aesthetic idea. This is defined as 'that representation of the imagination which induces much thought, yet without the possibility of any definite thought whatever i.e. *concept*, being adequate to it, and which language, consequently, can never get quite on level terms with'.[24] In *The Kantian Sublime* I have argued that there is indeed a plausible link between Kant's notion of the aesthetic idea and the experience of sublimity.

Weiskel's position, however, is not entirely adequate. This is not due to any internal tension in his account of the metonymic mode, but rather to difficulties which pertain to his overall approach—encompassing the metaphorical sublime as well. The first of these consists in the fact that Weiskel approaches his reconstructive task in isolation: that is to say, without situating the sublime in relation to criteria of aesthetic discourse generally. Hence, whilst he putatively explains what is involved in an experience of the sublime, his explanation serves to break up the sublime into two successive acts of judgement—on the one hand, an appraisal of phenomenal or imaginative excess, and, on the other hand, an appraisal which derives metaphorical or metonymic significance from the former. The result of this is not dissimilar to that of Kant's own theory—nature and art become merely the indirect vehicle for metaphysical or moral insight. Now, in the context of the current postmodern scepticism as to the viability of distinctive aesthetic categories, this

[21] Weiskel, *Romantic Sublime*, 29.   [22] Ibid.
[23] Louis Wirth Marvick in his *Mallarmé and the Sublime* (State University of New York Press, Albany, 1986), 70.
[24] Kant, *Critique of Judgement*, 175–6.

may be felt to be a strength of Weiskel's account, rather than a weakness. He shows how such a quasi-distinctive 'aesthetic' category can be deconstructed in terms of a play-off between presence and absence in an economy of cognitive energy. Against this, however, one can retort first that Weiskel's own principle of economy is simply too crude. It may be, for example, that in our interactions with the world we do broadly strive to achieve states of equilibrium, but Weiskel reduces this to quasi-mechanistic terms in so far as loss of meaning at one cognitive level must be compensated for by gain of meaning elsewhere in a constant total 'field' of mental energy. This, however, does no justice to the complexity and subtleties of gain and loss in our *embodied* engagement with the world. Such a model would only be of use in relation to the sublime if there were no better explanation of the experience available. Indeed, even if there were not, Weiskel's approach would face one remaining crucial difficulty. For, as I noted earlier, the very basis of his approach is an attempt to restate Kant's notion of the sublime as a 'mental movement', i.e. as defined by a transition from a feeling of pain or privation to one of pleasure. However, whilst Weiskel's approach by-passes some of the difficulties which this raises for Kant, it is open to a psychological counter-example of the most obvious kind. For surely we can experience the sublime without the necessary mediation of an occurrent state of privation or displeasure. Indeed, if someone insisted that in their experience of sublimity there was never the least sign of such a state, how could we hope to refute them? The real problem with Weiskel's approach is that he is trying to assimilate a feature which looms large in Kant's account but which is, in fact, psychologically contingent and looms large only because it is Kant's own way of coming to terms with the theory of the sublime dominant during his own times— namely that of Burke. Weiskel's psychological approach, in other words, is organized around what is, in fact, a historical contingency in Kant's theory. I shall, therefore, now hope to formulate a more satisfying approach based on Kant's essential insights.

III

Let us begin the process of reconstruction from Kant's point concerning the 'idea of reason' which compels us to comprehend any given phenomenal item in its totality. This insight reflects a truth whose validity does not depend on Kant's philosophical idealism. For if we were not compelled to comprehend phenomenal items in their totality, i.e. in such a way that none of their major parts (as encountered in immediate proximity to the body) were beyond our powers of perception, recall, or projection in imagination, then we would simply be unable to control or successfully negotiate such items. Comprehension in this sensible sense, in other words, is a most fundamental dimension of our being-in-the-world. Now, in normal circumstances this capacity will be exercised 'at a glance'. We do not need to go through any process of perceptual exploration or mental representation; we simply recognize that a phenomenal item's size or the effects of its power are amenable to such comprehension. With vast or mighty items, however, matters are more complex. It may be that we simply recognize them as being beyond our powers of perception and sensible representation 'at a glance'. But this does not mean that the item, thereby, becomes utterly unintelligible or hostile to our hold on the world. The reason for this is that we know that—no matter how formless or devastating it seems—the item is finite. We know that its size or effects must reach a stop at some point or other. This means, in other words, that its totality can be comprehended as an idea, i.e. in rational terms at the level of thought. This rational capacity for articulating items which cannot be wholly grasped in sensible terms is one with which we are fully familiar, but when do we realize it in the fullest sense? The answer is—in the experience of the sublime. For here the extraordinary scope of thought is made vivid by sensibility's limits in relation to vast or mighty nature. There is nothing metaphorical about this. For our engagement with nature here means that the scope of thought is exemplified at the concrete as well as the abstract level. Indeed, there is a harmonious continuity wherein perceptual and imaginative exploration engender rational insight.

This analysis of the sublime can also be applied, with modifications, to the realm of human artifice. We know that such artifice is of extraordinary scope. But we only fully realize this insight when our powers of perception and/or imagination are confronted by the appropriate sort of artefact. The criteria of appropriateness here are varied. The most obvious one is where vast or mighty artefacts overwhelm us with their sheer size or power or complexity, or, of course, a combination of these. Sometimes an artefact can do this in virtual terms, when it represents or evokes such qualities. There is also an expressive mode of sublimity which is evaluative in character. This occurs when some work of art transcends the category of the 'good' and overwhelms us with its greatness. The way form and subject-matter is treated awakens a sense of the work's universal relevance—its capacity to illuminate innumerable episodes in different lives, and different times and places. Here, in other words, the innumerable imaginative possibilities which the work opens up makes the existential scope of artistic expression vivid to the senses. We acknowledge the work as a product of genius, in the fullest sense of that term.

Now, at the heart of these ways of articulating the sublime lies Kant's basic strategy. This consists in construing the experience as a presentation of rational insight, achieved through some phenomenal item's capacity to exceed sensible comprehension. What Kant needs to stress—but does so only in hints—is that through this encounter the item brings different capacities in the human subject into a felt harmony. Specifically, our capacity for sensible comprehension is, despite the overload placed on it, in harmony with rational comprehension. it is this harmony which parallels that of the imagination and the understanding which is achieved through beauty. We are thence entitled to regard it as an aesthetic mode of pleasure.

With these points in mind, I shall now consider some issues which have been raised in relation to my strategy. The first is set forth by Mary McCloskey as follows.

Crowther's analysis of the sublime, like Kant's, takes our admiration of what we find sublime in nature and in art as admiration of, or rejoicing in, human capacities. [However,] Phenomenologically what we admire in the ocean, mountains and wild animals is their dignity, majesty, presence and, exuberance, and what we take, ourselves to be admiring in great as distinct from good art, is the powerful character of the work, and only secondarily and, derivatively, the capacities of the artist. I find it puzzling to be committed to the view that we are deceived in this.[25]

McCloskey's point about art here can be dealt with simply. My analysis of the sublime artwork does focus on the character of the

---

[25] Review of *The Kantian Sublime*, in *Philosophy* (Oct. 1990), 382.

work itself. Some works articulate their material in such a way that the relevance of the articulation overwhelms us by its universal applicability. It is this which makes vivid the extraordinary scope of artistic expression. In such an experience the particular artist's capacities are, indeed, of derivative and secondary significance. In relation to art, in other words, McCloskey has simply misinterpreted my position.

There is also an element of misinterpretation in McCloskey's response to my position *vis-à-vis* the sublimity of nature. Here, however, rather more complex issues are involved. I do indeed subscribe to the 'puzzling' view that it is not the object of nature as such which is sublime. But this does not amount to the same position as Kant's, namely that it is our rational capacity and not the object at all which is sublime. In this respect it will be recalled that throughout this chapter I have argued that Kant gives an undue emphasis to the role of reason. Our pleasure in the sublime does not consist in a mere sense of wonder or exhilaration at the scope of rational comprehension. Rather it flows from a felt harmony of sensibility—and thence nature—with the exercise of this capacity. Let me now relate this to McCloskey's difficulty. For her it is 'puzzling' to hold that it is not the object itself which is sublime. Indeed; but if an approach on broadly these puzzling lines were not correct, we would simply be returned to the starting-point of the whole inquiry—namely what explains our pleasure in vast and mighty objects. My approach answers this by occupying the middle ground between McCloskey's and Kant's positions. The object is special, we admire and rejoice in it because, unlike most phenomenal items, it brings our capacities for sensible and rational comprehension into harmony. We do, in other words, admire the object, but for what it does—and not simply for what it is.

This, however, brings us to a more fundamental question. Why, if the above analysis is true, does it seem to us that it is the object alone which we are enjoying? Why aren't we always explicitly aware of what it is doing to us, and what we are doing to it. An answer to these queries can be sketched on the following broad analogy. The enacting of a complex existential task may seem pleasurable in itself, but if we knew in advance that the task could never be successfully and definitively completed, the process of enactment would be pointless and frustrating. From this, it follows that a belief as to the successful outcome is a pre-condition of our taking pleasure in the process of enactment. Psychologically speaking, its trace informs the process, *even though we might not be explicitly aware of it during that time*. Our pleasure in the sublime parallels this. We could not enjoy the vastness or power of phenomenal items without being able to comprehend them as totalities in rational terms. It is the trace of this which enables us to cope with the item's excess in relation to sensible comprehension. We may be explicitly aware of our pleasure's origins, but this does not have to be the case. In the case of this latter eventually, it will seem as though we are taking a pleasure in the object alone. Indeed, the prevalence of this attitude should hardly surprise us. For the capacities for sensible and rationale comprehension are absolutely basic to our hold on the world. Their exercise is a matter of habit, rather than an explicitly conscious project.

Let me now address another problem—with some interesting ramifications—which McCloskey has raised in relation to my reconstruction of Kant's theory. This consists in the claim that, whilst grounding the experience of the sublime on what is 'overwhelming',[26] I offer no criterion for this term. This also links up with the broader fact that I offer no arguments (to replace Kant's deeply unsatisfactory ones) for the intersubjective validity of judgements of the sublime. Professor Eva Schaper has further suggested (in conversation) that this gap in my approach omits something so central to Kant's philosophical aims that it is misleading to regard my approach as a 'reconstruction' of his theory. I shall deal with these related points in turn.

First, my interpretation does offer criteria of the 'overwhelming'. In relation to nature, these involve phenomena which are excessive in the sense that their size, or the scope of their power, cannot be grasped in terms of some perception or set of sensible representations which leaves none of their major parts or (in the case of mighty objects) effects beyond our capacity for recall or projection. (In this chapter I have, of course, further refined this, by clarifying our criterion of a part.) Now, the interesting thing is that by interpreting the overwhelming in these terms, the road seems clear to a justification of their intersubjective validity. It could proceed along the route mapped out by Kant in his Deduction of judgement of taste. His position there hinges on the claim that we must suppose

---

[26] Review of *The Kantian Sublime*, in *Philosophy* (Oct. 1990), 382.

the imagination and understanding of human beings to combine in the same general proportions, otherwise communication between such beings would not be possible. Kant's development of this in relation to taste is (as I showed in *The Kantian Sublime*) unacceptable. However, it can be developed in relation to judgements of sublimity. This is because such judgements hinge on an object's being found overwhelming in relation to the body's capacities at the level of perception, imagination, and recall, but not at the level of rational comprehension. The sublime, in other words, is not directed at fine cognitive discriminations (as is the case with taste). Rather, it invokes comprehension in the sense of 'getting a hold of' and 'making intelligible'. Now, there may be people with prodigious gifts of recall, imagination, and reason, but unless there were some basic common ground or norms of comprehension, communication between human beings would not be possible. This norm of comprehension is central to the sublime. What it amounts to is that, given some vast or mighty object, we can recognize—generally at a glance—whether it is so overwhelming as to exceed the perceptual and imaginative capacities of even the most gifted human being. Likewise we know, in advance, that no matter how big or mighty it is, it has its limits, and this fact can be comprehended by any rational person. The upshot of this is that a judgement of the sublime can have a provisional claim to universal validity as the basis of the phenomenon's objective properties. But this is only provisional. For, whilst an overwhelming item can be objectively described as overwhelming, this does not, in itself, entitle us to claim it as sublime. Some such items can simply be monotonous. The problem here is that for an item's overwhelming properties to engage us, there must be something special about the particular way it exemplifies these. Hence, *contra* McCloskey, the 'overwhelming' as applied to the sublime is not a matter of personal idiosyncrasy, but the circumstances in which it attracts aesthetic attention are. We may be drawn by the complexity of the object's overwhelming properties, or by some dominating colour or shape; we may simply like the endless repetition of its parts, or, in the opposite direction, the object's apparent simplicity. The crucial point is that our imaginative engagement with the item is stimulated by the relation between an item's phenomenal properties and an experiential context. The item must be configured in such a way as to make it striking or out of the ordinary in relation to our customary experience of items of that kind.

These considerations show, then, that the justification of judgements of sublimity ultimately comes up against the same difficulties presented by attempts to justify the intersubjective validity of judgement of the beautiful. (This is especially true of sublimity ascribed to works of art.) The best way of dealing with these issues is on that comparative basis outlined in relation to art in Chapter 4: that is, an aesthetic judgement has claim to intersubjective validity if it can be defended by comparison and contrast between the aesthetic object and other such objects. In the case of the sublimity of nature, the provisional basis of such a claim is at least provided by objective features. Indeed, this foundation makes it more likely that consensus can be reached on cases of the sublime than on cases involving most other aesthetic ascriptions. (I shall return to the issue of objectivity towards the end of the last chapter in this work.)

The question which must finally be faced, then, is whether this inability to establish the claims of judgements of sublimity on anything other than a provisional status means that my approach is at best neo-Kantian, rather than—as I have described it—a reconstruction of his approach. There is, of course, no shame in being described as a neo-Kantian, but the approach I have taken to his theory is, in fact, a genuine case of reconstruction. The reason for this hinges on some complex issues which I will now very briefly outline.

First, Kant's fundamental goal in his Critical philosophy is to offer justification of, in the broadest sense, claims to objective knowledge. To do this he begins by clarifying the self's knowledge of its own relation to the world. Now the odd thing is that, viewed in relation to these aims, Kant's aesthetic theory in general is a very ambiguous enterprise. For, whilst it addresses the human subject's relation to the world at the level of feeling, this level does not involve claims to objective knowledge. Rather, the pure aesthetic judgement has a claim to intersubjective validity which is based on the co-operation of the faculties involved in cognition. However, as I argued earlier, this does not, without bringing in empirical considerations, allow Kant to establish the pure aesthetic judgement's claim to universal validity. If it is this strategy which defines the Kantian approach to aesthetics, then that approach is a failure. But, of course, there is much more to Kant's Critical philosophy than simply its goal. His great originality lies in the method whereby he strives to attain it. At the heart of this strategy is the notion of *synthesis*. Unlike his philosophical predecessors, Kant does not posit a passive relation between human subject and world. Rather, the world as it appears in experience is a function of the intellect's organizational activity in relation to sensibility and imagination. Now, in relation to judgements of beauty and sublimity, experience is also grounded in synthesis. Specifically we are dealing with two different ways in which phenomena engage our sensible and imaginative capacities, and our organizational rational ones. It is precisely on the basis of this set of relations that I have developed Kant's theory. My approach, therefore, is a genuine case of reconstruction, in so far as it is grounded on the fundamental methodological principle of Kant's Critical philosophy.

This principle has further significance for the specific purposes of this study. In Chapter 1 I stressed the primacy of body-hold—the fact that perception is a function of the senses and cognitive capacities co-ordinated as a unified field, on the basis of an awareness of the scope and significance of embodiment. Now, Kant does not have a comprehensive theory of embodiment. However, his notion of synthesis is something of a counterpart to body-hold, in so far as it involves a reciprocal interaction of forms of intuition and categories of the understanding, co-ordinated by the transcendental imagination. What Kant, in effect, does is to articulate body-hold abstractly in terms of its basic logical components. He thus commits an analytic error of the type noted in relation to Derrida in Chapter 1. Rather than construing synthesis as a function of our basic embodied reciprocity with the world, he sees the form of the phenomenal world (including the body) as a function of synthesis. Embodiment's privileged role in perception is thus denied.

However, whilst Kant fails to grasp the ontological priority of the body, his notion of synthesis is, nevertheless, of great importance. This is because it foregrounds precisely those elements within body-hold (namely our capacities to attend, comprehend, and retain and project in imagination) whose interaction is a necessary feature of any act of perception. Hence by grounding his aesthetic on synthesis, he ties aesthetic experience to constants in the human condition.

Having, then, discussed Kant's theory of the sublime and its ramifications at length, I shall now (in the next two chapters) consider it in relation to Lyotard's interpretations of Postmodernism.

8

The Kantian Sublime, the Postmodern, and the Avant-Garde

In this short chapter I shall evaluate J.-F. Lyotard's enormously influential use of Kant's theory of the sublime. First, let me briefly reiterate my revision of Kant's position on this subject. Clearly there are objects which are so vast or powerful as to completely overwhelm our powers of perception and imagination. We can, nevertheless, comprehend them as overwhelming totalities in rational terms. (Indeed, we can frame the rational idea of infinity itself—even though we could never hope to have sense-perceptions or images which would adequately present such an idea.) Given, then, the fact that the overwhelmingly vast or powerful object can be comprehended in rational thought, we feel ourselves, accordingly, as transcending the limitations imposed by our embodied existence. Now, it should be noted that whilst this reformulation of Kant's theory does hinge on an enriched awareness of the scope of our rational powers, it does not commit us to the view that our rational being is located outside the spatio-temporal world. Neither does it entail that we must regard rational comprehension, rather than the object itself, as sublime. This is because it is not every object which succeeds in overwhelming our perception and imagination, in a way that vivifies the scope of our rational comprehension. We are, therefore, quite entitled to call objects which stimulate this privileged effect sublime.

Stated in these terms, Kant's theory can encompass the domain of human artifice,[1] without much further modification. If some human artefact is of colossal size or of terrifying power, or employs images which successfully invoke a sense of such over-

This chapter originally appeared as 'The Kantian Sublime, the Postmodern, and the Avant-Garde: A Critique of Lyotard', in *New Formations* (Jan. 1989).

[1] For a more detailed account of this see ch. 7 my *The Kantian Sublime: From Morality to Art* (Clarendon Press, Oxford, 1989).

whelming properties, then this can serve to make vivid the extraordinary scope of human artifice itself. Something, in other words, which is encountered as problematic from the viewpoint of sense-perception enables the rich scope of a rational capacity—in this case, artifice—to become all the more manifest and enjoyable.

With these points in mind, we can now turn to the important links made by Lyotard between the Kantian sublime, and our understanding of the avant-garde and Postmodernism.

As Lyotard's arguments are both complex and highly generalized, I shall first attempt a (necessarily lengthy) interpretation and summary of their salient points, as follows. First, Lyotard holds that the function of painting since the quattrocento has been to document the socio-political and religious order of things, by means of the laws of perspective—thus enabling the audience to identify both with the order represented and with the artist's mastery of it. This tendency continues even into the nineteenth and twentieth centuries in the guise of various 'realist' styles (interpreting the term 'realist' here very broadly). However, this conventional form of art faces two difficulties. First, it conceals the shifting and elusive nature of visual reality itself, by presenting a world of stable and secure law-governed existents—a 'natural' order of things. This, according to Lyotard, means that 'it intends to avoid the question of reality implicated in that of art'.[2] Second, the development of photography and film has, in any case, surpassed and thereby vitiated the documentary function of art. Indeed, the development of photography points in the directions of a wholly transformed aesthetic sensibility, in so far as the images created by mechanical reproduction have a 'hardness' that points towards their origins in scientific and technological endeavour. As Lyotard puts it, 'The ready made in the techno-sciences presents itself as a potential for infinite production, and so does the photograph.'[3] The technologically produced image, in other words, points towards technology's capacity for unlimited progress and development. Its hard beauty is thus rendered ambiguous and unstable. We no longer have artefacts that can be judged by the consensus of established taste.

[2] J.-F. Lyotard, *The Postmodern Condition: A Report on Knowledge*, trans. Geoff Bennington and Brian Massumi (Manchester University Press, Manchester, 1984), 75.
[3] J.-F. Lyotard, 'Presenting the Unpresentable: The Sublime', *Artforum* (Apr. 1982), 3.

It is with the impact of photography and technoscientific culture, then, that we find the historical beginnings of a postmodern sensibility—wherein our conceptions of art and the aesthetic are transformed. However, it is in his tracing of the path of this development that Lyotard is most difficult to follow.[4] It must be stressed, therefore, that what follows is a very liberal interpretation of his argument. The story seems to proceed as follows. Conventional 'realist' art was under threat even before the impact of photography. Since the late eighteenth century a 'Modernist' avant-garde mode of art had been developing, which recognized that painting cannot simply be the reflections of a given order of things. These painters ask, in effect, the question of 'what is painting?'. Lyotard elaborates this as follows.

'Modern painters' discovered that they had to represent the existence of that which was not demonstrable if the perspectival laws . . . were followed. They set about to revolutionise the supposed visual givens in order to reveal that the field of vision simultaneously conceals and needs the invisible, that it relates therefore not only to the eye, but to the spirit as well.

Thus they introduced painting into the field opened up by the aesthetics of the sublime—which is not governed by a consensus of taste.[5]

Hence Lyotard's claim that 'it is in the aesthetic of the sublime that modern art (including literature) finds its impetus and the logic of avant-garde finds its axioms'.[6]

It is interesting that Lyotard invokes the sublime here, on the basis of Kant's theory. But why Kant? In this respect, Lyotard rightly points out that, in Kant's terms, 'We can conceive the infinitely great, the infinitely powerful, but every presentation of an object destined to "make visible" this absolute greatness or power appears to us painfully inadequate. Those are Ideas of which no presentation is possible.[7] Such ideas, however, can be suggested or alluded to by visible things.

---

[4] The problems accrue mainly to his linking of both Modernism and Postmodernism to the sublime, and in his use of the term 'avant-garde'. We customarily associate this latter term with 20th-c. painting—especially abstraction—and at times Lyotard seems to be using it in this way. However, at other times he seems to use it more broadly, in a way that encompasses the Romantics. This, interestingly, is not a wholly arbitrary usage, in so far as the term 'avant-garde' seems to have been first used, in relation to the arts, in the 1830s.
[5] 'Presenting the Unpresentable', 4.   [6] *The Postmodern Condition*, 77.
[7] Ibid. 78.

Kant himself shows the way when he names 'formlessness, the absence of form,' as a possible index to the unpresentable. He also says of the empty 'abstraction' which the imagination experiences when in search for a presentation of the infinite (another unpresentable) this abstraction is itself like a presentation of the infinite, its 'negative presentation'. He cites the commandment, 'Thou shalt not make graven images' (Exodus), as the most sublime passage in the Bible, in that it forbids all presentation of the absolute. Little needs to be added to those observations to outline an aesthetic of sublime paintings.[8]

Lyotard's reasoning here is based on the fact that because Modernist works can be 'formless' or 'abstract' (in comparison with conventional representation), this enables them to allude to the 'unpresentable' and 'invisible'. But whilst we know what Kant regards as 'unpresentable' (namely ideas of totality), it is rather more difficult to determine what Lyotard means by such a term. Some light is cast on this by a further crucial distinction which Lyotard makes between two forms of sublimity. The first of these is 'melancholic'—a 'nostalgia' for presence, wherein an emphasis is placed on 'the powerlessness of the faculty of presentation, on the nostalgia for presence felt by the human subject, on the obscure and futile will which inhabits him in spite of everything'.[9] Lyotard's meaning here, is, I think, best clarified by the artists he mentions in relation to this mode of sublimity—Fuseli, Friedrich, Delacroix, Malevich, the German Expressionists, Proust, and de Chirico. In the paintings or writings (or both) of these artists, we find a Romantic striving for a deep level of subjectivity—a striving for communion with an absolute self which can be conceived as existing, but which cannot be directly encountered in perception. On Lyotard's terms, it is this unpresentable and 'invisible' level of spiritual being which elements of formlessness or abstraction in their painting or writing allude to.

Now, as I have shown, for Lyotard the aesthetics of sublimity defines 'Modernist' painting. However, the nostalgic mode of sublimity just outlined (even though it continues into the twentieth century) is not an adequate response to the changes and aesthetic instability brought about by the impact of photography. As Lyotard puts it,

It allows the unpresentable to be put forward only as the missing contents; but the form, because of its recognisable consistency, continues to offer to

---

[8] *The Postmodern Condition*, 77.   [9] Ibid. 79.

the reader or viewer matter for solace and pleasure. Yet these sentiments do not constitute the real sublime sentiment, which is an intrinsic combination of pleasure and pain.[10]

However, there is another mode of sublimity in art—'novatio' (sometimes encountered in combination with the nostalgic), which does constitute an adequate response to photography, and changing sensibility, through the fact that it asks the question 'what is painting?' (or literature etc.), in a direct and uncompromising manner. Here, an emphasis is placed 'on the increase of being and the jubilation which result from the invention of new rules of the game, be it pictorial, artistic, or any other'.[11] What Lyotard seems to have in mind here are the radical stylstic changes that take place in the transition from Impressionism to Cézanne and Cubism, and which are consummated by the rise of abstraction from about 1910 onwards. In relation to Cézanne, the Delaunays, and Mondrian, for example, we are told that 'Their sublime was fundamentally not nostalgic and tended towards the infinity of plastic experiment rather than toward the representation of any lost absolute. In this, their work belongs to the contemporary industrial, techno-scientific world.'[12]

We are now in a position to grasp Lyotard's fundamental claim, which is that 'Postmodernism . . . is not modernism at its end, but in the nascent state, and this state is constant'.[13] As we have seen, for Lyotard Modernism in art involves an orientation towards the sublime. However, 'nostalgic' works do not fulfil their sublime potential. The fulfilment of such potential is achieved, rather, by those works of 'novatio' which make the nature of art explicitly problematic through striving to present it as a possibility of infinite (and thence unpresentable) experiment and development. Since, therefore, this avant-garde sublime anticipates the sensibility of a contemporary culture which is permeated by a sense of techno-science's infinite possibilities, we must regard it as a nascent state of Postmodernism—rather than the mere highpoint of an outdated Modernist sensibility.

Lyotard's theory, then, is an attempt to legitimize avant-garde art in relation to the needs and structure of contemporary Postmodern culture. The Kantian sublime provides the mediating

---

[10] Ibid. 81.   [11] Ibid. 80.   [12] 'Presenting the Unpresentable', 5.
[13] *The Postmodern Condition*, 79.

link. His arguments, however, raise a great number of difficulties. I shall confine myself to the more salient ones.

First, Lyotard's account of the function of conventional 'realist' art is derived from communication-theory—a theory devised primarily to explain the workings of mass-media. However, art even of the most blatantly realist sort is surely not reducible to the transmission of 'messages' about the order of things. Lyotard, in effect, turns away from a crucial distinction made by Kant himself—namely between *fine art* and that *mechanical art* which is created simply by following some technical rule, for the purpose of conveying information. If we accept this familiar distinction, then Lyotard's claim that photography renders realist art obsolete loses its force. A realist work may not communicate information about its subject-matter as efficiently as a photograph could, but from an aesthetic point of view this is irrelevant. As I have argued in Chapters 3 and 4, what interests us is *how* the work represents, and not what it represents. We look for changes and transformations of the subject-matter, for technical and stylistic innovations, and reappraisals of the past. Indeed, the question 'what is painting' is, in effect, asked by any work in any genre, in so far as it counts as an original development—an expansion of the medium's possibilities.

Lyotard's use of the Kantian sublime also has its worrying aspects. Clearly, he is not using it without qualification. The distinction between the mathematical and dynamic modes is not utilized; he ignores Kant's reservations about sublimity in art; and he makes no reference to the supersensible—an awareness of which (it will be remembered) is, for Kant, the source of the pleasurable aspect of the sublime. This last point directs us towards a crucial flaw in Lyotard's approach. Consider the following passage.

The sublime is not simply gratification, but the gratification of effort. It is impossible to represent the absolute, which is ungratifying: but one knows that one has to, that the faculty of feeling or of imagining is called upon to make the perceptible represent the ineffable—and even if this fails, and even if that causes suffering, a pure gratification will emerge from this tension.[14]

But why should such gratification emerge? Presumably because, although the idea of painting being infinitely developable is an

---

[14] 'Presenting the Unpresentable', 5.

unpresentable idea, one has at least shown something of this possibility through transforming the rules of painting. If, however, this jubilant transformation of painting can gratify us, why should there be any question of us (or the artist) striving to present what is unpresentable? It may be that, exceptionally, our enjoyment of innovation is accompanied by a sense of painting's infinite possibilities of development, but even if this does occur, it is only contingently related to our enjoyment—in other words, our enjoyment of innovation is one experience, and our sense of infinite possibility is another. This means, of course, that we would here be dealing with two psychologically successive, but logically distinct, experiences, rather than a single experience. But if the sublime is a genuine and distinct mode of experience, we must surely demand that its complex elements have at least a logical bearing on one another.

Now, the way round this problem would be to invoke the reconstructed version of Kant's theory proposed earlier on in this study. However, this leads to further problems for Lyotard's two modes of the sublime, 'nostalgia' and 'novatio'. I argued that the term 'sublime' is aptly applied to art when it is of colossal size or terrifying power, or employs form or imagery which successfully invokes such overwhelming associations. This, I would also suggest, broadly reflects our customary usage of the term 'sublime' in relation to art. Lyotard's modes, however, do not fit this usage, and do not, indeed, square with the historical role he assigns to them. In respect of 'nostalgia', for example, to use the term 'sublime' to describe any artists who incline towards colouristic painterless, or whose writings show that they aspire through their painting towards some spiritual reality, is so general as to be useless. It could embrace artists as far apart as El Greco and Malevich. Matters lie similarly with 'novatio'. As I suggested a little earlier, any innovatory work, in effect, asks the question 'what is painting' through its expanding the possibilities of the medium. Lyotard, of course, might well say that radical avant-garde artists ask this question more directly and insistently, but it is difficult to see what is gained by this. For (as I also noted earlier) whilst *some* superlative avant-garde works may evoke an overwhelming sense of the medium being latent with infinite possibilities of development, this is surely a striking exception rather than a rule which defines what counts as authentically avant-garde. Indeed, there is no intrinsic reason why the best non-avant-garde works should not also sometimes achieve this.

I have argued, then, that Lyotard's linking of the Kantian sublime to avant-garde art and the postmodern sensibility is unsuccessful. Ironically, the real direction in which Lyotard's theory of the avant-garde is tending is towards an aspect of Kant's aesthetics which he does not explicitly consider—namely the theory of genius.[15] As we saw in Chapter 3, for Kant, the art of genius is that whose primary quality is originality—it is that art which cannot simply be reduced to the following of established rules of creation and artifice. Since, however (as Kant also admits), there can be 'original nonsense', the art of genius must be 'exemplary', that is, it must involve not just a breaking with old rules but also the invention of *new* ones. Now, in the light of this theory we can locate Lyotard's account of the avant-garde within a rather more amenable theoretical context. For, with the rise of Romanticism— and more so with the advent of the Modernist avant-garde—there has been a reorientation of art towards the unpresentable, by means of the wholesale and continuing invention of new rules for art. This unpresentable is the creative individuality of the artist—a phenomenon which is constituted and manifested not simply in the work as such, but rather (as we have seen in Chapters 3, 4, and 5) in its relation both to the tradition with which it is breaking, and to the space of possibility which it is opening up. To enjoy the creative individuality of the artist's rule transformations, in other words, we must bring to bear knowledge which is not directly presented in the work itself. This, however, does not entail anything like that striving for the unattainable which Lyotard sees as a definitive characteristic of the sublime.

Now, it is important to make a qualification at this point. Kant himself uses genius as one of the means for defining fine art as a category. He does not use the term in any historical sense. My point, however, is that whilst all art of any quality may entail genius in Kant's sense of the term, it is only with the rise of Modernism that the wholesale invention of new rules for art seems to be the fundamental dynamic of artistic change. Kant's theory of genius, then, would have given a more useful theoretical framework for locating the main features in terms of which Lyotard

[15] See *The Critique of Judgement*, trans. J. C. Meredith (Clarendon Press, Oxford, 1973), esp. Bk. i, §§46 and 47.

defines the avant-garde. This would, of course, involve the abandoning of the exact links which Lyotard wishes to make between the avant-garde, the sublime, and the postmodern, but such abandonment would move Lyotard only in the direction of greater plausibility.

I want finally to suggest that whilst Lyotard's overall connective philosophical strategy is flawed, another aspect of his work has shown how the Kantian sublime might be linked at least to the idea of a distinctive contemporary postmodern sensibility. What this sensibility involves was given its fullest evocation in an exhibition organized by Lyotard at the Centre Georges-Pompidou in Paris, in 1985. The exhibition was entitled *Les Immatériaux*. This will form the subject-matter of my next chapter.

9

Sublimity and Postmodern Culture
Lyotard's Les Immatériaux

> . . . one should see the quest for the sublime . . . as one of the
> prettier unforced blue flowers of bourgeois culture. But this
> quest is wildly irrelevant to the attempt at communicative
> consensus which is the vital force which drives that culture.
>
> Richard Rorty.[1]

At the time of its staging in Paris in 1985, Lyotard's *Les
Immatériaux* elicited little more than polite non-committal reviews
from the English-speaking artworld. In this chapter, however, I
want to consider some of the philosophical issues which *Les
Immatériaux* raises in relation to postmodern art and postmodern
culture generally. Specifically, I will hope to pick out its shortcomings *vis-à-vis* aesthetic and political issues, and develop its implications in a direction which points to sublimity having the kind of
significance which Rorty (in the epigraph above) denies.

Let me start with Lyotard's own overall attitude to *Les
Immatériaux*, which is that it should be regarded in its totality as
an artwork.[2] This would seem, at first sight, to be very much in
the vein of 1970s conceptual art, i.e. 'high modernism' (to use a
term applied to Lyotard by Fredric Jameson). However, if *Les
Immatériaux* relates to Modernism it is as its *Götterdammerung*.
As Lyotard points out, 'Its purpose is to introduce the visitor into
the "dramaturgy" of postmodernism.'[3] Indeed, a publicity leaflet

This chapter is forthcoming in *Judging Lyotard* ed. Andrew Benjamin (Routledge,
London).
[1] Richard Rorty, 'Habermas and Lyotard on Modernity', in *Habermas and
Modernity*, ed. Richard Bernstein (Polity Press, Cambridge, 1985), 161–75. This ref.,
p. 174.
[2] See e.g. Bernard Blistene's interview with Lyotard, in *Flash Art*, no. 121 (Mar.
1985).
[3] 'Les Immatériaux: An Interview with Jean-François Lyotard' (in French),
CNAC Magazine, no. 26 (Mar.–Apr. 1985), 12–16. This ref., p. 13.

for the Exhibition tells us, 'It's neither pedagogical or demagogical . . . Our objective is to rouse a sensitivity which already exists in all of us, to make one feel the strange in the familiar, and how difficult it is to imagine what's changing.'

The basis of this sensitivity arises from the fact that, in post-modern times, reality is no longer simply *perceived* in terms of substantive, self-contained, material surfaces. It is, rather, *deciphered* as the intersection of various complex levels of meaning. Hence the Exhibition is organized on the basis of communication theory's notion of the 'message'. This involves the interplay of five factors: (1) the origin of the message (*maternité*), (2) the medium of support (*matériau*), (3) the code in which it is inscribed (*matrice*), (4) what is referred to (*matière*), (5) the destination of the message (*matériel*). The many different ways in which each of these five factors is involved in our deciphering of contemporary reality are explored through a physical layout of thirty-one zones (some subdivided) yielding a total of over sixty sites. There is no one route through this labyrinth. Rather the visitor is free to wander, wearing radio-controlled headphones which offer 'commentaries' in the form of music, poetry, literature, philosophy, and other readings, which change as one moves from zone to zone. For the sake of brevity I shall describe only one of the five factors explored through this complex, namely *matériau* (the support of the message). The aspects of *matériau* considered include the human body, sexuality, the human form reproduced on video, maps, the raw materials of industry, and new materials used in artistic production. What emerges from these presentations is that the surfaces which support the messages of contemporary life are unstable, elusive, and undergoing rapid transformations. This is not just to say that technoscientific advances are transforming reality, but that we are acutely conscious of, and made radically insecure by them. As Lyotard puts it,

The word 'human' as substantive adjective, designates an ancient domain of knowledge and intervention which the technosciences now cut across and share; here they discover and elaborate 'immaterials' which are analogous (even if they are in general more complex) to those examined and detected in other fields. The human cortex is 'read' just like an electronic field; through the neurovegetative system human affectivity is 'acted' on like a complex chemical organisation . . .

As a result of this, the ideas associated with the one of 'material' [i.e.

matériau], and which lend support to the immediate apprehension of an identity for Man, are weakened'.[4]

These remarks indicate the very essence of *Les Immatériaux.* Every familiar aspect of reality—even that of the embodied self— now proves to be infinitely analysable and transformable into a web of microscopic and macroscopic processes and relations (i.e. 'immaterials'). Although these 'immaterials' sustain lived-reality, they have hitherto been undiscovered or ignored. With the techno-scientific advances of postmodern times, however, they are thrust to the forefront of our consciousness. It is this awareness of infinite analysability and transformation which *Les Immatériaux* evokes, with startling success.

Now, traditionally, an aesthetic sensitivity to infinity (or to the suggestion of it) has been understood in terms of the 'sublime'. This notion can (indeed must) be applied to *Les Immatériaux*, though I shall defer justification of such a claim until the final part of this chapter. Provisionally, however, one might say, in relation to *Les Immatériaux*, that our appreciation of infinite analysability or transformability does not (as is usually the case with the sublime) arise from an encounter with objects which are, or which suggest, physically overwhelming size or power. Rather it arises when our powers of perception and imagination are overwhelmed by the complexity of those processes and relations which make the surfaces of everyday reality possible, but which normally pass unnoticed or undiscovered. The sublime, in other words, arises here from a deconstruction of the familiar into that which normally functions subliminally. Our postmodern sensibility can, therefore, be aptly described as 'sublimicist'. It is interesting, however, that whilst *Les Immatériaux* itself unmistakably points in this sublimicist direction, and whilst the sublime figures crucially in Lyotard's philosophical writings on Postmodernism, he does not, nevertheless, explicitly discuss sublimity in the lengthy catalogue material for *Les Immatériaux*. This is particularly unfortunate, as the problem of the sublime lies, I think, at the heart of several problems and possibilities which the exhibition raises. It is to these which I now turn.

First, the question of art. Those works which Lyotard includes

[4] J.-F. Lyotard, 'Les Immatériaux', *Art and Text*, no. 17 (Apr. 1985), 47–57. This ref., p. 49.

in *Les Immatériaux* are either very much in the tradition of avant-garde abstract–conceptual art—for example, Moholy-Nagy, Flavin, Ryman, Fontana, Malevich, Duchamp—or ones which utilize new 'hi-tech' processes and materials—for example, Stephen Benton, and Doug Tyler's holograms. What are not included are those recent (to use a very misleading label) 'Neo-Expressionist' works by the likes of Morley, Baselitz, Schnabel, or Clemente, and which, of course, are generally regarded as postmodern. In relation to such 'eclectic' works, Lyotard has said, 'they've lost all sense of what's fundamentally at stake in painting. There's a vague return to a concern with the *enjoyment* experienced by the viewer, they've abandoned the *task* of the artist as it might have been perceived by a Cézanne, a Duchamp, or by any number of others, such as Klee, for instance.'[5] Lyotard's claims, here, are based on that general theory of the sublime and the postmodern nature of the avant-garde as such which I analysed in the previous chapter. It is now worth reiterating his difficult argument before considering its ramifications for *Les Immatériaux*.

The argument proceeds broadly as follows. The Modernist era dates from the Enlightenment onwards, and in art is characterized by an aesthetic of the sublime. In Lyotard's words,

'Modern painters' discovered that they had to represent the existence of that which was not demonstrable if the perspectival laws . . . were followed. They set about to revolutionise the supposed visual givens in order to reveal that the field of vision simultaneously conceals and needs the invisible, that it relates therefore not only to the eye, but to the spirit as well.[6]

Hence the Modernist painter asks, in effect, the question, 'What is painting?' An experience of this sort of work is sublime—combining pain and pleasure—in the sense that through striving to present the 'invisible', the painter is striving after something which, in visual terms, is unpresentable. Now, the problem with much Modernist work is that this rigorous questioning of the nature of painting is not carried through. 'It allows the unpresentable to be put forward only as the missing contents, but the form because of its recognisable consistency continues to offer to the . . . viewer

[5] Blistene's interview with Lyotard.
[6] J.-F. Lyotard, 'Presenting the Unpresentable: The Sublime', *Artforum* (Apr. 1982), 64–9. This ref., p. 67.

matter for solace and pleasure. Yet these sentiments do not constitute the real sublime sentiment, which is an intrinsic combination
of pleasure and pain.'[7] However, there is an alternative to this
'nostalgic' mode of the sublime, and it is found in the work of the
authentic avant-garde. In relation to the work of Cézanne, the
Delaunays, and Mondrian, for example, we are told that 'Their
sublime was fundamentally not nostalgic, and tended towards the
infinity of plastic experiment rather than towards the representation of any lost absolute. In this, their work belongs to the contemporary industrial techno-scientific world.'[8]

On these terms, then, whereas the Modernist painter seeks to
suggest the spiritual realm and ends up stopping us short at a con-
soling beautiful surface, the avant-garde artist questions painting in
a way that disrupts and disturbs, thus suggesting the (visually
unpresentable) possibility of painting as infinitely developable.
This, allegedly, anticipates the postmodern sensibility which *Les
Immatériaux* seeks to evoke. Unfortunately, the difficulties raised
by Lyotard's arguments are enormous. I shall confine myself to the
following. First, it is extremely ironic that in his book *The
Postmodern Condition* Lyotard defines Postmodernism as an
incredulity towards meta-narratives, i.e. towards discourses which
seek to legitimize themselves through 'making an explicit appeal to
some grand narrative, such as the dialectics of the Spirit, the
hermeneutics of meaning, the emancipation of the rational or
working subject, or the creation of wealth'.[9] However, Lyotard's
account of the triumph of the avant-garde's authentic sublimicism
over Modernism's nostalgic aesthetic of the sublime is itself very
much an emancipatory 'grand narrative'. This means, in other
words, that Lyotard's exclusion of 'Neo-Expressionist' work is,
paradoxically enough, based on a persistence of modernist attitudes. Now, in response to this, Lyotard might argue as follows.
The task of *Les Immatériaux* in highlighting a postmodern sensibility is neutral rather than prescriptive—it seeks simply to evoke a
change in sensibility which has already taken place. If, therefore,
avant-garde works are included in the Exhibition to the exclusion

---

⁷ J.-F. Lyotard, *The Postmodern Condition: A Report on Knowledge*, trans. Geoff
Bennington and Brian Massumi (Manchester University Press, Manchester, 1984),
81.
⁸ Lyotard, 'Presenting the Unpresentable', 68.
⁹ Lyotard, *The Postmodern Condition*, p. xxiii.

of others, it is simply because of the fact that they anticipate or embody the postmodern sensibility highlighted by *Les Immatériaux* in a way that the other works do not. This neat response, however, would not be consistent with the general high moral tenor of Lyotard's writings on art. In relation to those excluded 'Neo-Expressionist' artists who mix styles, we are told that such 'eclecticism' is 'the corruption of painting's honour'[10] and 'strips artists of their responsibility to the question of the nondemonstrable. That question is, to me, the only one worthy of life's high stakes . . .'.[11]

On these terms we must see Lyotard's exclusion of 'eclectic' works as based on the fact that they fail to satisfy the demands of authentic painting, i.e. the task of asking the question, 'what is painting?' This would mean that Lyotard's attitude to art in *Les Immatériaux* involves a conflation of two rather different approaches. On the one hand, there is an empirical theory about a changed sensibility founded on technoscientific advance; and, on the other hand, there is a prescriptive grand narrative about avant-gardism as authentic painting. Now, because both these approaches challenge the existence of a status quo and point in the direction of infinite development, Lyotard assumes that both involve the same sublimicist sensibility. Hence, if we identify Postmodernism with the sensibility of technoscientific culture, and if avant-garde painting shares this, then we are entitled to regard the avant-garde as postmodern too.

However, Lyotard is, I think, mistaken as to the affinity between his two approaches, in so far as whilst the technoscientific culture of *Les Immatériaux* is indeed sublimicist, avant-garde painting is manifestly not. One might say that whilst the radical innovations achieved by the avant-garde show that painting can be developed in an inexhaustible number of directions, such works do not, however, explicitly attempt to present this unpresentable space of infinite possibility; rather, each new work simply demonstrates that the idea of totalized, 'definitive', absolute painting is nonsense— there is always something more to be done. This basic recognition involves nothing like the perceptual and imaginative struggle involved in trying to grasp all the aspects and levels of analysis offered through technoscientific approaches to (for example) the body. The sensibility highlighted by *Les Immatériaux*, in other

---

[10] Lyotard, 'Presenting the Unpresentable', 69.   [11] Ibid.

words, is sublimicist, but the avant-garde works favoured by Lyotard are not. In effect, Lyotard refuses to follow where the deconstructive argument of *Les Immatériaux* leads. For surely, if the pseudo-autonomous surfaces of lived-reality are sustained by complex levels of immateriality, then we must expect this also to be the case with art—that its claims to authenticity are grounded on a complex interrelation of concealed social and political factors, and epistemological closures. This would mean that an art-practice which addressed itself to the deconstruction of art's supposed autonomy or authenticity would be very much in keeping with the sensibility of *Les Immatériaux*.

Ironically enough, the works which do genuinely embody such a sublimicist tendency, and thus warrant the term 'postmodern', are the very ones which Lyotard excludes (and which I shall discuss at length in the next two chapters). For example, whilst a great deal of recent 'Neo-Expressionist' painting is merely eclectic, its finest achievements are not. In the work of Malcolm Morley, Georg Baselitz, and Anselm Kiefer, for example, convenient categories such as 'realist', 'expressionist', 'landscape', even the notion of 'good painting' itself, are questioned and made strange. We experience 'art' not as a well-defined notion with definite limits and criteria, but rather as an insecure and shifting totality, where categories constantly interweave and are transformed. Previous to works such as these, 'art' has been easy to assimilate. A few paradigms of each 'ism' give us the material for picturing to ourselves the whole domain of 'fine' art. The works of Morley, Baselitz, and Kiefer, however, through their crossing of boundaries, involve us in a struggle to locate them. We compare and contrast to see how far they satisfy such and such a stylistic label (for example, expressionist), only to find that through such analysis the label itself now seems flexible and of only relative validity. Thus the very moorings which hold our easy notion of art together are loosened and pulled apart. On these terms, whilst the avant-garde work simply demonstrates the fact that painting cannot be limited, the works of Morley, Baselitz, and Kiefer involve us in a painful struggle that shows the very notion of art itself to be so complex as to strain our perceptual and imaginative capacities to the utmost. We thus have painting which is genuinely sublimicist and which exemplifies the postmodern sensibility of *Les Immatériaux*.

The second main line of critique which I shall take in relation to

Les Immatériaux again involves a problem of exclusion. It is the Exhibition's declared objective not to be pedagogical, demogogical, or historical. However, without the politico-historical dimension, the technoscientific culture of *Les Immatériaux* appears as a self-perpetuating, self-justifying spectacle. We have a sensibility that is founded on the uncontrolled and unquestioned drive towards a technoscientific achievement. The questions which the Exhibition explicitly asks of the visitor (through the accompanying catalogue) concern only the nature of the changes taking place in contemporary life, and by-pass the issue of their validity. However, just as Walter Benjamin observes that the aestheticization of politics ends in war, could we not say that the postmodern aestheticization of technoscience will tend likewise—in the direction of *nuclear* war? Against this Lyotard might assert the putative 'art' status of *Les Immatériaux* and claim that, whilst the Exhibition might have political implications, these are for the particular visitor to assess on his or her own terms. *Les Immatériaux* itself attempts only the neutral task of evoking an already existent sensibility, rather than the prescriptive task of criticizing it.

The problem with this response (a response which, I think, Lyotard is implicitly committed to) is twofold. First, it assumes that having the status 'art-object' in itself is in conflict with explictly raising political questions. This, of course (as I showed in Chapter 4), is not necessarily the case. Indeed, it assumes the validity of the unjustified 'grand narrative' about authentic, autonomous painting noted earlier. However, even if we allowed Lyotard his grand narrative, there would be a further, even more glaring, problem, in so far as it is surely the case that the new sensibility which *Les Immatériaux* addresses itself to also pervades the political domain. By this, I do not simply mean the way that technoscientific methods have revolutionized patterns of political communication and determined the image of politicians, but rather the way in which new modes of political sensibility have arisen. Are not, for example, feminism, the anti-nuclear movement, and Green politics all embodiments of an incredulity towards the patriarchal and alienated grand narratives of superpower politics? Are they not, thus, on Lyotard's own terms, exemplars of postmodernity? An inclusion of zones or sites alluding to these transformations of political reality, in other words, would have fitted into *Les Immatériaux* without disrupting its supposedly neutral 'art' status at all. We would thus have had a reflective dimension to counter-balance the sense of technoscience as uncontrolled spectacle. A space for asking the most fundamental questions would have been opened up.

The final critical issue which I wish to raise is connected with the above points. It concerns the question of what positive political implications we can draw from *Les Immatériaux* as a whole. In *The Postmodern Condition*, Lyotard states that 'consensus does violence to the heterogeneity of language games. And invention is always born of dissension. Postmodern knowledge is not simply a tool of the authorities; it refines our sensitivity to differences and reinforces our ability to tolerate the incommensurable.'[12] However, this does not (as Lyotard thinks) in itself point in the direction of justice. For if specific language games and the forms of life grounded upon them have their own internal criteria of validation, and are incommensurable with each other, then participants in one game may well simply seal themselves into it, and respond with cold war or aggression to those who participate in other games. Here the sensitivity to difference could lead, as Meaghan Morris aptly puts it, to 'a state of permanent bellicosity . . . where Might is Right'.[13]

Nevertheless, *Les Immatériaux* marks, I think, an important change from Lyotard's earlier position. The second volume of the Catalogue, for example, extends the sublimicist approach of the Exhibition to the purely linguistic level. Fifty or so concepts relevant to *Les Immatériaux*, such as Body, Desire, and Code, are considered by a team of theorists, and shown to have displaced and shifting meanings. This suggests that what characterizes Post-modernism is not so much sensitivity to mere heterogeneity and difference, but rather a sensitivity to *différance*—in something like Derrida's sense of that term, i.e. the immaterials which are concealed by, but which sustain, the pseudo-autonomous surfaces of lived reality parallel those unstable and overlapping meanings which are concealed by, but which sustain, the pseudo-autonomous discourses of the human sciences. On these terms, immaterials do not constitute absolutely heterogeneous sub-levels of reality. Rather, there are important overlaps and analogies between them,

[12] Lyotard, *The Postmodern Condition*, p. xxv.
[13] Meaghan Morris, 'Postmodernity and Lyotard's Sublime', *Art and Text*, no. 16 (Summer 1984), 44–67. This ref., p. 53.

and the possibility of constant transformation. Now, can a sensitivity to such *différance* point us more securely in the direction of justice? I would suggest that it can, if we rectify a difficulty in
Lyotard's overall theory.

The problem is this. As *Les Immatériaux* shows, our sense of
reality has been defamiliarized and rendered insecure, through
technoscientific immaterialization. What has not been shown, however, is why this should be found pleasurable, rather than alienat-
ing in the extreme. In relation to a parallel problem in his theory
of avant-garde art, Lyotard invokes a Kantian notion of the sublime,[14] and it is something like this (as I suggested earlier on)
which we need in order to make sense of *Les Immatériaux*.
Unfortunately, Lyotard's adaptation of Kant's theory is itself problematic. For example, we are told that

The sublime is not simple gratification, but the gratification of effort. It is
impossible to represent the absolute, which is ungratifying, but one knows
that one has to, that the faculty of feeling or imagining is called upon to
make the perceptible represent the ineffable—and even if this fails, and
even if that causes suffering, a pure gratification will emerge from the tension.[15]

But *why* should a 'pure gratification' emerge? Lyotard presents
our reaching for the sublime as Sisyphean—something one has to
do for no reward but the effort. But effort without pay-off is
surely mere frustration. Lyotard, in other words, explains the negative side of the sublime's ambiguous pleasure, but not the positive
side. Lyotard could attempt to meet this objection by saying that
we enjoy the way avant-garde works and technoscientific change
transform the rules of painting and sensibility, respectively.
However, against this one must argue (as I did against Weiskel in
Chapter 7) that if the sublime is to be a distinct form of experience
sui generis, it must be because there is some intrinsic connection
between its negative and positive aspects. This is not true of

---

[14] In his paper 'The Sublime and the Avant-Garde' (*Artforum* (Apr. 1984),
36–43), Lyotard also invokes Burke's theory of the sublime in relation to avant-
garde art. His basic idea is that such art is fundamentally an event—a shock which
affirms the Moment, in a way that allays our fear of all moments coming to an end.
In Ch. 6 I developed the implications of this aspect of Burke's thought in a rather
different direction. In any case, given the technoscientific and epistemological orientation of *Les Immatériaux*, it is Kant's theory of the sublime which is more immediately relevant.

[15] Lyotard, 'Presenting the Unpresentable', 68.

Lyotard's projected response. For (on the one hand) to be over-whelmed by the infinite possibilities of painting and technoscience, and (on the other hand) to enjoy innovation in those fields, is, logi-cally speaking, to have two different experiences—no matter how psychologically proximal their occurrence might be. If, therefore, we are to have a theoretically adequate notion of the sublime, we must—in a way that Lyotard does not—show some logical kinship between its negative and positive components. We must, in effect, argue that in our cognitive relation to certain kinds of objects, a deficiency in one aspect of cognition serves to clarify and empha-size the richness of another aspect; or (to put it in a different way) that the positive aspect presupposes the negative aspect in order for its scope to be fully manifest.

Happily (as I showed in Chapter 7), Kant himself offers a more viable approach. His basic position is that whilst some phenome-non may be so vast or destructive as to overwhelm our capacity to grasp it in perceptual or imaginative (i.e. sensory) terms, we can nevertheless encompass it in thought. We can even form an idea of infinity itself, despite being unable to experience a sense-perception or mental image which would fully embody that idea. Given this, Kant suggests that in such cases the very inadequacy of our sensory cognition makes the scope and superiority of rational comprehen-sion—the 'supersensible' side of our being—all the more striking. Our sensory pain gives way to a pleasure in reason.

Let me now reiterate how this approach should be modified. First, the idea of our rational being as wholly 'supersensible' (with all the difficulties that such a notion would entail) can simply be discarded, in so far as it is an outcome of Kant's broader, philo-sophically dubious, transcendental Idealism. This would enable us to make the more modest claim that the inadequacy of sensory cognition to certain kinds of phenomena serves to vivify the scope of our powers of rational comprehension. In day-to-day existence such powers are exercised more or less unnoticed. In the experi-ence of the sublime, however, they are strikingly manifest, and this is the source of a profound satisfaction, in so far as through it we enjoy a felt transcendence of the limitations of embodiment. Now, whilst Kant confines such experiences to vast or mighty objects, we can again modify his position to encompass those which are com-plex. Hence, whilst *Les Immatériaux* shows that reality is under-pinned by immaterials of infinite complexity, and whilst, indeed, we cannot fully comprehend this complexity in terms of sense-perceptions or images, we can, nevertheless, conceptualize it as a surface sustained by infinite complexity. Reason circumscribes that which overwhelms the senses. It is this vivification and affirmation of rational comprehension which overcomes the possibility of alienation.

Given this analysis, then, the sublimicist sensibility of *Les Immatériaux* emerges as the source of an *aesthetic* pleasure. We can describe it in these terms because, on the one hand, it is fundamentally a kind of vigorous, reciprocally enhancing 'play' between two different aspects of cognition, and, on the other hand, it is the kind of thing which can be enjoyed for its own sake—rather than for its practical or theoretical utility in relation to the lifeworld. This latter feature, of course, is usually labelled as 'disinterestedness'. Now, the fact that such an experience is disinterested in terms of its logical grounds does not prevent it from having, in certain contexts, a further, more practical significance. It is, indeed, a failure to realize this which accounts for the current hostility to notions of the aesthetic felt by many contemporary theorists of Postmodernism.

However, suppose the sublimicist sensibility is brought to bear diachronically and synchronically on notions of socio-political import, such as that of 'community'. In relation to the first of these aspects, the sublimicist sensibility would regard any given community as a surface of only provisional validity. It would try (and fail) to imagine all the historical transformations which brought the community to its present stage, and all the realistic transformations which it might possibly undergo. From the synchronic viewpoint, such a sensibility would attempt (and again fail) to perceive or imagine all the individuals and groupings in the community with their different and sometimes changing experiences and interests. Now, although in both cases sensory cognition is overwhelmed by the data it seeks to grasp, our possession of the *idea* of the community—our capacity to grasp it in rational terms—is made all the more vivid, and, thereby pleasurable. The side-effects of such sublimicizing are rather interesting. First, in even attempting to grasp the diachronic and synchronic complexities of community existence, we are sensitizing ourselves to its transformatory possibilities, and to the nature of its unstable diversities. Indeed, the fact that such a politically useful sensitization arises in the context of an aesthetic project, i.e. one that is disinterested, means that our own partiality to particular transformations and groupings will not have as much sway as it would if we had undertaken the project for the explicit purpose of socio-political understanding. It may, in other words, teach us to be fairer in our political judgements. Similarly, whilst we may attempt to view the community diachronically and synchronically in the way described as part of our ordinary political praxis, the difficulty of the task may simply frustrate us—thus leading to despair or dogmatism, or even violence. However, as part of a sublimicist experience, our sensory cognition's inadequacies lead on to a pleasure in our rationality. This means, of course, that the generation of such politically significant awareness in a pleasurable aesthetic context, rather than through the frustrating hurly-burly of politics itself, will provide an incentive for cultivating and deepening such awareness which might otherwise be lacking. Given these facts, one might hope and expect that through the sublimicization of political contexts, the aesthetic factor will help develop a political sensibility that is more deeply aware of possible transformations of existing society, yet, at the same time, is averse to solutions that violently erase the different interests of groups and individuals. Sublimicism, in other words, can point towards, and prepare us for, critical tolerance. Such tolerance, of course, is an essential feature of any notion of justice or consensus.

In conclusion, I would briefly like to relate the foregoing argument to a broader debate. Jürgen Habermas has suggested that the problem of modernity can in part be resolved through a reintegration of aesthetic experience with the lifeworld. As he puts it,

. . . as soon as such an experience is used to illustrate a life-historical situation and life problems, it enters into a language-game which is no longer that of the aesthetic critic. The aesthetic experience then not only renews the interpretation of our needs in whose light we perceive the world. It permeates as well our cognitive significations and our normative expectations and changes the manner in which all these refer to one another.[16]

Now, as Martin Jay has pointed out,[17] Habermas does not really clarify what form such a reintegrative project might take. What

[16] Jürgen Habermas, 'Modernity—An Incomplete Project', in *Postmodern Culture*, ed. Hal Foster (Pluto Press, London, 1985), 3–15. This ref., p. 13.

[17] In his essay 'Habermas and Modernism', in *Habermas and Modernity*, ed. Bernstein, 125–39. See esp. p. 133.

Habermas is sure of, however, is that the deconstructive postmodern approach will not help, in so far as 'Nothing remains from a
de-sublimated meaning, or a destructured form; an emancipatory
effect does not follow'.[18] Against this I would claim not only that
the sublimicist sensibility highlighted by *Les Immatériaux* has an
emancipatory effect through its affirmation of reason, but that it
can make a substantial contribution to precisely that reintegrative
task which Habermas specifies in the first passage quoted. For, as I
have shown, sublimicist pleasure not only arises from the impact of
technoscience, but has grounds which are distinctively aesthetic in
character, and which are yet able, in the right context, to promote
deeper political awareness.

However, it is important as a final point to qualify this opti-
mism, by a reiteration of the second critical issue which I raised in
relation to *Les Immatériaux*. Left to itself as an unquestioned, self-
justifying drive, the sublimicist aestheticization of technoscience
will tend towards nuclear war. This is why it must be accompanied by a sharpened political consciousness—towards which, as I
have attempted to show, a sublimicist sensibility can actively contribute. In this latter respect, of course, it has hitherto been left to
Fascism and authoritarian Communism to aestheticize the mere
means of political expression and repression, through their mass
parades, and glorifications of warfare. Sublimicist aestheticization,
in contrast, will involve the deconstructive interrogation of socio-
political reality itself, thus favouring a sensibility of a critical tolerance. Aesthetics will, thereby, by returned to the lifeworld, but this
time by, and into, the right hands.

This completes my analyses of the sublime. As we have seen,
both Burke and Kant's theories have profound relevance to the
understanding of the postmodern sensibility. In the Introduction to
this book, I argued that such a sensibility is orientated towards
shock (in the very broadest sense). We see now—as we saw in relation to our responses to art—that the pleasure of the sublime is
not just some affective jolt. Rather it brings elements of body-hold
into heightened reciprocity, and affirms our dignity as rational
embodied beings. True, there are dangers—aesthetic, moral, and
political—in such experiences; but these can be countered by a
proper mode of critical awareness.

[18] Habermas, 'Modernity—An Incomplete Project', 11.

Having (in Part One) discussed our experience of art generally, and (in Part Two) the contemporary status of the sublime, it now remains for me to bring these and related issues together in relation to the understanding of postmodern art.

PLATE 1. Malcolm Morley, *S.S. Amsterdam at Rotterdam*
Acrylic on canvas (1966) 62 × 84 in.

PLATE 2. Anselm Kiefer, *Die Meistersinger*
Oil and straw on canvas (1982) 112 × 152 in.

PLATE 3.
Julian Schnabel, *The Sea*
Oil and crockery on wood
(1981)
104 × 156 in.

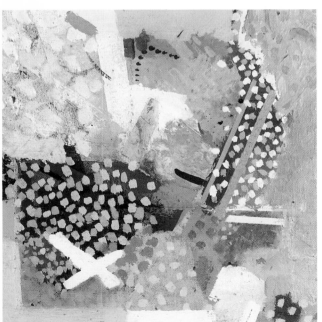

PLATE 4.
Peter Suchin,
With Yellow Cross
Acrylic and collage
on chipboard (1980)
12 × 12 in.

PLATE 5.
Peter Suchin, *The Golden Code* (1986)
Acrylic on wood
26.5 × 22.5 in.

PLATE 7. Thérèse Oulton, *Counterfoil*
Oil on canvas (1987)
92 × 84 in.

PLATE 6. Thérèse Oulton, *Second Subject*
Oil on canvas (1987)
92 × 84 in.

Part Three

10

Postmodernism in the Visual Arts

A Question of Ends

The question of Postmodernism in the visual arts has been dominated by a number of themes, notably the idea that art, its history, and its theory, have come to an end; and that Postmodernism is largely the product of a force external to art—namely, the market. It might be argued that, for the most part, these themes have been set forth and received with rather more enthusiasm than understanding (the works of Victor Burgin are perhaps a case in point here). However, in the writings of the philosopher and art critic Arthur Danto, the themes are linked in a more coherent and incisive way as part of an interesting discourse concerning the end of modernity in the visual arts. In this chapter, therefore, I shall use a critique of Danto's theory as a means of answering the question of Postmodernism in the visual arts. Specifically, in section I, I will outline Danto's theory at length, and will argue that it is not philosophically decisive. In sections II and III, I will go on to offer a more plausible alternative reading of modernity and postmodernity; and in section IV, will offer a final refutation of Danto's claim that (through being rendered posthistorical in the postmodern era) art has come to an end.

I

The premise of Danto's arguments concerning the end of art is that the advent of cinematography precipitated a traumatic crisis in the artworld. This crisis centred on the fact that, whilst art had always taken itself to be essentially bound with imitating the world, it was now recognized that cinematography could achieve this in a more

This chapter was published under the same title in *Postmodernism and Society*, ed. Roy Boyne and Ali Rattansi (Macmillan, London, 1990).

total way. Twentieth-century Modernist art, therefore, turned towards a kind of self-interrogation. As Danto puts it, 'In its great philosophical phase, from about 1905 to about 1964, modern art undertook a massive investigation into its own nature and essence. It set out to seek a form of itself so pure as art that nothing like what caused it to undertake this investigation in the first place could ever happen to it again.'[1] This interpretation is, according to Danto, confirmed by the fact that Modernist movements seem to be in perpetual conflict with each other. Again, in his words, 'There have been more projected definitions of art, each identified with a different movement in art, in the six or seven decades of the modern era, than in the six or seven centuries that preceded it. Each definition was accompanied by a severe condemnation of everything else, as *not* art.'[2] On these terms, then, the discontinuity and conflict between modern movements should be taken as signifying the fact that all were involved in a search for art's essence, and that all were offering different, mutually exclusive, answers.

Now, for Danto, this search ends at a quite specific point—namely in Warhol's Pop Art, and, in particular the exhibition at the Stable Gallery in 1964 where the infamous *Brillo Boxes* were shown for the first time. Since Warhol's Boxes were ostensibly indistinguishable from real Brillo cartons, the question of what differentiates artworks from real things was posed in the most naked and unambiguous fashion, or, as Danto has it, 'its true philosophical form'. And the answer emerged as follows. It is only an atmosphere of theory which differentiates artworks from other things. The essence of art does not consist in some perceptible property or set of properties, but rather in art's institutional setting. Broadly speaking, the artwork is what the artist designates as such, on the basis of some theory about art.

Now, this answer—and its reiteration in Minimal and (one presumes) Conceptual art—effectively brought the internal logic of Modernist art's quasi-philosophical questioning to fulfilment. But this created a hiatus. As Danto puts it, 'the institutions of the art world continued to believe in—indeed to expect—breakthroughs, and the galleries, the collectors, the art magazines, the museums and finally the corporations that had become the major patrons of

---

[1] A. Danto, *The State of the Art* (Prentice Hall, New York, 1987), 217.
[2] Ibid.

the age were also awaiting prophets and revelations'.[3] Danto's point, then, is that the radical innovations of Modernist work had by the late 1960s and 1970s found a market, and thence created a demand for art that was innovative and new. But what came next was a mere pluralism—a repetition or refinement of preceding styles (be they representational or abstract) and a willingness to accept these on their own terms, rather than on a partisan basis of mutual exclusivity. Indeed, in the terms of Danto's argument this is an entirely logical development, in so far as once Modernist art has worked through to and declared art's essence, there is nothing new for art to do. It can only rework old ground. The advent and triumph of Neo-Expressionism in the 1980s is simply a special case of this. According to Danto, 'Neo-Expressionism raised, as art, no philosophical question at all, and indeed it could raise none that would not be some variant on the one raised in its perfected form by Warhol.'[4] Neo-Expressionism, then, is to be seen as an exaggerated and empty response to the art market's demand for innovation. It provides, as it were, a show of newness, but, in terms of strict artistic criteria, can only be an inflated repetition of what has gone before.

The central substantive claims of Danto's position, then, are these. In response to the usurping of its mimetic functions by cinematography, Modernist art became energized by an internal 'logic' necessarily progressing towards the revelation of art's real essence—an essence that would not be assimilable in terms of other forms of communication. In Warhol's Pop Art this progression issues in its logical culmination. The essence of art is, in effect, declared as institutional. This self-congruence of art with its own essence is the culmination of art history. After it there can be nothing new in a distinctively artistic sense. On these terms, in other words, postmodern art is essentially *posthistorical*. Art, in effect, has come to an end.

Having outlined Danto's theory, I shall now make some observations concerning its strengths, and some philosophical points concerning its weaknesses. Its strength lies in two basic achievements. First, Danto has pinpointed a crucial fact—namely that in the modern epoch art practice has been taken to its logical limit. For, once what counts as art is determined by artistic intention alone—

---

[3] Ibid. 205.   [4] Ibid. 209.

rather than by possession of specifiable phenomenal characteristics—then we have reached a point beyond which there can be no new kinds of artwork. Anything and everything is admissible in the context of artistic theory and intention. The second strength of Danto's theory is that this first point enables him to explain exactly why postmodern art is fundamentally empty and a product of market forces. Rather than simply declaring it as regressive or the result of a general cultural 'slackening' (Lyotard), he provides a model wherein the origins of the slackening can be traced to art's progression towards logical exhaustion at the end of the modernist era. Postmodern art is empty because it is posthistorical.

However, whilst Danto thence offers a superficially plausible explanation of the origins and nature of Postmodernism, it is not, I think, an ultimately satisfying one. For even if we allow Danto's claim that twentiety-century Modernism consists fundamentally in a necessary progression towards the logical limit of art, there is no reason why we should regard the attainment of this limit—as Danto clearly does—as a restriction upon the creativity and historical development of art. What is lacking here is an argument to establish that creativity and artistic advancement are necessarily connected to the having of new ideas about what counts as the essence of art. For example, we might not count something as creative and quality art unless it does embody some new and novel feature, but this feature does not have to take the form of an embodiment of new ideas about what kind of items should be counted as art. It could rather take the form of a new style of handling, or the refinement of an existing style to an optimum degree. Indeed, it is the pattern and structure of just these sorts of developments which are the key elements in the history of art. The fact that, on Danto's reading, Modernist art fixes on a particular sort of innovation bound up with quasi-philosophical questioning could simply be regarded as a kind of extended detour from the standard preoccupations of art. Indeed, the fact that this detour leads to the logical limits of art acts only as a restriction on the scope of art which is explicitly orientated towards the question of what counts as art. On these terms, in other words, the logical limit reached by Modernist art does not exhaust the possibilities of artistic creativity and advancement as such. Hence, we are not compelled on philosophical grounds to regard postmodern art as essentially posthistorical.

The second major area of difficulty raised by Danto's approach concerns his very reading of twentieth-century Modernism as a kind of quasi-philosophical endeavour. For one must ask whether there is anything which *compels* such a reading? As I interpret him, Danto might offer us two putatively compelling reasons. First, there is the fact that Modernist movements offer, in effect, different and mutually exclusive definitions of what counts as art—and hence embody rival philosophical viewpoints. Now, in relation to this, whilst it is true that the twentieth century has seen more conflicting philosophical theories of art than any other, these have generally been put forward by philosophers rather than artists. Indeed, whilst many Modernist artists have rejected the worth of traditional art in relation to modern experience, very few have claimed that it—or the work of rival modern movements—should not be regarded as art at all. What we find, rather, is a willingness to expand the field of art, rather than to restrict it to one style or one kind of artefact. Danto, in other words, wholly ignores the crucial bonds of practical and theoretical continuity which link modern movements. Now, the second reason which Danto might argue as justifying his reading of Modernism concerns the traditional supposed function of art. He claims that because the advent of cinematography finally vanquished art's mimetic function, art was led into a necessary progression towards the discovery of its essence. This, however, makes some pretty simplistic assumptions about the life which art traditionally plays in our culture. It is certainly true—as Aristotle noted—that mimesis seems to have an intrinsic fascination for human beings, but one might argue that the fascination with mimesis for its own sake has rarely been regarded as art's definitive function. Mimesis has rather been seen as a means to the end of various salutary effects—such as moral improvement, or the expression of feeling. Hence, one might see the impact of photography and cinema not as precipitating a crisis of philosophical questioning, but rather as a liberation. Artists were now free to orientate their work towards salutary effects that eluded more conventional techniques of representation.

I am arguing, then, that Danto's approach to the question of twentieth-century Modernism and Postmodernism is not philosophically decisive. In particular he overlooks possible dimensions of practical and theoretical continuity and salutary effects which might link Modernist and, indeed, postmodern movements together. In the following section of this chapter, therefore, I shall continue my critique of Danto by constructing an alternative historical interpretation which takes full account of the dimension of continuity.

II

Modernist art in the twentieth century has moved in two dominant directions. On the one hand, in, say, Fauvism, Futurism, Expressionism, and Surrealism, we find a revisionary approach towards representation which seeks to reappropriate it for the needs of modern experience. On the other hand, in, say, Suprematism, Neo-Plasticism, and Abstract Expressionism, we find a tendency towards purely abstract form. Now, these two tendencies are linked in two crucial respects. First, virtually all of them embody to greater or lesser degree a debt to Cézannesque and Cubist form or space. That is to say, they employ a formal vocabulary which tends to reduce form to more basic geometric shape, and/or which distributes such forms in a hyper-pictorial space, i.e. one which accentuates the two-dimensionality of the picture plans, and diminishes the sense of three-dimensional illusion. Hence, whilst Modernist movements tend in different stylistic directions, they do so on the basis of a root vocabulary derived from Cézanne and Cubism.

Now, although this vocabulary is one that departs from, and to some degree subverts, conventional forms of representation, it is not one which radically subverts the notion of high art, as such. Picasso and Braque's Cubism, for example, reappropriates and relegitimizes traditional genres such as the still life, the nude, and the portrait, in terms of an aggressive subjectivity. Indeed, even in Cubist collage—where alien physical material is incorporated into the work—such material is thoroughly mediated. Any oppositional sense of its physical reality is lost within the totality of the overall artistic composition. Again, in the case of Surrealism's dislocations of form, these do not subvert art as such, but rather draw on the precedent of Romantic and Symbolist Fantasy, in order to evoke repressed depths of subjectivity. The function of Cubist space, in other words, is not to posit an antithesis to high art but rather to refocus it in terms of a liberating affirmation of the subject.

It is this affirmative dimension which provides the second, and most important, bond between twentieth-century Modernists. It even encompasses those American Abstract Expressionists who radically break with Cubist space after 1945. Barnett Newman, for example, declared that 'Instead of making *cathedrals* out of Christ, man, or "life", we are making it out of ourselves, out of our own feelings'.[5] Compare this with the following set of statements.

When we invented Cubism, we had no intention of inventing Cubism. We simply wanted to express what was in us.[6]   (Picasso)

Without much intention, knowledge, or thought, I had followed an irresistible desire to represent profound spirituality, religion and tenderness.[7]

(Emil Nolde)

We . . . create a sort of emotive ambience, seeking by intuition the sympathies and the links which exist between the exterior (concrete) scene and the interior (abstract) emotion.[8]   (Umberto Boccioni)

The truly modern artist is aware of abstraction in an emotion of beauty . . .[9]

(Piet Mondrian)

. . . what interests me is the intensity of a personality transposed directly into the work; the man and his vitality . . . what manner he knows how to gather sensation, emotion, into a lacework of words and sentiments.[10]

(Tristan Tzara)

On these terms, then, Newman's declaration that he and his contemporaries are making 'cathedrals' of 'our own feelings' is a statement that captures a profound theme running throughout Modernist art—namely that the artwork receives its ultimate authentification as a vehicle for expression of *feeling*. What *sort* of feeling is expressed here varies (as the foregoing statements show) from artist to artist. In some it is bound up with aesthetic experience and religious sentiments; in others it is linked to the artist's affective response to technological change and utopian political ideals. But what all these have in common is the view that what legitimizes modern art and gives it its worth is some kind of elevating expressive effect embodied in its creation and reception. I shall hereafter call this view the 'legitimizing discourse' of art.

There are now two crucial points to be made. First (*contra*

---

[5] H. Chipp, *Theories of Modern Art* (University of California Press, Los Angeles, 1968), 553.
[6] Ibid. 210.   [7] Ibid. 146.   [8] Ibid. 297.   [9] Ibid. 321.
[10] Ibid. 387.

Danto), far from Modernist art movements being engaged in a kind of war between mutually exclusive definitions of art, there exists a surprising degree of continuity between them at the level of both phenomenal appearance and theoretical justification. Second, the legitimizing discourse of Modernist art also gives it continuity with more traditional idioms. For, since the Renaissance at least, the *raison d'être* of art in Western culture has been insistently tied to its elevating effects. As J.-J. David puts it, 'the purpose of the arts is to serve morality and elevate the soul'.

What demarcates Modernist art from such sentiments as these is the different readings of morality and elevation which it involves, and the different pictorial means which it operates. But the fundamental point is the same: art has its justification as a vehicle of—in the broadest terms—ethical and aesthetic improvement and elevation. If, therefore, we are to talk of a 'logic' of modernity in the visual arts at all, it can only be in the loose sense of a *radical transformation of the existing legitimizing discourse of art*. This, however, should not be seen as a logic of 'necessary' progression; neither must it be viewed as a matter wholly internal to art itself. For in Modernist art the different senses of elevation operative in the works of different artists and the means by which they are achieved are frequently enmeshed in complex responses to broader societal changes. Danto, then, is led astray in historical terms by his failure to look at the continuity of Modernist art in its sociocultural context.

There is, however, one point in the growth of Modernism which does seem more amenable to Danto's narrative. This is to be located in certain aspects of Pop Art—such as Warhol's *Brillo Boxes*—and in the development of Minimal and Conceptual art in the 1960s and 1970s. The former tendency seems to insist on collapsing the distinction between art and life, whilst the latter tendencies (respectively) seem to declare—in the most strident terms—that the minimum conditions for something being an artwork are mere objecthood, or embodying an 'idea' about what counts as art. Now even if (with Danto) we view these as quasi-philosophical statements about the definition of art, they point in a rather different direction from that which Danto's interpretation would lead us to expect. For if, as I have argued, the central feature of Modernism is a radical transformation of the legitimizing discourse, then the fact that certain movements after 1960 seem to break with this carries with it the implication that we have here the beginnings of a break with modernity itself. What Danto's narrative of quasi-philosophical questioning really signifies, in other words, is not the underlying 'logic' of modernity, but the transitional point at which modernity begins to pass into postmodernity. In the next section of this chapter, therefore, I will develop this interpretation by showing how the critique of the legitimizing discourse can be construed as a definitive feature of Postmodernism in the visual arts.

III

The key artist in understanding the transition from modern to postmodern is Malcolm Morley. In the late 1950s and early 1960s Morley was working in an Abstract Expressionist idiom much indebted to Barnett Newman. However, around 1965 he began producing works such as *S.S. Amsterdam at Rotterdam* (Plate 1). Now, at first sight, in utilizing imagery derived from the mass-media—in this case a commonplace postcard—it might seem that Morley is linking himself to those aspects of Pop Art which overtly celebrate the virtues of mass-culture. This, however, would be a very superficial reading. For Morley's 'Super-Realism' lacks any sense of the hedonism, humour, or gentle irony which generally characterizes Pop Art's relation to its sources. The internal resources of an image such as *S.S. Amsterdam*, rather, declare it as more serious and critical through the very insistency with which it manifests its own origin in an image derived from mechanical reproduction. (Even the margin of the postcard is, in fact, worked into Morley's image.) This impression is consolidated by knowledge of how the work is created. In this (and kindred works of the late 1960s) Morley has small-scale photographic-based material blown up into poster size. He then inverts the image, divides it up into a series of grid squares, and transcribes it—one square at a time (with the rest covered up)—in acrylic paint on to a canvas. Thus the process of making the work is reduced to the level of quasi-mechanical reproduction. We have a framed picture offered in the 'big' format characteristic of 'high art', but whose status as high is subverted by the image's banal content. Other levels of negation are also operative. For here, a mechanically reproduced image (the postcard) is the original, whereas the high-art format painting is only a *copy* of this original. Indeed, whilst the common prejudices of the general public equate 'good' painting with verisimilitude ('it could almost be a photograph'), here the 'good' painting is achieved by quasi-mechanical reproduction, rather than the virtuoso fluency of the skilled hand.

Morley's Super-Realism, in other words, is a critical practice which highlights, questions, and thwarts our expectations of art as a 'high' cultural activity. It addresses not so much the Minimalist and Conceptualist preoccupation with the minimum conditions for something to be counted as art, but rather the legitimizing discourse whereby art is justified as a vehicle of elevation and improvement. To some degree, this is anticipated in the blatant parodies of Duchamp, but in Morley's case the critical dimension is, as it were, painted into the image. We have not so much a kind of external 'anti-art' as art which internalizes and displays the problematics of its own socio-cultural status.

Now, in the work of a number of other Super-Realist artists in the late 1960s and early 1970s—such as the paintings of Audrey Flack and Chuck Close or the sculptures of Duane Hanson—a broadly similar critical dimension is operative. However, the great bulk of work in this idiom has a much more superficial orientation. For, as the Super-Realist tendency spread, it began to address itself to more traditional concerns and become simply a style. In the work of John Salt or Richard Estes, for example, we find close-up images of such things as cars or flashy shop frontages, which, whilst being derived from photographs, present themselves as ostensibly virtuoso performances. Super-Realism becomes the means for intricate, aesthetically dazzling compositions on the grand scale. The work of Morley and the other innovators, in other words, is reappropriated within the legitimizing discourse. Indeed, Super-Realism of this sort has overwhelming market appeal through its combining both the traditional and Modernist exemplifications of this discourse. On the one hand, its flashy verisimilitude appeals to the traditional prejudices that art should uplift through its complexity and virtuosity; on the other hand, because such works look so much like photographs, they still seem odd—vaguely outrageous even—thus feeding on the demand for fashionable novelty and unexpectedness that is created by Modernism.

One might trace a similar pattern in relation to the development and consumption of the tendency that began to displace Super-Realism in the late 1970s—namely 'Neo-Expressionism'. Again, the case of Malcolm Morley proves decisive here. Around 1970 he began to ruffle the surfaces of his photographic-derived works, by working them in more broken brushstrokes. Of especial interest here is *School of Athens* (1972). This work is a copy of a photographic reproduction of Raphael's original. Raphael's work—in both content and handling—affirms art's status as a dignified and uplifting activity akin to the pursuit of those timeless essential truths which are the vocation of the great philosophers depicted in the painting. It is the quintessential icon of the very notion of high art itself. Morley's treatment of Raphael's work, however, makes the artistic enterprise look earthy and contingent. This is achieved not only through the disruptions effected by the loose handling, but through the fact that Morley leaves a transcriptional mistake intact in the 'finished' work (namely a horizontal line of grid squares, that is manifestly asynchronous with the rest of the composition). Indeed, it becomes acutely difficult to locate Morley's *School of Athens* within the customary discourse of art history itself. Is it a copy; is it Expressionist; is it a parody; is it Surrealist; is it classicist? Perhaps all—yet none of these.

Such dislocation effects are even more manifest in Morley's more recent works. In *Day of the Locust* (1977), for example, Morley not only completely mixes up such categories as Expressionist and Surrealist, but blatantly parodies that notion of 'stylistic development' which is so central to art history. Morley injects motifs drawn from his earlier work but malforms them and screws them up. One must also note a further crucial dimension to this and kindred works. Morley does not simply overload us with images of breakdown and catastrophe, but rather tangles these up in a way that makes it difficult to disentangle strands of depicted reality from strands of fiction. He does not offer an illusion of real space, but neither does he open up a surreal space of pure fantasy. We are left, rather, in a state of insecurity that seems to bear witness to painting's inadequacy in relation to articulating the complexity and/or horrors of contemporary existence. This felt inadequacy, in other words, arises from a pictorial compromisation of the legitimizing discourse. A critical dimension of this sort is to be found in other innovative 'Neo-Expressionist' artists of the 1970s and 1980s, notably Anselm Kiefer, Georg Baselitz, and Philip Guston.

Kiefer, for example (see Plate 2), moves from large claustrophobic interiors that hint at unseen powers and violence, to devastated landscapes linked with symbols or inscriptions that allude more directly to catastrophe, and, in particular, the disasters of German history. In these works, the very overload of scale, catastrophic excess, and an insistence on the physical means of the medium itself, expressly thematizes painting's inadequacy in relation to life.

Now, whilst Morley, Kiefer, and others make Neo-Expressionism into a critical practice, their work created a stylistic precedent and climate which enabled less incisive, more market-ori-entated Neo-Expressionisms to flourish. In relation to the work of Julian Schnabel (see Plate 3), Sandro Chia, and Francisco Clemente, for example, the term 'Neo-Expressionism' is a catch-all phrase that picks out a discourse of painterly excess, and unbridled eclecticism. The overload of paint and imagery connects with its audience fundamentally at the level of private and arbitrary associ-ation. If a dimension of public or collective significance is lacking in these works, it is taken as a signifier of the artist's profundity or depth of being. The viewer is invited to compensate for his or her own lack of experience by vicarious identification with the com-plex signs borne by the canvas. By engaging with the work, in other words, the viewer is elevated and improved.

I am arguing, then, that there are two fundamentally different aspects to Postmodernism in the visual arts. First, in the late 1960s and 1970s, there developed a kind of art which is sceptical about the legitimizing discourse of art as a vehicle of elevation and improvement. Now, whereas radical modern movements such as Cubism and Surrealism redeploy traditional genres such as still life, and fantasy, as a means of elevating subjectivity, artists such as Morley and Kiefer radically question the affirmative discourse of high art, as such. They do so either by incorporating (in an *apparently* unmediated fashion) that which is most directly antithetical to high art—namely mechanically reproduced imagery; or by the-matizing (within the particular work) the inadequacy of artistic categories, and, indeed, art's inability to express the complexities and catastrophes of concrete historical experience. We have, in other words, a new form of art whose very pictorial means embody a scepticism as to the possibility of high art. By internaliz-ing this scepticism and making it thematic within art practice, *Critical* Super-Realism and *Critical* Neo-Expressionism give art a *deconstructive* dimension. Such work embodies the same kinds of strategy which inform contemporary post structuralist approaches to discourse in general. They can, therefore, be defined as the definitive postmodern tendency. However, this deconstructive approach also created a market demand which was rapidly met by *Secondary* (uncritical) Super-Realisms and Neo-Expressionisms. These works served directly to reinvigorate the legitimizing discourse of art by tapping the traditional expectation of virtuoso performances and 'profundity' and the modernist appetite for the odd and the outrageous. Now, in the latter half of the 1980s the Critical aspect of postmodern art has reached a crisis point. It is to a consideration of this phenomenon, and some broader questions, that I now turn in the final section of this chapter.

IV

Much art practice of the late 1980s involves a kind of ironic deconstruction that recognizes and internalizes its own inevitable assimilation by the market. In the Neo-Geo abstractions of Phillip Taafe, for example, we find parodies and subversions of Modernist colour-field painting and 'Op' Art. Barnett Newman's high Modernist *Who's Afraid of Red, Yellow, and Blue?* finds its riposte in Taafe's send-up '*We Are Not Afraid*'. Likewise, Peter Halley's Neo-Geo electric cell and conduit paintings parody the high-falutin claims of Rothko-style colour-field painting by stating it and containing it in terms of banal imagery drawn from the technological base of postmodern culture. Again, the 'sculpture' of Jeff Koons and David Mach questions conventional notions of taste and representation, through creating assemblages of quirky and comical ingenuity. Mach's *101 Dalmatians*, for example, turns Disney's hounds loose on the domestic environment. The disturbing sense of gravitational precariousness created by Barnett Newman's *Broken Obelisk* or Richard Serra's *Delineator* is here achieved through a Dalmation balancing a washing-machine on its nose.

Now, in all these Neo-Geo paintings and sculptures a dimension of deconstruction is present, in so far as art's pretensions to elevation or improvement are called into question or shifted to the level of the humorous. But the very good humour of this strategy and the ludicrousness of its means bespeaks an overtly self-ironical and self-negating level of insight. We can deconstruct, but the legitimizing discourse and the market will still have us—so let's have fun with the whole situation while we can. This comic fatalism is of some broader significance, in so far as it marks the point where Critical Postmodernism recognizes its own limits. Any art objects set forth with internal critical intent will be assimilated by the legitimizing discourse and market forces, and redistributed in the form of a *style*. This fate is promised as soon as the attempt to criticize the legitimizing discourse of art is made internal to art itself. For here the deconstructive tendency succeeds in fulfilling the legitimizing discourse despite itself.

To see why this is so, one must invoke the experience of the sublime, in terms of its two main expositors—Kant and Burke. Having already discussed both theories at length in preceding chapters, I shall state their positions briefly. In the Kantian version,[11] when we encounter some phenomenon which overwhelms, or threatens to overwhelm, our imagination or emotions, this can sometimes issue in a kind of rational counterthrust. In such a case, we recognize and comprehend that which overwhelms or threatens to overwhelm us. Indeed, the very fact that a phenomenon which so manifestly defeats our sensible capacities can nevertheless be articulated and thence, in a sense, contained by reason, serves to vividly affirm the extraordinary scope and resilience of rational selfhood. I would suggest that an affirmative response on something like these lines is embodied in our engagement with certain aspects of Critical Postmodernist art. Consider, for example, the overwhelming disaster motifs and dislocational effects of Critical Neo-Expressionism. These signify art's essential inadequacy in relation to expressing the complexity and immensity of the real world and its problems. However, the very fact that such a profound insight can be articulated within the idioms of art serves, paradoxically, to vivify the extraordinary scope of art itself as a mode of rational artifice. The disaster of failure to signify is, as it were, contained and redeemed by the achieved signification of this failure within the visual means of art. The artist offers an affirmative and elevating experience of a kind of artistic sublimity.

Burke's existential theory of the sublime can also be applied to

[11] For a much fuller discussion of the general relation between art and Kant's theory of the sublime, see my *The Kantian Sublime: From Morality to Art* (Clarendon Press, Oxford, 1989), ch. 7.

the Critical dimension of postmodern art (and, indeed, avant-garde art in general). According to Burke, prolonged states of inactivity and monotony are deleterious to our organic constitution. In order to counter this, we need to experience mild shocks—which will stimulate our sensibilities, but without involving any real sense of pain or danger. Experiences of this sort are provided by such things as vast or destructive objects encountered from a position of safety, or by human artefacts which outrage or thrill us in some way. Now, as I showed in Chapter 6, Burke's argument can be transposed into contemporary terms, on the basis of our response to patterns of work and social existence in a society characterized by the division of labour. In such a society the reified and monotonous pattern of life demands a compensating substitute for real experience. The shocks and thrills provided by media news items, or such things as violent adventure films and the like, fulfil this function. It is this vein of compensatory affective response, I would suggest, which is tapped by Critical Postmodernism. In the case of Critical Super-Realism and Neo-Geo, for example, we have works which engage us fundamentally in terms of affective jolts—through thwarting of parodying expectations based on our intercourse with high art of the traditional or Modernist kinds. They have a shock or surprise value which rejuvenates and heightens our very sense of being alive. The means may be banal or ludicrous, but in the midst of social monotony and accelerating standardization, the 'whatever-will-they-do-next' aspect of artistic innovation is a life-enhancing force. Its affective jolt, indeed, may even thematize the notion that the individual creator *can* resist the forces of reification to some degree—however trivial.

I am arguing, then, both that the Critical dimension of postmodern art has ended up on a kind of comical recognition of its own limits; and that this kind of result was implicit in the very attempt to deconstruct art from within. Such a practice tends towards elevating experiences of the sublime in either the Kantian or Burkean modes. This interpretation raises two questions. First, is there any way in which Critical Postmodernism in the visual arts can avoid assimilation by the legitimizing discourse and market forces; and second, if it cannot, does this not mean that Danto is at least right in his claim that Postmodernism is posthistorical? Let me address the former question. First, as I have already argued, internalized deconstruction is assimilated by the legitimizing discourse in terms of the sublime. But what about those cases where the critique is conducted from a more external viewpoint?

A good example here is the work of the feminist artist Mary Kelly. In her *Post Partum Document*, Kelly seeks to break out of the patriarchal power structures which have regulated what is admissible as art and what is not. The work consists of a series of largely documentary displays charting biographical facts about, and theoretical interpretations of, her relationship with her son—from earliest infancy to earliest childhood. Now, the problem with this work (and, indeed, the problem faced by 'conceptual art' in general) is that the level of sensuous, essentially visual meaning is almost entirely eliminated. It might, of course, be argued that the removal of this dimension is an extremely positive feature, in so far as it is art's sensuousness which appeals to the market and which provides the essential spectacle for the male gaze. However, on these terms, Kelly's work merely throws out the baby with the bathwater. For to remove the appeal to distinctively visual meaning is to render the notion of visual art itself superfluous. Collapsing the boundary between art and documentation in this way simply eliminates art. Interestingly, however, Kelly—as is the case with most conceptual artists—is not willing to allow her *Post Partum* work to be judged as a series of theoretical statements, for its units are mounted so as to be hung in accordance with the presentational formats of conventional art. Thus the work takes on its deconstructive edge through the play-off between its primarily non-artistic content, and its conventional art format of presentation. Again, however, whilst this thwarts our normal expectations as to what should be counted as art, the fact that it is mounted as an-object-for-contemplation serves to contain the shock response. We feel that this is just the avant-garde thrilling us with the outrageous and extending our horizons once more. Our sensibility is, once, more, elevated and improved.

That the legitimizing discourse should exert so profound a pull in relation to even the most (superficially) antithetical works is hardly surprising. For, whilst the concept 'art' is a social construct of Western culture, it is not merely a construct. The reason why it needs to be constructed is to pick out the fact that certain kinds of artefacts bring about certain positive effects *through the mere contemplation of them*. It is the fact that certain artefacts can be valued in this way that necessitates the concept 'art'. The legitimizing discourse, in other words, legitimizes not just this art and that, but the very concept of 'art' as such.

I shall now finally return to Danto's implicit equation between postmodern art and posthistoricality. It will be remembered that, for Danto, the reason why this equation is justified is that Modernist art—in the form of Warhol's *Brillo Boxes*—brings about a congruence between art and the statement of its essence. Thereafter there cannot be anything artistically new—only a rehash of old forms. Now, whilst I rehearsed the philosophical objections to this claim in section I, it is worth looking at again in the light of my alternative historical account of Modernity and Postmodernity. First, I have tried to show that there is some continuity between the late Modernism of Warhol, Minimal art, and Conceptual art, and the Critical varieties of postmodern Super Realism and Neo-Expressionism. All these tendencies are energized by the philosophical implications of art. The difference between them consists in the fact that, whereas the late Modernists question the logical scope of art and take it to and beyond its limits, the Critical Postmodernists question the social reality of art (i.e. the status of the legitimizing discourse) from within. This latter fact is itself a concrete illustration of how postmodern art—working within and loosening up the limits of already established idioms (i.e. 'Realism' and 'Expressionism')—is authentically critical and historically innovative, rather than the mere product of market demands.

Now, of course, I also argued that whilst Critical Postmodernism shakes up and questions the legitimizing discourse, it does not escape it; but this fact in no way restricts its historical possibilities. For, as I further suggested, the legitimizing discourse is the very basis of our having a concept of art at all—indeed, it is the very basis of our interest in art's historical development. To escape the legitimizing discourse, in other words, would involve giving up art. One might expect, therefore, that future postmodern art will become less obsessed with criticizing the legitimizing discourse, and will instead orientate itself towards new ways of exemplifying it. To some degree this process is already under way. As we shall see in the next chapter, for example, Thérèse Oulton's paintings draw on tradition in a way that redirects rather than criticizes. They articulate primeval experiences of place and presence through a collectively accessible vocabulary of form, texture, and colour. Ross Blechner's sinister memorial paintings referring to

Aids victims likewise state private experience in a way that is collectively moving and enlightening. Here, in other words, we have the beginnings of a postmodern art that is profoundly creative, and which involves an elevating reappropriation of the *lifeworld*, rather than criticism or eclecticism alone.

In conclusion, then, one must concede only one major point to Danto—namely that all future art will have to work within the logical limits that were set out by late Modernism, and this will involve operating with genres and categories already defined. Even this, however, would only rule out the possibility of future authentic artistic innovation on the assumption that such innovation is sufficiently definable in negative terms, that is as simply creating something the like of which has not been created before. But, of course, this assumption is false. Historical innovation in art has always been determined in the context of creative breaks with, or refinements of, what has already been given. We do not want new artefacts that are simply unprecedented—but rather ones whose unprecedentedness casts new light on the traditions of art or on our broader relation to the lifeworld. Artistic innovation, in other words, in a complex relation between art and its past, rather than the kind of absolute philosophical break which Danto's reading makes of it. The moral is clear. Art lives . . . and will continue to do so whilstsoever artists see their world and, in particular, their discipline's history, from different viewpoints.

11

Creativity, Contemporary Art, and Critical Aesthetics

In the previous chapter (and indeed throughout this book) I have argued that the continued creativity of art is bound up with the specific work refining or innovating in relation to tradition. Likewise the experience of the sublime. It has been revitalized by shifts in respect of the items which occasion it, and the societal contexts in which it is experienced. Similar considerations apply to culture generally, and (not least) to the realm of philosophy itself. This is why most of my chapters begin with a critical analysis of some specific thinker, and then seek to correct and extend that viewpoint. In this way, philosophical progress is seen as overtly historical. It does not consist of simply matching up some theory arrived at in splendid isolation with some pristine, as it were *raw* reality. Rather, it is a refinement of our conception of reality, based on the interaction of concepts yielded by tradition and our present mode of inherence in the world. (This theme will be substantially articulated in the fourth volume of this project.)

However, given the importance which I assign to refinement and innovation in relation to tradition, this raises an important question. For, might it not be said that art—indeed, culture in general—has become posthistorical through, in effect, an *excess* of history: that the enormous contemporary flow of information reduces individuals and artefacts to a sum of the influences upon them? We are saturated by tradition. A view of this sort is closely associated with Roland Barthes' notion of the text, and its apparent relevance to contemporary eclecticism.

In section I of this chapter, then, I shall outline Barthes' notion of the text and its putative links to eclecticism in contemporary painting. However, I will then go on to criticize both these positions, by developing some ideas concerning embodiment (originally

broached in Chapter 1), and also the argument concerning critical
eclecticism from Chapter 10.

In section II I shall go on to argue (on the basis of ideas from
Merleau-Ponty) that there is a further and more positive creative
tendency in recent eclecticism, which thematizes painting's very
essence—in the reciprocity of the visible and the invisible. In section III I will relate some of these ideas to my notion of Critical
Aesthetics, and will bring together themes explored throughout this
book.

I

Barthes' notion of the text is meant to foreground the fact that our
intercourse with symbolic formations involves a cognitively
dynamic relation, rather than the passive deciphering of 'meanings'. In his words, 'The text is a productivity. This does not mean
that it is the product of a labour . . . but the very theatre of a production where the producer and reader of the text meet: the text
"works", at each moment and from whatever side one takes it.'[1]
The text, then, is not just a symbolic formation. Rather, it is an
inexhaustible zone of generation—a relation between what a producer has put into such a formation and what a receiver finds
there. This relation does not admit of definitive formulation or stabilization, because the terms which it relates (producer and
receiver) are *linguistic* subjects. Such a subject in any moment of
consciousness draws upon the resources of language in ways which
are enormously complex and linked to broader cultural and historical circumstances. The consequences of this are highly significant
vis-à-vis the possibility of creativity. As Barthes puts it,

the text is not a line of words releasing a single 'theological' (the 'message'
of the Author-God) but a multi-dimensional space in which a variety of
writings, none of them original, blend and clash. The text is a tissue of
quotations drawn from the innumerable centres of culture . . . His [the
author's] only power is to mix writings, to counter the ones with the others, in such a way as never to rest on any one of them.[2]

[1] Roland Barthes, 'Theory of the Text', in *Untying the Text: A Post-Structuralist
Reader*, ed. Robert Young (Routledge & Kegan Paul, London, 1981), 31–47. This
ref., p. 36.
[2] Roland Barthes, *Image Music Text*, trans. Stephen Heath (Fontana, London,
1982), 46.

Barthes suggests further that the author 'ought at least to know the inner "thing" he thinks to "translate" is itself only a ready-formed dictionary, its words only explainable through other words, and so on indefinitely'.[3]

In these remarks, Barthes is developing the implications of an approach to language similar to Derrida's. Although he deals specifically with literature, his remarks clearly apply also to other art forms. Any attempt at an authentic or unique configuration of signs in thought or in representation is merely a shifting play within that sign-system as a whole. It is a mixing of idioms already laid down. Recent 'postmodern' developments in the visual arts ostensibly manifest this very fact in so far as they self-consciously combine different stylistic tendencies or modes of representation and material in the space of a single picture. The work of Julian Schnabel and David Salle are cases in point here. Schnabel's expressionist handling of paint is combined with three-dimensional materials—such as crockery or charred wood—or with unorthodox support material such as velvet. Salle's imagery clearly combines a schematizing tendency derived from technical manuals or caricature with material derived from soft-porn magazines. The effect of such works upon the viewer is that of sensory overload. This can be interpreted in two ways: first, as simply pandering to a stereotype of complex eclectic consumer sensibility; or, second, as an attempt to impress the validity of the artist's personal fantasy upon the viewer, by a kind of artistic aggression. In either case, individual creativity has been reduced to that of remixing what is given, and calling it one's 'own' on that basis. In such a mixing, the elements which are combined do not undergo any kind of real qualitative change. What results is *just* a mixture.

Now, whilst this empty eclecticism seems to bear out Barthes' analysis, it is not decisive. For Barthes' whole understanding of subjectivity is itself deeply flawed. He—like Derrida—sees individuality as, in effect, a function of the signs which the individual manipulates. Putting it bluntly, we are more 'produced' by language than it is by us. Difference between individuals is a play of *différance* within the language which we occupy. This account, however (as I have shown at length in Chapter 1), *idealizes* the terms which it involves. It assigns no role to the fact and

---

[3] Ibid.

consequences of human embodiment. This role, nevertheless, is decisive. The very existence of language—or any symbolic formation—presupposes a substantive human subject, founded on real physical difference, rather than difference at the level of language use. A further argument to this effect is as follows.

Without the need for communication there would be no language; but the need for communication itself presupposes that there are finite beings who share a common world, yet see it from different viewpoints. This means, of course, that such beings are embodied. They are in a spatio-temporal continuum, but occupy different positions. Hence, to communicate involves the articulation of embodiment with a view to expressing both what is common in the experience of embodied subjectivity, and also what is distinctive about each embodied subject. This latter point needs particular emphasis. For an embodied self necessarily sees the world from a unique position. It shares a latent existential space—of bodily, linguistic, and social competences—with other such beings; but the world encompassed by this space does not stand still. It cannot be definitively fixed in place, or absolutely comprehended. Each embodied subject experiences contingent situations which demand new strategies, or the reworking of old ones. Indeed, even if the individual is a member of the most static and norm-governed social order, its unique position *qua* embodied subject means that it has a personal history. Each moment of awareness is not simply added to those which preceded it in an accumulating quantitative whole. Rather, the accumulation of moments constantly reconfigures the whole. The subject grasps its present interests. It relates the past to the present as the unfolding of its own history.

Now, this does not imply that the self is some figment, or play, or a mere social construction. It testifies rather to the hegemony of presence-to-body. The reason for this is that if the body's present hold in physical and latent existential space is to be maximized, it must be able to mobilize the resources of its past experience in a lucid way. It must be able to intuit itself as a unity. This means that any item which the subject encounters in perception, or articulates in language, is assimilated within this unity. The contents of the embodied subject's perception and consciousness are stylized: that is, they are given unique inflections by virtue of being absorbed into a unique personal history. Hence, when such a sub-

ject expresses itself—in language or by the creation of artefacts—
what is expressed can bear the imprint of this stylization. This is
not simply a quantitative 'mix' of existing idioms and techniques.
Rather it is a qualitative transformation of them. What is decisive
there is not what is expressed but *how* it is expressed. The style of
expression is a direct manifestation of the individual embodied
subject *qua* individual embodied subject. Such stylization *changes*
the significance of the material which it is giving expression to.

From this it can be concluded that so long as art is produced by
embodied subjects the possibility of creativity exists. This possibility is even realized in the midst of eclecticism in contemporary
painting. For, as we saw in the previous chapter, there is a deconstructive strain in that tendency which involves more than a mere
repetitive 'mix' or 'tissue' of pre-given idioms. Rather, it integrates
such idioms in visible presences which question the very possibility
of art's presence. This may be paradoxical, but it is not arbitrary.
It serves instead to exemplify the fact that, in the face of mass-cul-
tural pressures to identify and conform, or simply sell out to prevailing trends, the individual can criticize, resist, and, indeed,
achieve self-identification through the products of this resistance.
For example, although Malcolm Morley in works such as *Race
Track* parodies the idea of phases of artistic development, and
although his Super-Realism is a kind of negation of the artist's
'gesture', these works define themselves as 'Malcolm Morleys' by
the ingenuity and unexpectedness of this utilization of established
visual idioms. They manifest, in other words, the creative strategy
of the embodied individual.

However, this being said, might it not be true that art has
reached its limits? With the conceptual art of the 1960s and its
rejection of the concrete art-object, art in effect can be anything
which the artist chooses to designate as art. Can there be anything
new or creative after this limit has been reached? The answer to
this would be 'no' if, *but only if*, creativity were simply a negative
notion—sheer innovation and play in an absolute sense. But this,
in Kant's apt phrase, would simply allow 'original nonsense'. For
creativity to have real content it must be viewed in relation to
painting's foundational ontology—in a reciprocity of the visible
and the invisible. And this brings us to a key point of transition.
For, whilst poststructuralist scepticism concerning presence, meaning, and subjectivity has found its echo in, on the one hand, an

empty eclecticism, and, on the other hand, a genuinely creative but sceptical deconstructionism, there is, I would suggest, an element in contemporary painting which is in effect sceptical about the scepticism. The works I have in mind here are ones which, instead of questioning the very possibility of art, seem to return us to a reciprocity of the visible and the invisible which is foundational to painting as an art form. To show this, I shall now introduce a key theme from the late work of Merleau-Ponty. It was first broached in Chapter 1.

II

Merleau-Ponty observes in relation to Rembrandt's *Nightwatch* that

> We see that the hand pointing to us in the Nightwatch is truly there only when we see that its shadow on the Captain's body presents it simultaneously in profile . . . Everyone with eyes has at some time or other witnessed this play of shadows, or something like it, and has been made by it to see a space and the things included therein. But it works in us without us; it hides itself in making the object visible . . . The visible in the profane sense forgets its premises, it rests upon a total visibility which is to be recreated and which liberates the phantoms captive in it.[4]

The significance of painting, then, is that it generates some visible presence from a nexus of relations such as colours, tones, shapes, and textures. This invisible nexus, however, is not passed over unnoticed, as is the case with the invisible fabric of everyday perception. Rather, it is made symbolically thematic as that from which the specific visible presence is composed. Now, of course, the work may have been called into being by, and be addressed to, some socially determined function, but the reason why painting is so amenable to such broader usages is the fact that it gives them plausibility at the level of sensory existence, by generating them from what is fundamental to that level, namely the reciprocity of the visible and the invisible. Of course, in some cases the broader

---

[4] Maurice Merleau-Ponty, 'Eye and Mind', in *Aesthetics*, ed. Harold Osborne (Oxford University Press, Oxford, 1972). This ref., pp. 62–3. This key text is also to be found in a collection of Merleau-Ponty's writings entitled *The Primacy of Perception*, ed. and trans. James Edie (Northwestern University Press, Evanston, Ill., 1964).

social function of a painting will be so well served by this reciprocity that our awareness of it will be primarily in terms of its social
significance. We will engage with the visible ideological meaning at
the expense of the invisible means by which it is achieved. In other
paintings, however, what is made visible may emerge in a way
which draws attention to the means of its realization. The distinctive style of treatment of subject-matter will throw the world 'out
of focus'. The conditions of this (which, as we saw in Chapter 2,
Merleau-Ponty underestimates) are comparative, that is, they are a
function of the work's relation to tradition and broader ideology.
A painting will disclose itself fully as a painting only if it substantially refines or to some degree breaks with existing modes of handling the medium. This means that we relate the work to a second
network of 'invisible' *historical* relations, in addition to those phenomenal ones embodied in the material fabric of the work itself.
One might say that it is through being energized by reference to
this historical dimension that painting, through being appraised *as*
painting, becomes *art*.

   Now, the relation between the visible and the invisible is thema-
tized in the work of a number of contemporary painters. One
might cite in this respect the work of Leon Golub and Eric Fishl,
whose treatment of politically and sexually charged material
(respectively) explicitly thematizes a fundamental Merleau-Pontian
motif—namely (the usually 'invisible' fact) that he or she who
paints or sees is also part of the visual field. In Golub and Fishl's
works the viewer is directly addressed by the political or sexual
protagonists in the pictures. He or she is inscribed into the visual
presence as a kind of voyeur. This thematization clearly raises a
number of ethical issues, and I shall hope to address these elsewhere. For the purposes of the present study, however, I shall now
turn to two less figuratively orientated painters—Peter Suchin and
Thérèse Oulton. In their work the reciprocity of the visible and the
invisible is focused in a somewhat more concentrated way.

   First, then, Peter Suchin. Since 1980, his painting has not evolved
in a strictly linear stylistic progression. Rather, it moves between
two poles, each undergoing gradual mutation on the basis of their
interchange. At one extreme we find a work such as *With Yellow
Cross* (1980) (Plate 4). This conjoins relatively uniform pastel colour
fields with more differentiated polychromatic ones. These interact
within a Cubist space which echoes the truncated rectilinear format

of the painting's edges. The strategically placed cross provides the key form around which the other masses constellate in a unified visual presence. At the other extreme is *The Golden Code* (1987) (Plate 5). Here the polychromatic elements are more individually defined in terms of acicular forms—sometimes straight, sometimes curvilinear. These are concentrated in two loosely defined strata of formal activity at the top and the bottom of the painting, and in a third, and more wayward, diagonal stratum which connects them. Again, the composition defines itself as a singular presence through its elements constellating around a single formal device—in this case, a thistle of purple edged in yellow, to the top left of centre.

The bulk of Suchin's work is located between these two poles. In *Measured by Waste* (1986), for example, relatively uniform areas of banded colour in the top right and bottom left corners are counterposed by a diagonal swirl of interweaving forms that impart a quasi-illusionistic depth to the pictorial space.

Suchin's paintings declare their sources—conscious or subconscious—quite manifestly. In particular, names such as Tobey, Hodgkin, and Morley spring to mind. Indeed, the fact that Suchin paints only on board gives the painted surface a particularly vigorous affirmation—in accordance with one of the deepest impulses of modernist art. However, Suchin's work is much more than the sum of these and other influences. He has absorbed them into his own growth pattern—a kind of cerebral sensuality which is at once both virile and fecund. What makes this lyricism of special interest for the purposes of this study is that it not only delineates a quite distinctive generation of the visible from the invisible (as all *artistic* painting does) but also thematizes this relation in a more general way. Suchin's 'imagery' locates us in the ambiguous zone, where elements and relations hover before constellating into definite figurative presence. He arrests the visible in the very act of its emergence.

Similar considerations apply in relation to the work of Thérèse Oulton. Painterly debts, to such figures as Constable, Turner, Titian and Rembrandt, are clearly declared, but are qualitatively transformed into a distinctive vision. In her first major exhibition, *Fools Gold* (1984), works such as *Cinnabar*, *Copper Glance*, and *Midas Vein* evoke subterranean origins and processes. In *Mortal Coil* a braided silver cord connects distance and foreground, the intervals between which are defined by upwards-winding step-like forms. The density of silvered textures in the background, however, seems to close off the possibility of any emergence at a definite 'surface' level. One has a sense of place or presence—but one delineated at, and through, the ambiguous zones of its processes of becoming and mutation.

In her more recent work a lightening and diversification of palette has occurred. In paintings such as *Second Subject* (Plate 6) and *Counterfoil* (Plate 7) (both 1987), the step motif is accentuated and blocked off by a fan-like panoply of fibrous polychromatic forms. In these, as in all Oulton's paintings, texture is crucial. Whatever colour inflections may enliven their surface, these textures embody or insinuate layers of subterranean earth. This earth and its textured surfaces, with all its metallic glimmerings and fibrous qualities, declares itself as *presence which has emerged*.

I would suggest, then, that Suchin and Oulton's work brings about a twofold general thematization of presence. At the most immediate level, their complex allusive forms evoke presence as a *zone of emergence*, rather than as something which is closed and definite and simply *there*. This, however, is not allowed to be simply a play of relations. Rather, the compositional unity of the formal aspects, and hints of figurative meaning, constellate each pictorial manifold into an emphatically singular image of presence. This stabilization of presence, indeed, is further consolidated by the insistent—but not aggressive—painterly means whereby the image is realized. On these terms, in other words, visible presence is addressed not in the spirit of deconstruction—as the mere play of *différance* or as a system of arbitrary closures—but rather as a concrete achievement of the body's relation to the world.

Now, the second way in which Suchin and Oulton's work authentically thematizes visual presence is in the historical dimension. Our vision of the world is informed by a network of 'invisible' relations at the level of tradition and ideology, as well as in purely perceptual terms. As noted above, whilst Suchin and Oulton's works do not conceal their stylistic debt to tradition, they go beyond it through achieving a distinctive evocation of the emergence of the visible. On these terms self-presence becomes something more than the play of *différance*, or a position within an ideology. It is shown, rather, to spring from the concrete achievements of embodied being. No matter how we are pressured to repeat or conform, our existence as embodied subjects means that, in the final analysis, the individual always sees the world from a position which cannot be wholly colonized by the structures of broader social existence. Of course, a common language and the common conditions of such existence will tend towards the erasure of individuality. But this erasure cannot even approximate absoluteness. At times—such as now—when social and intellectual forces seem to be pressing in this direction, it is always open to the artist to return to the foundations of his or her medium. This return, of course, can itself never be absolute. But if it acknowledges its debts, and finds a distinctive way of rearticulating these foundations, it will have the character of both integrity and creativeness. Suchin and Oulton's work is of this kind.

III

In discussing creativity in contemporary art, I have been mobilizing the notion of a Critical Aesthetics. Such an approach focuses on the way art and aesthetic experience involve an interplay between what is constant and what is historically determined in our engagement with the world. By way of a conclusion to this chapter and my book as a whole, I shall now say a little more about all these themes.

First, whilst I have discussed the reciprocity of the visible and invisible primarily in relation to Suchin and Oulton's thematization of it, this reciprocity (as I showed in Chapters 1 and 2) is a basic structure in perception itself. Art, therefore, has the capacity to disclose different aspects of our most basic contact with the world. Suchin and Oulton focus on it in overt terms. Since, however, the reciprocity of the visible and the invisible is an essential feature of all art *qua* perceptual object, there are accordingly many other possible avenues of exploration. Poussin and Cézanne, for example, give lucid expression to those constants in the perceptual field which we learn abstractly as geometrical solids. However, whereas much of Cézanne's pictorial energy is directed towards articulating the relation between these solids, the mobility of the observer, and the limits of the picture plane, in Poussin they are part of a complex discourse of stability and change that gravitates around ideas of classicism and history. Poussin is the more representative artist here, in so far as the reciprocity of the visible and the invisible has (at least until the twentieth century) usually been bound up with the presentation of narrative meanings.

There are numerous other constants involved in art and aesthetic experience. In Chapter 5, for example, I described how violence in painting can gravitate around the disclosure of finitude. Indeed, a sense of the limits of our perceptual hold on the world, and of the redemptive possibilities of understanding, is at least implied in all serious art. It also, of course, features centrally in those experiences of the sublime discussed in Chapters 6, 7, 8, and 9. Another constant (central, in particular, to aesthetic empathy) is our need to recognize and articulate what we are as individuals through recognizing, identifying with, and learning from, the achievements of other people. The work of art facilitates all aspects of this, in so far as it involves the creation of a sensible manifold inseparably bonded to a symbolic content. It draws on capacities for synthesis such as imagination and rational comprehension which are necessary features of our cognitive relation to the world. More than this, it places such capacities in a mutually enhancing reciprocal relation.

However, all this being said, these (and other constants) are often present in art, only in an inert sense. For example, just as in everyday perception we rarely notice the network of 'invisible' background relations which declare some visual presence, so too in art. If a painting is mediocre or commonplace in some respect, we simply read it as a painting 'of' such and such a thing, and then pass on. It is only the work of originality—the one which refines or innovates—which solicits investigation as to the conditions of its visibility and their relation to other aspects of meaning. Likewise, it is only the original item which can engage our cognitive capacities in the heightened reciprocity of an aesthetic response. This means, of course, that as well as referring a work to constants in experience, we must also refer it to a comparative context. This is also true of the object of any experience. Not every overwhelming or mighty object, for example, is sublime. It is only those whose configuration is out of the ordinary in some respect which succeed in both engaging and stimulating our cognitive capacities.

Now, a question which has been left a little ambiguous in previous chapters is that of what constitutes a comparative context. In Chapter 5 I suggested that it was a function of personal experience and general cultural stock rather than specialized historical knowledge. To experience aesthetic empathy, for example, presupposes that the work is striking *vis-à-vis* our own personal experience of art, or in relation to general cultural expectations, but it does not presuppose any knowledge of the artist's intentions or the immediate conditions under which the work was produced. We may have such knowledge, but it is only a contingent feature in relation to the having of aesthetic experience. However, when it comes to questions of cultivation, rather different considerations come into play. For aesthetic responses are not static elements in a person's life. They answer to the individual's changing experience, and this means that the objects and relations which trigger them are subject to transformation. What once illuminated can become deadened by familiarity. This means that if our capacity for aesthetic experience is to be sustained in any healthy sense, we must develop it. Such cultivation involves opening ourselves not only to new works, but also to new sets of relations in terms of which works are situated. In effect, this will mean the formation of more detailed knowledge *vis-à-vis* art, its traditions and techniques, and broader implications.

The danger of this, of course (as I also noted in Chapter 5), is that cultivation in such a direction can tend to reduce the experience of art to that of historical understanding or social critique. The risk, however, is well worth taking for reasons in addition to those just mentioned. To show why this is so, I shall now reiterate and expand the central theme of this work as a whole. Its starting-point is the fact that our relation to the world—no matter how complex the influences upon it—gravitates around body-hold. In the sphere of art and the aesthetic in particular, constants inherent in embodied subjectivity enjoy enhanced activity. The pleasure arising from this is autonomous in the sense of being *logically distinctive*. This means that it does not presuppose reference to the immediate needs of our everyday practical existence, or our desire for instinctual gratification. Rather, it is a function of basic perceptual relations with the world. This does not imply some return to a closed realm of cosy 'spritual' values; for, as I have also argued, the whole aesthetic realm is driven by the need for transformation. Developments in, say, the history of painting, or the sensibility of the sublime, are needed in order to energize aesthetic responses. The reason for this is that our general cognitive capacities will only be stimulated into a heightened and pleasurable co-operation if they have something new to challenge them—something at odds (however slight) with preestablished ways of experiencing things. Suchin and Oulton's work, for example, thematizes the reciprocity of the visible and the invisible with far more perspicuity and poignancy than many other artists. Indeed, the fact that they achieve this *now*—at a time when scepticism about presence is at a general dogmatic premium—gives their work a much broader societal significance. Now, there are doubtless those—perhaps even the artists themselves—who would disagree with this interpretation, but the capital point is that interpretations of this type are contestable in terms of rational debate. Given a work which we find aesthetically engaging, one can affirm and defend one's response by showing how it generally improves on others and adds to the development of the medium. One can show what general cultural expectations the work thwarts or consolidates. Likewise, one can, on the basis of comparisons and contrasts, contest the responses and evaluations of others. This rational debate is not simply something exerted upon our aesthetic experience of the object. Rather, it can figure as an important part of that experience itself, in so far as the debate reinterprets the object, and shows it in terms of new aspects and possibilities.

I am arguing, then, that, in a Critical Aesthetics, the striving for objectivity in aesthetic judgement can facilitate the deepening of aesthetic experience itself. This is why the acquisition of detailed historical knowledge noted earlier is a risk well worth taking. Indeed, there is one final illuminating aspect to this. Aesthetic experience is profoundly bound up (as we have seen) not only with subjective responses but with the very conditions of embodied subjectivity itself—for example, the reciprocity of sensibility, imagination, and comprehension. The psychology of aesthetic response *qua* feeling, however, is deeply personal and (unless informed by an adequate theoretical discourse) will tend to stay rooted at that level. However, in striving for objectivity through grounding our judgements on historical knowledge, we are restoring the dimension of intersubjective significance. It can even inform the 'felt' character of the experience, in that we are here endeavouring explicitly to *share* with our fellow humans. And this is the decisive point. Objectivity in judgement—indeed, truth in art itself—is not a matter of conformity with, or matching up to, pre-existent norms or standards. It is rather a case of forwarding a work or critical assessment from which others can learn, and which enables them to experientially appropriate the aesthetic object (and thence the world) in a new way. Objectivity in judgement, in other words, is the projection of a shareable response. It represents a possibility of fulfilment, rather than the privation of passive acceptance. We are thus reintegrated with the lifeworld.

Now, in the foregoing paragraphs, I have described how aesthetic experience, whilst being in logical terms autonomous, is nevertheless historically mediated to a profound degree. I have further shown how it serves as a stimulant to rational and ethical interchange in the most positive senses. All in all, it is a realm of experience wherein through its complex syntheses we exist in the fullest sense, rather than in the alienated idioms of everydayness. (This theme will be explored in much greater depth in the next volume of this project, *Art and Embodiment*.)

Finally, then, whilst an understanding of Critical Aesthetics as I have formulated it is, of course, not presupposed in order to enjoy aesthetic experience, it is of vital significance in the way such experience is contextualized and deepened. As a clarification of the aesthetic, it shows that an area which has sometimes been regarded as subjective to the point of ineffability is, in fact, highly amenable to rational articulation. Indeed, this articulation is a stimulant to the furthering of aesthetic concerns in so far as it establishes the continuing possibility of creativity in the arts, and the humanizing effects of aesthetic experience. However, it also enables the aesthetic domain to be kept in a proper social perspective. For, whilst I have shown that the aesthetic can be legitimately pursued for its own sake, I have also shown (in Chapters 6 and 9, especially) how this should be squared-off against complex ethical and political considerations. We are thus led to the following conclusion overall. In its continuing orientation towards art, and its susceptibility to the sublime, the postmodern sensibility is not reducible to that of an alienated consumerism. Rather, the dimension of shock is a subjective outflow from both a renewed reciprocity—a sense of belonging—between the self and the world; and a dynamic historical transcendence towards it. Thus, the response to the decay of aura noted in the Introduction is, in fact, *a transformed experience of aura*. This experience is positive so long as it is subjected to proper theoretical articulation. Such a discourse sharpens our discriminatory powers, and enables the redemptive significance of the aesthetic to reverberate throughout experience. This is the continuing task of Critical Aesthetics.

Index